Third Edition

Islamic Studies

Level 10

Husain A. Nuri and **Mansur Ahmad**

ISBN: 978-1-936569-24-3

First Edition: 2010
Second Edition: 2011
Third Edition: 2013

Cover Design: Mansur Ahmad

Weekend Learning Publishers
5584 Boulder Crest St.
Columbus, OH 43235

www.weekendlearning.com
email: weekendlearning@gmail.com

Printed in China

Preface to the First Edition

After several delays and false starts, al-hamdulillah, the Level 10 book in the Weekend Learning series is now ready. During these long delays, several scholars and teachers reviewed the content of the book. Based on their feedback and critical evaluation, we decided to delete some of the lessons that we originally wanted to include and replace them with new topics. Several schools that used the pre-print version of the book in the 2009–2010 school year will find that we adopted some of their suggestions in the book. With all these changes, we hope this book will appeal to a wider section of readers. If these changes caused an inconvenience to any school, we extend our apology.

We would like to mention that the concept of this series of Islamic Studies books was conceived in 2002 when we were either teachers or principals in two weekend schools in two different states. We used several excellent textbooks and reference books. However, as teachers, we found there was no single textbook available that could meet our classroom needs. Some of the available books had either too many or too few lessons for an academic year. Some lessons were too long for an hour-long class, and some were too short. Some lessons were too difficult for the targeted age or too basic for higher levels. Some books were written without a 12-year curriculum in mind. Therefore the lessons in higher grades did not develop from the knowledge base of prior years. Sometimes extra emphasis was placed on one topic to the detriment of other important topics. Thus, we thought a balanced knowledge base was lost.

To offset this shortfall, we decided to develop a functional, comprehensive Islamic Studies curriculum for weekend schools in the West. We wanted a curriculum that would include everything that Muslim students growing up in the West would ideally need to know. We wanted to include topics based on the life experiences of students growing up in the West. Muslim children growing up in the U.S., Europe, and Australia are facing diverse challenges and conflicting pressures at school and in social settings. They are constantly influenced by the mainstream culture. We wanted Islamic lessons to address their issues from their perspective.

The curriculum alone would not be of any use without lessons based on the curriculum. The lessons had to be age-appropriate and suitable for the typical class duration of most schools. We began writing and editing the lessons over the next several years. Finally, in 2007 when we printed Islamic Studies Level 1 to Level 8 books in this series, they became instantly popular in many schools.

We are thankful to Allāh for giving us the ability to write these books. We pray to Allāh to accept our labor and make us successful in communicating the message of Islam. We hope Islamic schools and home schools in the U.S. and other countries will find these books useful. Any mistakes or errors in this series of books are our responsibility. We appreciate receiving meaningful comments and suggestions to improve these books.

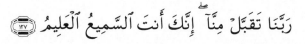

"Our Rabb! Accept from us, you indeed are the all-Hearing, all-Knowing." (2:127)

August 15, 2010

Husain A. Nuri
Mansur Ahmad

Preface to the Second Edition

All praise is due to Allāh alone. We are indebted to Him for this work and other works in this series. If it was not for His infinite grace, this work would never have been possible. It is because of His grace that in a relatively short period of time, the second edition of the book became due. The second edition provides the ability to improve the text, presentations, and layout without sacrificing the overall ease of use and appeal of the lessons.

We are grateful to Brenda Rusch for editing and proofreading the book on a short notice. She has not only eliminated basic grammatical, punctuation, and spelling errors, but also improved content flow, transitions and overall organization. We are also thankful to J. Maria Brown for reading the book and providing valuable suggestions. We thank all the teachers and home-schooling parents for adopting this book and other books in the series. We sincerely hope students, teachers, and parents will find the content of the book useful in their pursuit of knowledge. We welcome readers' thoughtful comments, criticism, and suggestions for the next edition of the book. May Allāh accept our small effort.

March 15, 2011   Husain A. Nuri
                                                                            Mansur Ahmad

Preface to the Third Edition

In the third edition of the book, we added a few clarifications in some of the chapters. We added these clarifications based on valuable editorial comments received from Muzahid Ahmad. We thankfully acknowledge his comments. We believe these clarifications made the lessons complete. We made minor layout changes without sacrificing the overall ease of use and appeal of the lessons.

We thank all the teachers and home-schooling parents for adopting this book and other books in the series. We sincerely hope students, teachers, and parents will find the content of the book useful in their pursuit of knowledge. We welcome readers' thoughtful comments, criticism, and suggestions for the next edition of the book. May Allāh accept our small effort.

September 15, 2013   Husain A. Nuri
                                                                            Mansur Ahmad

Table of Contents

APPENDICES

How to use this book effectively
Instructions for teachers and parents

The lessons in this book are designed to develop and reinforce understanding of Islam from the correct perspectives. The purpose is to help students understand the connection between the *deen* and the *dunya*. As with other books in the series, this book begins with a few topics on Allāh, and the Qur'ān. Relevant topics on the Qur'ān are included to give students a taste of serious studies on Islam. Keeping the importance of comparative religion in mind, a few topics were included. Several lessons are based on the life experiences and challenges of students growing up in the West.

The Level 10 book will ideally be used by high school students. In order to make the best use of the lessons, a teacher can adopt one of the following approaches. The teacher can ask the students to read the lesson before class and use class time for constructive discussion of the lesson. In this case, students will take the lead in the discussion, and the teacher will only facilitate the discussion. Another approach would be to assign a topic to a group of students to prepare and present to the class. The students will moderate the class discussion, and the teacher will only facilitate the discussion as needed.

A few lessons in the book are presented in table format. The content of each row and column should be carefully discussed.

Many of the lessons contain several Arabic āyāt. Ideally, the teacher or the students who are presenting the lesson should read the āyāt. It is not a requirement that the teacher should be a Hafiz of the Qur'ān, but it is advisable that the teacher know these āyāt well.

Homework lessons can be assigned to students or they can be used as discussion topics in the class.

Teaching Respect:

From an early age, students should be taught to show respect to Allāh, His Prophets, and His Angels. Teachers and parents are requested to mention the following:

Whenever the word Allāh appears in the book, please add the glorification, "*Subhāna-hu wa-Ta'ālā.*"

Whenever the word Muhammad, or other words indicating Muhammad, e.g., Rasulullah, the Prophet, or Nabi appears, please add the prayer, "*Salla-llāhu 'alaihi wa Sallam.*" We have used (S) in the book as a reminder of the prayer. Whenever students read the names of a prophet or an angel, please add the prayer "*Alai-hi-s Salām.*" This is noted by (A). Students should be taught to add the prayer "*Radi-allāhu 'an-hu*" for a khalifa or a male companion of Rasūlullāh (S). For a female companion, the prayer "*Radi-allāhu 'an-hā*" should be used. These are noted by (R) or (ra).

Suggestions:

Please provide your suggestions, corrections, and ideas to improve the book by sending an e-mail to the publisher at *weekendLearning@gmail.com*. It is a combined effort of the publisher, authors, teachers and parents to prepare our future ummah. May Allāh guide us all. Amin.

Understanding the Word "Allāh"

Objective of the Lesson:

Is the word "Allāh" a unique term in Arabic or is it a contraction of two or three words? This introductory lesson analyzes the use of the word "Allāh" among the Arabs, before and after Islam and connects it to other Semitic languages.

God

In this lesson, we will undertake an analytical study of the word "Allāh." How did the concept of a deity named "Allāh" originate in Arabia, particularly before the advent of Islam? Did Messenger Muhammad (S) introduce the term, or did he use an existing term to denote the one and only deity? Evidently these questions open up a whole new approach to understand "Allāh." To a Muslim child, the concept of Allāh as the One and Only Deity is not new. A Muslim child grows up with the knowledge of and belief in Allāh. However, the question remains: when we talk about "God" in English, does it mean Allāh or some other god? Many Islamic scholars argue whether Allāh can be appropriately translated into the English word "God." If so, does God, as understood in English, aptly represents Allāh—the One Deity all Muslims worship.

The purpose behind all of these questions is to help us understand the history of the word "Allāh." The history refers to the etymology of the term, how people used it, who did they mean when they used the term, how other religions used the term, and so on. To a Muslim, it does not matter whether He is Allāh or God—He is the One and Only Deity. The Qur'ān allows us to call upon God by any names, and urges us to call God by other qualifying names as well. Whatever name we use to call upon Allāh, He is the center of Islamic monotheism.

وَلِلَّهِ ٱلْأَسْمَآءُ ٱلْحُسْنَىٰ فَٱدْعُوهُ بِهَا

And to Allāh belongs all the finest names, therefore call upon Him by these names. (7:180)

Etymology: Miriam Webster dictionary defines etymology as the history of a linguistic form (a word) by tracing its development back to the time of its earliest recorded occurrence. Etymology also traces the transmission of the word from one language to another by analyzing the word in its component parts, by identifying its equivalents in other languages or by tracing it and its equivalents to a common form in an ancestral language.

Different opinions: Many Muslim scholars have discussed whether the term Allāh is a unique word or a contraction of two words. Most believe that the word "Allāh" is unique. It does not have any etymological example, and it is not a meaningful contraction of two or more words. According to them, the word "Allāh" is a unique term in Arabic that stands for a monotheistic deity. For example, the word "table" is a unique word, not formed by a contraction or an adaptation of other words. They believe explanations of the origin of the word "Allāh" reflect a false etymology.

Other scholars believe the word "Allāh" could be an adaptation of other words. This is an interesting theory worthy of further analysis. We will, therefore, try to examine the commonly mentioned etymologies of the word "Allāh" for the sake of academic interest.

Contraction of two words: Even if the word "Allāh" is believed to have been derived from the contraction of two words, His majesty and almightiness is not compromised. Some linguistics experts believe the term "Allāh" is derived from the contraction of two Arabic words:

al (meaning the), and

ilāh (meaning deity).

Here the word *ilāh* is a masculine word for deity. If the words are broken down, *al-ilāh* means "The God." The concept of "The God" was known to Arabs even before the Qur'ān was revealed. Several āyāt in the Qur'ān mention that if you asked the pagan Arabs who created the heavens and the earth, they would have invariably said, "Allāh."

وَلَئِن سَأَلْتَهُم مَّنْ خَلَقَ ٱلسَّمَـٰوَٰتِ وَٱلْأَرْضَ وَسَخَّرَ ٱلشَّمْسَ وَٱلْقَمَرَ لَيَقُولُنَّ ٱللَّهُ ۖ فَأَنَّىٰ يُؤْفَكُونَ ۝

And in case you ask them: "Who created the heavens and the earth, and subjected the sun and the moon?"— they will invariably say: "Allāh." Why are they then turning away? (29:61)

وَلَئِن سَأَلْتَهُم مَّنْ خَلَقَ ٱلسَّمَـٰوَٰتِ وَٱلْأَرْضَ لَيَقُولُنَّ خَلَقَهُنَّ ٱلْعَزِيزُ ٱلْعَلِيمُ ۝

And if you ask them: "Who has created the heavens and the earth?"— they will invariably say: "The Exalted in Might, the all-Knowing has created them." (43:9)

وَلَئِن سَأَلْتَهُم مَّنْ خَلَقَهُمْ لَيَقُولُنَّ ٱللَّهُ ۖ فَأَنَّىٰ يُؤْفَكُونَ ۝

And if you were to ask them who had created them, they would invariably say: "Allāh." Then why are they turning away? (43:87)

From these passages it appears that the word "Allāh" is a unique word standing for God. This is the viewpoint of the majority of the Muslim scholars.

However, other scholars argue that Arabs considered the word "Allāh" as a contraction of "al" and "ilāh", meaning "The God."

Interestingly, prior to Nabi Muhammad (S), no messengers came to the Quraish to teach them about Allāh.[28:46; 32:3] Therefore, the question arises as to how they came to know about *al-ilāh*. The answer is that the Arabs were accustomed to worshipping a "Supreme" God, "al ilāh" and credited Him with the creation of the Heavens and the Earth. Probably they learned about one God from Ismā'īl (A), who lived in Makkah long before the origin of the

Quraish tribe. The Arabs also worshipped multiple gods, who, they believed administered specific duties. Thus, the concept of monotheistic God was diluted into polytheistic gods.

At this point, it is important to note that one of the main pagan goddesses in Arabia was Allāt.[53:19] It is a contraction of three words: *al* + *ilāh* + *at*. You may already know that whenever the letter ت (ta) is added to the end of a noun or verb, it represents the feminine gender. For example, ka-ta-ba (ك ت ب) means (he) wrote, but ka-ta-bat (ك ت ب ت) means (she) wrote.

Thus, it is etymologically possible that the pagan Arabs believed 'Allāt' was a feminine counterpart of masculine Allāh. This is why some scholars thought the word "Allāh" was a contraction of two words.

Allāh as God and God as Allāh: People in the West, particularly people from other faiths, seem to be divided about whether their God is the same God whom Muslims worship. Is Allāh God, or is God Allāh? Despite the disagreements, it is not surprising to find that Muslims, Christians or Jews who speak native Arabic readily use the word "Allāh" to mean God. The term is used as a proper noun for God. In the Arabic translations of the Bible and the Torah, the word for God is nothing but Allāh. However, Allāh, as understood by Muslims, specifically refers to "The Only God." This One God is different from the Trinitarian concept of God in Christianity. The Trinity is a concept based on three gods merged into one god.

God in Semitic languages: In Arabic and Hebrew, the two Semitic languages, the word for God is closely related. In the very first book of the Bible, Genesis āyah 1:1 mentions God as Elōhīm, which is a plural of the Hebrew root word Elōah (הולא). Besides similarity in sound, the two names are similar in roots, spelling, and meaning. The root El (ל א) in Hebrew means God or divinity. In the Aramaic language, the language spoken by Jesus, the word for God is spelled *alep-lamed-heh* or A-L-H. This word closely corresponds to the Hebrew Elōah. The prefix "al-" in Arabic is similar to the suffix "–im" in Hebrew. The prefix "al-" is used in Arabic to emphasize "the," i.e., one specific being; but in Hebrew "–im" is a masculine plural suffix, grammatically used in singular form.

Allāh in Islam: In Islam, Allāh is neither a descriptive name nor a qualitative name. It is simply a proper name. In Arabic usage, Allāh is often described using the masculine gender "He," since in Arabic usage there is no neutral gender to describe Allāh. The feminine gender was not used as it would indicate gender of Allāh. Usage of the feminine gender would create confusion and would become problematic. For a long time, pagans believed Allāh's alleged progeny were all daughters.[16:57]

Many people from other religions think Allāh is a God "created" by Messenger Muhammad (S) or that he simply made use of an existing deity known by the name Allāh. The reason for this claim was the pagans knew about Allāh before Messenger Muhammad (S) arrived. For example, his father was Adbullah, which means servant of Allāh.

The fact remains that all past messengers, including Ādam, Nūh, Ibrāhīm, Yūsuf, Mūsā, 'Isā (A) and others, worshipped Allāh. Muslims often name their children after one of the qualifying names of Allāh, but a person is never named Allāh. It is His exclusive name.

1. In the Hebrew language, the word for God is represented by which of the following words?

    A.   Allāh.
    B.   Ishwar.
    C.   Elōah.
    D.   Khuda.
    E.   Rasul.

2. Which Arabic letter at the end of a word could mean it is a feminine gender?

    A.   Only the letter "ta" ت
    B.   Only the letter "ya" ي
    C.   Both the letters "ta" and "ya" ت ي
    D.   Letters "ta" and "ya" and "fa" ف ي ت
    E.   Letters "fa" and "ba" and "tha" ث ب ف

3. Read āyah 19:23. Which Arabic word in the āyah is a feminine term? Write the actual Arabic word.

    Qalat

4. Check the national flags from Middle Eastern countries, and identify which country's flag has the word "Allāh" in it.

    Iran, Syria, Saudi Arabia

5. Based on the lesson about the history of the name Allāh, which of the following choices is correct about the term "Allāh"?

    A.   It is a proper name not formed by a contraction of two or more words.
    B.   It is formed by a contraction of two words.
    C.   It is a derivative of the Hebrew Eloah.
    D.   It is a masculine word standing for God in Arabic.
    E.   None of the above.

6. In Arabic, the word *ilāh* stands for god, and *al-* stands for the definitive article. What are your thoughts about the word "Allāh" as a contraction of "al-" and "ilah"?

    Al-lah, Al-Dea Mi wa

7. In Arabic usage, Allāh is often mentioned using the masculine gender. Which of the following choices gives a valid reason for this usage?

    A.   Masculine use of gender is only for the matter of linguistic ease.

    B.   Neutral or abstract pronouns (it, that, etc.) would alienate God from man's life.

    C.   Feminine use of gender would be unconventional, as it might specifically indicate the gender of God.

    D.   Use of the masculine gender is conventional so nobody forms ideas about God's gender.

    (E.)   All of the above.

8. In the debate about whether Allāh is God or God is Allāh, which of the following choices would be correct from the perspective of a Muslim?

    A.   The term God cannot be accepted since it is used by Christians.

    B.   As long as God means "the only God," it is acceptable.

    C.   As long as both stand for a "monotheistic god," without reference to subordinate gods, it is acceptable.

    (D.)   Only (b) and (c).

    E.   Only (a) and (c).

9. In āyāt 53:19–20, the names of three goddesses are mentioned. Read the āyāt and write down the three names of the goddesses.

Allat , Al-Uzaa , Al-Manat

10. In āyah 4:48, the Qur'ān states some sin will not be pardoned. Read the āyah to answer the following.

Sin that will not be pardoned: _~~Killing~~ Shirk Allah does not forgive association with Him_

Sins that might be pardoned: _~~Satan lied~~ He forgives what's less than that for whom He Wills_

Al-Fātihah: *An Analysis of its Message*

> **Objective of the Lesson:**
>
> This lesson provides an analytical study of the introductory sūrah in the Qur'ān to show that the sūrah Al-Fātihah is not only the beginning of the Qur'ān, but also the essence of the Qur'ān. The analysis also shows why the sūrah is one of the finest prayers that people from all faiths can invoke.

One of the best-known sūrahs in the entire Qur'ān is Sūrah al-Fātihah. Muslims recite the sūrah several times a day during their obligatory prayers. The significance of the sūrah is tremendous. The sūrah is not only the beginning of the Qur'ān, but also the essence of the Qur'ān. In this lesson, we review the meaning of this sūrah and then try to analyze its inner majesty and literary style.

Time of revelation: Islamic scholars disagree about the exact chronological order in which the sūrah was revealed. Jalauddin Suyūtī indicated that it was revealed in the early part of the Makkan era. John Rodwell believed it was eighth in the chronological order of revelation. William Muir believed it was sixth in the chronological order of revelation. One of the Shī'ah Traditions indicates that 'Alī ibn Abū Tālib narrated that this sūrah was the first revelation. However, based on several adadīth reported by Bukhārī, Tirmidhī and Muslim, the first revealed āyāt were unmistakably the five āyāt of sūrah al-Alaq. It is possible that al-Fātihah was the first sūrah revealed in its entirety at that time. Thus, 'Alī's view that it was the "first" sūrah is valid with many theologians. In āyah 15:87, the Qur'ān says:

وَلَقَدْ ءَاتَيْنَكَ سَبْعًا مِّنَ ٱلْمَثَانِى وَٱلْقُرْءَانَ ٱلْعَظِيمَ ۝

And truly We have given you seven oft-repeated, and the Grand Qur'ān. (15:87)

Sūrah al-Hijr, where this āyah belongs, is a Makkan revelation. Thus, it again confirms that sūrah Fātihah was already revealed prior to the revelation of sūrah al-Hijr.

Names of the sūrah: The meaning of the title "al-Fātihah" is 'the opening.' The word is derived from the root *fataha*, which means 'to break open.' The meaning aptly points to an opening—a doorway or an avenue that leads readers to a path, which the sūrah later describes as the "Straight Path."

Due to the immense significance of the sūrah in Islamic theology, it is often symbolically described by many other names, which attests to its diverse importance and meaning. The two best-known names are *Fātihat Al-Kitāb* (literally, the opening of the book) and *Umm Al-Kitāb* (literally, the mother of the book). The word *umm* means mother. Symbolically, mother is the central body from which offspring originate. Thus, *Umm Al-Kitāb* means this chapter contains the essence of the entire Qur'an. It provides a summary of all the Qur'anic principles that are enunciated later in the rest of the Qur'an. Another name is *Sab'a Al-Mathānī* (literally, seven oft-repeated [āyāt])[15:87] because it is repeated several times during each of the daily prayers.

Sūrah al-Fātihah is also known as *As-Salāt, Al-Hamd, Ash-Shīfa, Ar-Ruqya* and *al-Kanz*. As-Salāt (the Prayer) signifies that sūrah al-Fātihah is a perfect invocation as well as part of our daily prayers. *Al-Hamd* (the Praise) signifies man's gratitude towards Allāh and also the realization of his dependence on Him. *Ash-shīfa* (the cure) suggests that sūrah al-Fātihah provides the remedy for all spiritual diseases and devotional imbalances. The name *Ar-Ruqya* (the Charmer) implies that the sūrah acts as a charm to thwart evil and provides protection against Shaitān and his instigations. Lastly, sūrah al-Fātihah is called *Al-Kanz* (the Treasure) by virtue of the sūrah containing an endless treasure of knowledge.

Umm Al-Kitāb: The most significant title of the sūrah is *Umm Al-Kitāb*. This title points out that the sūrah al-Fātihah is an abridged version of the fundamental principles enunciated in the Qur'ān. These principles are as follows:

1. Oneness and uniqueness of Allāh,

2. Originator, sustainer, and sovereign of the entire universe,

3. Everything in the universe is dependent upon Him,

بِسْمِ ٱللَّهِ ٱلرَّحْمَٰنِ ٱلرَّحِيمِ ۝	1. WITH the name of Allāh, most Gracious, most Rewarding.
ٱلْحَمْدُ لِلَّهِ رَبِّ ٱلْعَٰلَمِينَ ۝	2. The Praise belongs to Allāh, the Lord of all the worlds;
ٱلرَّحْمَٰنِ ٱلرَّحِيمِ ۝	3. the Rahman, the Rahim;
مَٰلِكِ يَوْمِ ٱلدِّينِ ۝	4. Master of the Day of Judgment.
إِيَّاكَ نَعْبُدُ وَإِيَّاكَ نَسْتَعِينُ ۝	5. You alone we do worship, and to You alone we ask for help.
ٱهْدِنَا ٱلصِّرَٰطَ ٱلْمُسْتَقِيمَ ۝	6. Guide us on the Straight Path—
صِرَٰطَ ٱلَّذِينَ أَنْعَمْتَ عَلَيْهِمْ غَيْرِ ٱلْمَغْضُوبِ عَلَيْهِمْ وَلَا ٱلضَّآلِّينَ ۝	7. the path of those upon whom You have bestowed favors; not of those upon whom wrath is brought down, or of those gone astray.

4. Human beings are ultimately responsible and accountable to Allāh,

5. Allāh is the Master of Day of Judgment,

6. Allāh is the only deity man can worship,

7. Allāh is the only source that can really guide and help,

8. The principle of guidance comes from the institution of sending messengers,

9. The messengers brought guidance and were rightly guided,

10. Islam is the continuation of the same divine teachings brought by other messengers,

11. The followers of the messengers were rightly guided,

12. In recognition of Allāh's blessings, man surrenders to Him,

13. Guidance is not automatic, so the believers must continuously seek guidance to remain on the Straight Path,

14. Non-believers can hope to gain guidance by requesting "Guide us to the Straight Path,"

15. Those who do not follow the Straight Path go astray, and upon them wrath is brought down.

Sequential progress: There is a clearly defined sequential progress in the sūrah. A renowned Muslim scholar, Abdel Haleem, identified the sequences as:

(a) **Invocation** – first four āyāt

(b) **Affirmation** – fifth āyah

(c) **Petition** – sixth and seventh āyāt

Invocation: The first four āyāt of the sūrah are an Invocation. It is meant to glorify the Lord, acknowledge His almightiness and express sincere gratitude. It shows that man's relationship to Allāh is that of dependence for everything. In the first part, when the sūrah says, *All praise belongs to Allāh*, it is stated without any reference to the reader or worshipper. In other words, the statement is not made from a specific viewpoint; it is neutral. It does not matter whether the praise is made by man, by worshipper, by angel or by nature—the praise belongs to Allāh. The first part also recognizes Allāh as the Master of the Day of Judgment.

Affirmation: Affirmation is the next logical step after the Invocation. The second part includes āyah number five, which states: *You alone we do worship, and to You alone we ask for help.*

Only when man approves and acknowledges the first part can the second part follow naturally. In other words, if man does not accept and agree to the Invocation part of the sūrah, he cannot logically conclude the second part. Of all things, who is logically most worthy to be worshipped? Who is most worthy of being sought for help? Obviously, the answer lies in the first part of the sūrah. The being most worthy of worship is Allāh, Lord of the Universe, the Most Beneficent, Most Merciful and Master of the Day of Judgment.

Now that man recognizes that there is a Day of Judgment, he must prepare for the Day by surrendering to Allāh. He affirms that Allāh is the only deity worthy of worship. Look at how man affirms his statement. The object "you" (*iyyāka*) is repeated twice—first before the verb, *naʿbudu* (literally, we worship) and again before another verb, *nastaʿīn* (literally, we ask for help). This placement of *iyyāka* is significant, because it places emphasis on the word "you," and, thus, excludes everything else from being a deity.

إِيَّاكَ نَعْبُدُ وَإِيَّاكَ نَسْتَعِينُ ۝

The Invocation is stated in the third person. But in the Affirmation, the worshipper appears on the scene. He not only worships Allāh, but also seeks

His help. The shift from third person to second person, a beautiful Qur'ānic style, begins a two-way process where man worships Allāh, and, in return, he expects help from Him. Allāh is not only the recipient, but He is also a giver.

Petition: In the third and final sequence, man makes a petition. In the second part of the sūrah, man recognizes that Allāh is the only One worthy of worship and of asking for help, but in the third part he actually makes a request: a request for guidance. The guidance requested is spiritual guidance, but the request is made in the image of a straight path (*sirātal mustaqīm*). It appears that man is standing at a crossroad and is not sure which path will ultimately beneficial.

The petition for guidance recognizes that Allāh knows which path will lead to a blessed destination and which path will lead to destruction.

The Straight Path: Continuing with the third and final sequence of the Petition, we now see that man is recognizing that there are fundamentally two kinds of paths. There are some inherent characteristics of both paths, which he explains later. The worshipper wants to follow the Straight Path. This path is not only the surest path, but also the shortest to the destination. The worshipper also knows this path was tested by others and was proven right.

Even if it is argued that the worshipper does not know whether the path was tested earlier, he submits to Allāh to guide him on the path that He has blessed. Thus, even in the petition, the worshipper is humble enough to leave the decision to Allāh. He simply points out that three criteria should be available on the path. These criteria are a check-and-balance mechanism so that he can understand that the path is indeed the Straight Path. The Straight Path is:

(i) Blessed and favored by Allāh,

(ii) The path that will not incur anger,

(iii) The path that will not lead him astray

Style of the sūrah: The sūrah contains 29 words in Arabic. These are written in seven short āyāt in rhymed prose. In the first āyah, the proper name of God is mentioned as Allāh. Then it mentions two of his most significant attributes—Most Beneficent, Most Merciful. The translation does not capture the entire essence of *ar-rahmān* and *ar-rahīm*. The translation cannot capture the inherent beauty of the soft-sounding consonants in the first part of the sūrah or the contrasting higher intonation in the later part, particularly when it talks about those who incur anger and those who go astray.

When the seventh āyah talks about anger (*ghadab*) and astray (*dalla*), we note the use of two heavy-sounding letters *gahyn* (غ) and *dād* (ض). These letters, used twice in the āyah, were not used in any of the preceding āyāt. There is nothing wrong with the usage, but symbolically the letters seem to intensify the gravity of the situation.

غَيْرِ ٱلْمَغْضُوبِ عَلَيْهِمْ وَلَا ٱلضَّآلِّينَ ۝

The entire sūrah also carries a high degree of voicing and nasality, which not only produces a pleasing effect when recited, but also slows the reciter down from quickly pronouncing the words. The rhymes comes at crucial moments — "...īm" and "...īn" —making the reader pause before proceeding to the next āyah.

In conclusion, we pray to Allāh to guide us on the Straight Path, the path of those upon whom He has bestowed favors; not of those upon whom wrath is brought down, and not of those who have gone astray.

1. According to the lesson, into how many sequences can Sūrah al-Fātihah be divided?

    A.   One sequence.
    B.   Two sequences.
    C.   Three sequences.
    D.   Four sequences.
    E.   Seven sequences.

2. Under the "affirmation" sequence of Sūrah al-Fātihah, what two affirmations are made by the reciter?

    A.   Guidance and blessings.
    B.   Guidance and removal from anger.
    C.   Guidance and help.
    D.   Removal from anger and protection from going astray.
    E.   Help and worship.

3. In the "Petition" section of Sūrah al-Fātihah, what is the most significant request of the reciter?

    A.   Help.
    B.   Guidance.
    C.   Forgiveness.
    D.   Blessings.
    E.   Removal of anger.

4. Which of the following choices correctly identifies the key aspect(s) of the Straight Path?

    A.   The Straight Path is already tested by others.
    B.   The Straight Path is a blessed path.
    C.   The Straight Path is the path to success.
    D.   All of the above.
    E.   None of the above.

5. What are the two heavy letters used in the seventh āyah of Sūrah al-Fātihah, but not used in the other āyāt of the sūrah?

    A.   Letters غ and ض
    B.   Letters ق and ض
    C.   Letters ع and ل
    D.   Letters غ and ح
    E.   Letters ي and ح

6. Which of the following inferences can be drawn from the fact that the Straight Path was blessed earlier?

    A.   Islam is a continuation of the Straight Path shown to earlier generations.
    B.   All past messengers walked on the Straight Path.
    C.   Believers in the past were all blessed.
    D.   Allāh sent guidance to all communities in the past.
    (E.)   All of the above.

7. In which āyah of Sūrah al-Fātihah does the mode of address change from the third person to the second person?

    A.   Third āyah.
    B.   Fourth āyah.
    (C.)   Fifth āyah.
    D.   Sixth āyah.
    E.   Seventh āyah.

8. The literary style of Sūrah al-Fātihah shows that it contains a certain number of key Arabic words. How many key words are used in the sūrah?

    A.   20 words.
    B.   25 words.
    (C.)   29 words.
    D.   35 words.
    E.   50 words.

9. What are the three aspects specifically mentioned about the Straight Path in Sūrah al-Fātihah?

    (A.)   Blessed path, will not incur anger, and will not lead astray.
    B.   Judgment, guidance, and lack of anger.
    C.   Blessed path, will not incur anger, and will not help.
    D.   Help, mercy and praise.
    E.   Anger, mercy and forgiveness.

10. Are there several paths that can lead people to Jannah? Explain your answer with clear evidence.

There is only one path, The straight path.

Al-Fātihah *vs* The Lord's Prayer

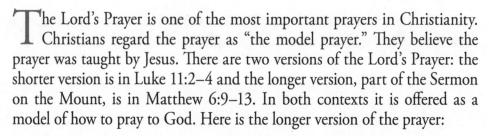

Objective of the Lesson:

The Lord's Prayer is one of the most important prayers in Christianity. The prayer is often compared to Sūrah al-Fātihah. This lesson provides an analytical study of both prayers to highlight the objectives and scope of each prayer.

The Lord's Prayer is one of the most important prayers in Christianity. Christians regard the prayer as "the model prayer." They believe the prayer was taught by Jesus. There are two versions of the Lord's Prayer: the shorter version is in Luke 11:2–4 and the longer version, part of the Sermon on the Mount, is in Matthew 6:9–13. In both contexts it is offered as a model of how to pray to God. Here is the longer version of the prayer:

[9] Our Father, who art in Heaven, Hallowed be thy name.

[10] Thy kingdom come. Thy will be done on earth, as it is in heaven.

[11] Give us this day our daily bread.

[12] And forgive us our debts, as we forgive our debtors.

[13] And lead us not into temptation, but deliver us from evil: For thine is the kingdom, the power, and the glory, for ever. Amen.

Many Christian scholars have often compared Sūrah al-Fātihah to the Lord's Prayer with two objectives: (1) To show that the Lord's Prayer is a superior prayer and (2) to belittle Islam. They have argued that Sūrah al-Fātihah was "modeled after the Lord's Prayer" and it is a weak model. However, Muslims have traditionally showed no interest in comparing these two prayers, and have had no problem accepting that these two prayers have some similarities. In fact, they would readily accept the similarities since they believe the Qur'ān affirms all past scriptures, including the Bible.

Our purpose here is to compare the prayers to show the inherent differences and similarities in the scope and magnitude of the prayers.

Sūrah Al-Fātihah	The Lord's Prayer
Sūrah al-Fātihah is the first chapter of the Qur'ān.	The Lord's Prayer is placed within the New Testament.
Sūrah al-Fātihah encapsulates the entire essence of the Qur'ān.	The Lord's Prayer does not contain the essence of the Bible.
The central theme of the petition to God is "Guide us on the right path."	The petition to God begins with "Give us this day our daily bread." No spiritual motives are seen in the petition.
The petition is for guidance. Guidance is forward-looking, required by anyone in any action—whether moral or spiritual.	The petition is about specific items like bread and forgiveness of debts. The word 'debt' is used in the sense of wrongdoings.
Guidance on the right path encompasses guidance in all matters. It is a broad appeal aimed at covering every step and action in life.	The petition not to fall into temptation is one of the possible traps in life. Deliverance from evil is excellent, yet the issue of guidance is missing.
The praise belongs to God—in His entirety.	The praise is only of His name.
Praise emphasizes the attributes of God being Rabb. The quality of Rabb is one who is Master, and the one who Sustains, Provides, Rules, Rewards, Creates, and Maintains.	Praise is limited to identifying God as "father." Thus, it describes the relationship between God and man as that of father and son.
God is referred to as Lord of all the Worlds.	Nothing is specified about His absolute almightiness. He is "who art in Heaven"—thus, seems to be remote in Heaven.
Praise emphasizes God being Gracious, Merciful, and Master of the Day of Judgment.	Praise is limited to His name.
Lord of all the Worlds—the farthest world, billions of light years away, and this world, closest to us. Thus, God is also close to human beings.	"Who art in Heaven" distances God from the earth and from humans.
We ask for help—it encompasses all areas and all aspects in man's life.	Prayer asks for specific things: bread, forgiveness of sins, forgiveness of wrongdoings and prevention of temptation.
God is referred to as Lord of all the Worlds. He is a universal God. He is not the God of Muslims or the God of Arabs.	Referring to God as "Our Father" confines Him down to the limits of Christianity. "Father" is the exclusive mode of address in Christianity.

Some notes: The Lord's Prayer addresses God as "Father," thus describing the relationship between God and man as that of father and son. It subtly hints of the Christian belief that Jesus is the Son of God. Muslims would have a serious problem with accepting God as "father"—a word that suggests biological ties. A father definitely has his father. Does God as "father" have His father too? On the other hand, by addressing God as "Father," Christianity suggests that mankind is a single brotherhood. The same concept is also present in Islam as the Qur'ān says mankind is a single community.[2:213]

The phrase "Thy kingdom will come. Thy will be done" means that the true goal of human dwelling on earth is to establish justice, and to create happiness and success. The Qur'ān conveys a similar message. The purpose behind placing Ādam on earth was for mankind to serve as khalīfah. A khalīfah would serve as a representative of Allāh, thus helping to establish His principles on earth. To that effect, establishing justice is one of the central principles in Islam.

Praying for daily bread, forgiveness of debts (meaning wrongdoings) and not to being lead into temptation seems to address certain specific needs and problems of people. Here the prayer's limited scope prevents the worshipper from seeing the bigger picture. The bigger picture is guidance on the Straight Path, to achieve good in this life and good in the Hereafter.

It is true that increasing resources and curtailment of wrongdoings would bring much good to humanity. In sūrah al-Fātihah, prayer for guidance on the right path has a twofold petition—(a) guidance in earthly matters, and (b) guidance in spiritual matters. Both matters are ever-changing and ever-evolving in human life; therefore, guidance is an ongoing process. As human beings continue to receive guidance, both their earthly and spiritual matters will be resolved.

The Lord's Prayer does not address the ultimate destiny of human beings. On the other hand, al-Fātihah recognizes the Day of Judgment and seeks guidance in order to face the Day successfully. Al-Fātihah describes man's destiny on this earth as well as in the Hereafter.

The prayer for not leading us into temptation and for delivering us from evil is a wonderful appeal. The Qur'ān teaches us to shun the evil and temptation that lurks in every phase of human life.

Conclusion: We should remember that The Lord's Prayer has a different purpose and objective. Its scope is different from the scope of Sūrah al-Fātihah. As previously mentioned, Muslims are not interested in comparing the superiority of one prayer over another. Each prayer has continued to support and motivate the followers of each religion for thousands of years.

1. In which two books in the Bible is the Lord's Prayer mentioned?

    A.   Matthew and John.
    B.   Matthew and Luke.
    C.   Genesis and Mark.
    D.   Exodus and Leviticus.
    E.   Psalms and Luke.

2. Christians could use sūrah Fātihah as their prayer without any objection as it does not violate any of their fundamental teachings.   True / False

3. A Muslim could use the Lord's Prayer, but there is one element in the prayer that would be difficult for a Muslim to readily accept. What is that?

    A.   Asking for daily bread.
    B.   Asking for forgiveness of wrongdoings.
    C.   Asking not to fall into temptation.
    D.   Addressing God as "father."
    E.   All of the above.

4. Both Sūrah al-Fātihah and the Lord's Prayer make important petitions to God. What are the main petitions of each prayer?

    A.   In al-Fātihah it is about praise. In the Lord's Prayer, it is about guidance.
    B.   In al-Fātihah it is about guidance. In the Lord's Prayer, it is about the Right Path.
    C.   In al-Fātihah it is about guidance. In the Lord's Prayer, it is about daily bread.
    D.   In al-Fātihah it is about relief. In the Lord's Prayer, it is about guidance.
    E.   In al-Fātihah it is about forgiveness. In the Lord's Prayer, it is about wrongdoing.

5. The Lord's Prayer makes a petition to God to provide a few things. Which choice below lists the correct request?

    A.   Daily food and daily clothing.
    B.   Daily bread and forgiveness of wrongdoings.
    C.   Daily bread and forgiveness of future sins.
    D.   Daily food and daily survival.
    E.   Daily food and wealth without debt.

6. How is praise of the Lord different in Sūrah al-Fātihah and in the Lord's Prayer?
    A.   In al-Fātihah, all praise is to the Lord, but in the Lord's Prayer, praise is to the Father.
    B.   In al-Fātihah, all praise is to the Lord, but in the Lord's Prayer, praise is to His name.
    C.   In al-Fātihah, all praise is to the Father, but in the Lord's Prayer, praise is to the Lord.
    D.   In al-Fātihah, all praise is to Heaven, but in the Lord's Prayer, praise is to the Father.
    E.   In al-Fātihah, all praise is to Heaven, but in the Lord's Prayer, praise is to His name.

7. What four specific things does the Lord's Prayer ask for:

A. ....

B. ....

C. ....

D. ....

8. How is the essence of Sūrah al-Fātihah different from the essence of The Lord's Prayer?

A. Al-Fātihah sums up the entire essence of the Qur'ān, The Lord's Prayer sums up the Bible.
B. Al-Fātihah sums up the entire essence of the Qur'ān, while The Lord's Prayer does not sum up the Bible.
C. Al-Fātihah sums up the entire essence of the Qur'ān, while The Lord's Prayer sums up the Tawrat.
D. Al-Fātihah sums up the entire essence of the Qur'ān, while The Lord's Prayer sums up the Zabur.
E. Al-Fātihah sums up the essence of Rasūlullāh (S), while The Lord's Prayer sums up the teachings of Jesus.

9. Explain the significance of praying for guidance, as in Sūrah al-Fātihah, over seeking protection from falling into temptation in The Lord's Prayer.

....

....

....

10. Explain how the phrase *Rabbul 'alamīn* describes Allāh compared to God being in Heaven in the Lord's Prayer.

....

....

Muhkam and Mutashābihat Āyāt

Objective of the Lesson:

The Qur'ān has fundamentally two different types of āyāt. This lesson provides a basic understanding of the two types of āyāt that will help students appreciate the scope of the Qur'ānic message with greater ease.

As with all good essays or books of literature, the Qur'ān has its own unique style and approach. The author of the Qur'ān is Allāh and He has employed certain methodologies to convey a divine message for humanity. Since the message of the Qur'ān is universal and for all periods of time, it must be told in a manner best suited for people across different geographical regions, times, cultures and intellects. The message of the Qur'ān must also be able to address unique socio-political and economic circumstances arising from different periods of time. In order to achieve this objective, the Qur'ān employed a distinctive linguistic style and explained the style to benefit readers.

Types of ayats: In āyah seven of Sūrah Al-e-'Imrān, the Qur'ān says its āyāt are of two types. Some of the āyāt are fundamental or decisive, and other āyāt are allegorical. Let us read the āyah:

هُوَ ٱلَّذِىٓ أَنزَلَ عَلَيْكَ ٱلْكِتَٰبَ مِنْهُ ءَايَٰتٌ مُّحْكَمَٰتٌ هُنَّ أُمُّ ٱلْكِتَٰبِ وَأُخَرُ مُتَشَٰبِهَٰتٌ فَأَمَّا ٱلَّذِينَ فِى قُلُوبِهِمْ زَيْغٌ فَيَتَّبِعُونَ مَا تَشَٰبَهَ مِنْهُ ٱبْتِغَآءَ ٱلْفِتْنَةِ وَٱبْتِغَآءَ تَأْوِيلِهِۦ وَمَا يَعْلَمُ تَأْوِيلَهُۥٓ إِلَّا ٱللَّهُ وَٱلرَّٰسِخُونَ فِى ٱلْعِلْمِ يَقُولُونَ ءَامَنَّا بِهِۦ كُلٌّ مِّنْ عِندِ رَبِّنَا وَمَا يَذَّكَّرُ إِلَّآ أُو۟لُوا۟ ٱلْأَلْبَٰبِ ۝

He it is Who has revealed the Book, where some āyāt are decisive, these are the Mother of the Scripture, and others are allegorical. Then as to those in whose hearts there is perversity, they in fact follow the allegorical part of it seeking trouble and seeking to give it interpretations. But no one knows the interpretation of it except Allāh. And the trustworthy in knowledge would say: "We believe in it—the whole (of it) is from the presence of our Lord." And no one minds (this rule of interpretation) except those who possess understanding. (3:7)

If you read the Arabic āyah, the fundamental or decisive āyāt are stated to be *muhkam* āyāt. The word *muhkam* is derived from *hakama,* meaning "to govern," "to have power over," "to command," or "to direct." *Muhkamat* āyāt are clear, plain, perspicuous and devoid of any ambiguity. These āyāt are further qualified as being the Mother of the Scripture, or *Umm al-Kitāb.* By stating these āyāt as *Umm al-Kitāb,* the Qur'ān states the fundamental and decisive nature of the āyāt. These āyāt carry a definite meaning, and, consequently, provide a singular, unambiguous message. The word *umm,* although translated literally as "mother," implies the essence, basis, principle or matrix.[13:39; 43:4]

Other āyāt are called allegorical āyāt or *mutashābih* āyāt. The word is derived from *shabbah* (literally, to liken). In 39:23, Allāh calls the Qur'ān *kitāban mutashābihan,* i.e., a book conformable to itself or repeated itself. The word *mushābihāt,* therefore, means something that has a metaphorical, figurative, or allegorical meaning. The allegorical or figurative āyāt are those that are likely to provide more than one plausible explanation.

Three criteria: Based on the analysis above, we can now see the differences between *muhkamat* and *mutashābihat* āyāt.

Muhkamat:

- Carry a fundamental, unambiguous message.
- Have one precise meaning.
- Are the source from which other principles can be derived.

Mutashābihat:

- Deep meanings of the āyāt are known only to Allāh.
- Āyāt require further explanation.
- Āyāt have more than one level of understanding.

Examples of muhkamat: Here are some examples of *muhkamat* āyāt:

Every soul will taste death. (3:185; 21:35; 29:57)

O you who believe, fasting is prescribed for you as it was prescribed to those who preceded you so that you may attain taqwa. (2:183)

They ask you as to what they should spend. Say, 'whatever good things you spend, it is for the parents and the kins and the orphans and the needy and the wayfarers.' Whatever good you do, Allāh indeed knows it. (2:215)

These āyāt are clear, precise and unambiguous in their meanings. In the Qur'ān, the āyāt dealing with legal matters, such as inheritance, marriage, divorce, halāl and harām, prohibition, alcohol, gambling, and so forth. belong to the muhkamat category.

Examples of mutashābihat: Here are a few examples of *mutashābihat* āyāt:

He is established on the Throne of Power... (7:54)

If We had sent the Qur'ān on a mountain, you would surely have seen it falling down, breaking due to fear of Allāh...(59:21)

We certainly conferred upon Dāwūd grace from Ourselves. You mountains! Turn with him and the birds. (34:10)

On that day We shall roll up the heaven like the rolling of the scroll of writing... (21:104)

Rules of interpretation: *Muhkam* and *Mutashābih* āyāt provide key guidelines for interpreting the Qur'ān, and more importantly, for interpreting the messages in a manner that would reflect upon its own teachings. Readers of the Qur'ān will run the risk of misunderstanding some of its messages if they fail to understand the significance of *Muhkam* and *Mutashābih* āyāt.

Based on the *Muhkam* and *Mutashābih* ruling of a āyah, we can understand whether its message is clear and uniform or whether it speaks in dual tones. The ruling explains the extent of the interpretation of a āyah based on analogy or reasoning. The ruling also explains whether the interpretation of a āyah, based on the current knowledge of the commentator, is valid with respect to the teachings in other āyāt. The example below illustrates this point.

Medical science has understood the details of human embryology only recently. The Qur'ān has accurately explained some of the details more than 1,400 years ago. Any commentary of these āyāt written a thousand years ago was bound to be limited by the knowledge available at that time. Today, these commentaries may appear to be shallow, inconsistent, and off the mark. Similarly, our understanding of many āyāt will undergo changes in another hundred years with the further advancement of knowledge and technology.

The rulings of *Muhkam* and *Mutashābih* also clarify how much variation in the basic teachings of the Qur'ān can be accommodated, and the potential danger is in these interpretations.

---

from hadith

It is reported that Rasūlullāh (S) said, "that which is lawful is plain and that which is unlawful is plain, and between them are doubtful matters about which not many people know." (Bukhari and Muslim)

Earlier, we learned that the allegorical or figurative āyāt are those that are liable to provide more than one plausible explanation. The question is: while interpreting the allegorical āyāt, can the interpretation override the teachings of *muhkam* āyāt? How far does the interpretation of the allegorical āyāt go?

Let us look at the following example where the āyāt command us to eat only that meat on which Allāh's name has been pronounced, and not to eat the meat if the name was not pronounced at the time of slaughtering.

Then you eat of that on which the name of Allāh has been mentioned, if you are believers in His message. (6:118)

And do not eat of that on which Allāh's name has not been mentioned, for it is surely a disobedience. And certainly Shaitān will inspire their allies to dispute with you; and if you obey them, you will surely become polytheists. (6:121)

The command in the āyāt is clear and decisive, therefore *muhkam* in nature. If the ruling is not to eat any meat on which Allāh's name has been not been pronounced at the time of slaughtering. If the ruling of these two *muhkam* āyāt is ignored while reading a third āyah, we will put us in jeopardy. Now let us read the third āyah:

This day the good things have been made lawful for you. And the food of those who have been given the Scripture is lawful for you, and your food is lawful for them... (5:5)

When this āyah is read without further analysis, it seems that the Qur'ān has allowed us to eat food of the People of the Book without any qualification. Is every meat available in Western supermarkets and fast food restaurants halāl for Muslims? What about those meats that are prepared by stunning the animal, a method clearly prohibited in the Qur'ān.[5:3] What about a swine prepared by the People of the Book—is that permissible too?

The ruling in āyah 6:118 and 121 is clear that if Allāh's name was not pronounced at the time of slaughtering, the meat is not permissible. How does one balance all these āyāt correctly?

The food of the People of the Book is lawful only if the meat is prepared by properly slaughtering the animal, and the name of God is mentioned at the time of slaughtering. This instruction can be found in the scriptures of the People of the Book (for details, see the Level 9 book).

The purpose of *mutashābihat* is not to obscure the meaning of the Qur'ān, but to provide a crucial function in the interpretation of its messages. If there is any ambiguity in understanding one of the messages of the Qur'ān, the rulings given in the *muhkam* āyāt must settle the dispute.

Caution about mutashābihat: Those who do not follow the guidelines above for *muhkam* and *mutashābihat* āyāt will create trouble or dissension (*fitnah*) by arbitrarily interpreting (*ta'wil*) the Qur'ān based on their own desires, and by relying solely on the *mutashābihat* āyāt without referencing the supportive unambiguous āyāt. People who tend to do this are said to have perversity in their hearts. Their main intention is to align the divine message to their own ways of thinking and gain support for what they are doing. This caution is applicable to Muslims, who follow the Qur'ān as much as it is applicable to non-Muslims who interpret specific āyāt of the Qur'ān to malign the religion.

No one but Allāh knows: Āyah 3:7 says that no one knows the hidden meanings of the *mutashābihat* āyāt except Allāh. It is true that some of the aspects of heaven and hell, resurrection, attributes of Allāh, eternal life, purposes of creation, and so forth are conveyed in allegorical terms, often simplified in common language. Yet the true meaning or realities of these things are beyond the grasp of human understanding.

Does this mean human beings will never understand the *mutashābihat* āyāt or that the Qur'ān is unintelligible? How do we address this issue when we read āyāt 41:3, 43:2 and 44:58, where the Qur'ān says it is easy to understand? The answer is given in the āyāt when the Qur'ān praises those who believe the entire message is from Allāh. From this we can see that Allāh strongly recommends reading and interpreting the Qur'ān holistically, i.e., relating to and connecting to the message in its entirety.

Only the steadfast in knowledge and those who possess understanding will believe in the whole of the message through proper study and research.[38:29; 47:24] The last sentence in āyāt 38:29 fortifies the fact that people who possess understanding can comprehend the *muhkam* and *mutashābih* āyāt. On the subject of *mutashābihat*, we can conclude that the greater the efforts extended to understand the message of the Qur'ān, the greater the reward.

1. Which of the following choices correctly states the symbolic meaning of the Muhkam āyāt of the Qur'ān?

 A. They are the figurative āyāt.
 B. They are the mother of the book.
 C. They are the most ambiguous āyāt.
 D. They are the mother of the believers.
 E. All of the above.

2. Which of the following statements is correct about Muhkam and Mutashābihat āyāt?

 A. Muhkam āyāt can override the meaning of the Mutashābihat āyāt.
 B. Mutashābihat āyāt can override the meaning of the Muhkam āyāt.
 C. Muhkam āyāt are figurative in nature, and therefore can have various meanings.
 D. Mutashābihat āyāt were composed by Rasūlullāh (S).
 E. Mutashābihat āyāt are highly allegorical, and therefore can be ignored during readings.

3. According to the Qur'ān, which type of people will follow only the Mutashābihat āyāt?

 A. Those who love reading the Qur'ān.
 B. Those who love critical analyses of the Qur'ān, e.g. the scholars.
 C. Those who want to create trouble and dissension.
 D. Those who want to formulate the Shariah.
 E. Those who want to create harmony and peace among different faiths.

4. According to the Qur'ān, who knows the actual meaning of the Mutashābihat āyāt?

 A. No one knows except Allāh.
 B. All scholars.
 C. All messengers and all angels.
 D. Those who are steadfast in knowledge.
 E. Those who understand the Shariah.

5. In which sūrah is the ruling about Muhkam and Mutashābihat āyāt given?

 A. Sūrah Baqarah.
 B. Sūrah An-Nās.
 C. Sūrah At-Taubah.
 D. Sūrah Al-e-'Imrān.
 E. Sūrah An-Nahl.

6. Which of the following classical theologians understood all of the Mutashābihat āyāt?

    A.   At-Tabari—since his commentary of the Qur'ān is most voluminous.

    B.   Ibn Kathīr—since he is well recognized as one of the finest commentators of the Qur'ān.

    C.   Imam Abu Hanifa—since he promulgated the first Madhhab in Islam.

    D.   Umar Ibn Al-Khattab—the Companion of Rasūlullāh (S).

    (E.)   None of the above.

7. Since Allāh made the whole Qur'ān easy to understand (26:195; 44:58), which of the following choices is correct about Mutashābihat āyāt?

    A.   They can be understood within the context and limits of current knowledge, provided that the Muhkam āyāt are not ignored.

    (B.)   They can be understood if a person is thoroughly educated in science, arts, literature and religion.

    C.   They can be understood if a person studies Hadith thoroughly.

    D.   They can be understood thoroughly if Muhkam āyāt are closely followed.

    E.   They can be understood if the Qur'ān is memorized.

8. All Islamic rules should be derived from Mutashābihat āyāt.   True / False

9. Āyāt dealing with various aspects of the Awakening, Heaven, and Hell are:

    A.   Muhkam āyāt.

    B.   Mutashābihat āyāt.

    (C.)   Both Muhkam and Mutashābihat āyāt.

    D.   Neither Muhkam nor Mutashābihat āyāt since they deal with aspects of the Hereafter.

10. Which of the following statements about Muhkam and Mutashābihat āyāt is true?

    A.   The ruling about Muhkam and Mutashābihat āyāt make interpreting and understanding the Qur'ān easier.

    B.   The ruling about Muhkam and Mutashābihat āyāt introduce a limit for the interpretation of the Qur'ān.

    C.   The ruling about Muhkam and Mutashābihat āyāt help commentators of the Qur'ān.

    D.   The meanings of Mutashābihat āyāt are followed by those who want to create confusion and division among Muslims.

    E.   All of the above.

Al-'Asr: *The Formula of Success*

Objective of the Lesson:

Besides being a magnificent sūrah, Al-'Asr also provides a mathematical equation for the success of mankind. This lesson provides a brief summary of the sūrah with an analysis of the success formula.

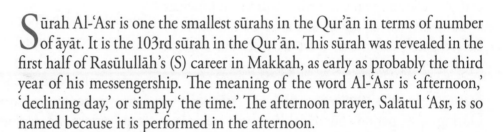

Sūrah Al-'Asr is one the smallest sūrahs in the Qur'ān in terms of number of āyāt. It is the 103rd sūrah in the Qur'ān. This sūrah was revealed in the first half of Rasūlullāh's (S) career in Makkah, as early as probably the third year of his messengership. The meaning of the word Al-'Asr is 'afternoon,' 'declining day,' or simply 'the time.' The afternoon prayer, Salātul 'Asr, is so named because it is performed in the afternoon.

Volumes have been written on this short but very majestic sūrah. This sūrah actually summarizes all of the moral and spiritual duties of human beings. The sūrah does not mention anything about the Hereafter, but there seems to be a suggestion of man's final destiny that cannot be overlooked when the meaning of the entire sūrah is fully grasped.

Notice in this sūrah there is no mention of the word Allāh or God, no mention of the need to worship, no mention of the word Muslim, no mention of Islam, no mention of Rasūlullāh (S) and no mention of any of the core pillars of Islam. Yet, this sūrah is so piercing in its force, so breathtaking in its appeal and so awe-inspiring in its message that whoever reads it cannot help but to humble their heart with the deepest respect for its abiding message.

Notice, too, that if this sūrah were not from the Qur'ān, it could easily have been from any other revealed scripture. The message of the

	With the name of Allāh, most Gracious, most Rewarding.
بِسۡمِ ٱللَّهِ ٱلرَّحۡمَٰنِ ٱلرَّحِيمِ ۝	
وَٱلۡعَصۡرِ ۝	1. Consider the Declining day.
إِنَّ ٱلۡإِنسَٰنَ لَفِى خُسۡرٍ ۝	2. Surely man is indeed at loss,
إِلَّا ٱلَّذِينَ ءَامَنُواْ وَعَمِلُواْ ٱلصَّٰلِحَٰتِ وَتَوَاصَوۡاْ بِٱلۡحَقِّ وَتَوَاصَوۡاْ بِٱلصَّبۡرِ ۝	3. Except those who believe and do good, and exhort one another to Truth, and enjoin one another to perseverance.

sūrah is such that even a non-Muslim could accept its teachings without any hesitation and without violating his or her own religious adherence. It simply talks about mankind's destiny in life. At the end of the lesson you will realize this sūrah provides a mathematical equation of man's overall success. Before going any further, let us read the original Arabic version and the translation of the sūrah.

Economic environment during revelation: During the period Sūrah al-'Asr was revealed, the atmosphere in Makkah was predominantly oligarchic. In an oligarchic society, the wealth and power are controlled by the chieftains of the tribe, and the Makkan chiefs wielded unassailable power. In the Makkan society, a few became the inheritors of power, and they reigned economically supreme over all others. Only they benefited from wealth and might. The key to their power and economic supremacy was centered around the Ka'bah and their status of being its custodians.

During seventh century Arabia, the Quraish rendered the Ka'bah the largest center of polytheism. They filled up the Ka'bah with a large number of idols worshipped by various tribes. By allowing these gods inside the Ka'bah, the Quraish endorsed and approved the religious practices of other tribes. If they had not allowed the idol gods inside the Ka'bah, the annual hajj in Makkah probably would not have thrived. The hajj season helped bolster their economy.

Besides the economic boost they received during the annual pilgrimage, the Quraish oligarchy was further intensified by their successful trade with Syria in the north and Yemen in the south.[106:2]

Social environment during revelation: Along with economic supremacy, the Quraish continued to exploit the social environment. The rich continued to get richer and the poor continued to get poorer. The women were largely seen as objects of lust, deprivation and exploitation. Female children were often buried alive since the birth of a girl was viewed as a social stigma.

Timing of the day: Sūrah Al-'Asr beautifully uses the timing of the day to convey its message. In Juz 30 of the Qur'ān, four other sūrahs have a title bearing names of various parts of the day: Fajr (s. 89), Al-Lail (s. 92), Ad-Duhā (s. 93), and Al-falaq (s. 113). If you read these sūrahs, you will clearly notice the time of day is used in each sūrah to create a solemn prelude to the resultant theme.

Particle of oath: Except for sūrah Al-Falaq, the rest of the four sūrahs mentioned above begin with the oath particle *waw* (و). The opening letter *waw* (و) is called *waw al-qasam*, i.e., particle of oath. The particle is a literary device used to gain the attention of the listener and the reader. The oath particle also creates suspense and makes the audience or the readers pay full attention to the message that follows the oath.

First two āyāt: The first two āyāt of sūrah Al-'Asr uses the time of day to remind people that if 'time' is wasted in life, and the prime duties in life are not done, it will result in enormous loss. There can be many different definitions and interpretations of 'time.' For our purposes, all we can say is that time is an aspect of nature that cannot be reversed. Once it is gone, it is gone forever.

The term *al-'asr* attempts to arouse a thoughtful reminiscence of the life of a person who has aged and now stands at the end of his or her life. From this point onward, a person has only a short time left in life but can look back at his or her past days. Obviously, person to person, the timing of *al-'asr* is different. But sooner or later, a person is bound to realize that time has sneaked upon him or her too quickly while the key objectives of life remained unattended. The person realizes that he or she is at a loss (*khasir*). Notice the āyah is not talking about a particular group or nation—believer or non-believer —it is referring to mankind (*insān*). The āyah is making a point here—strongly, forcefully—implied by the word *inna*.

Without any question, all human beings are surely at a loss. Why the loss? Are the objectives in life to fulfill earthly desires, have wealth, earn name and fame, gratify needs or to lead a calm, quiet, and peaceful life? Is there anything above and beyond these earthly objectives? The sūrah does not answer these questions—thus it creates tension in our minds. It creates suspense in our hearts. We may think we have achieved so much in life, but how can it be that we are at loss?

The loss (*khasir*) literally means to wander away from the right path, to be deceived or to suffer a loss. The use of this word brings those key factors that would eventually determine the ultimate course of human beings in the Hereafter to the forefront.

Four key activities: After pointing out a loss for everybody, the third and final āyah of the sūrah affirms four key activities that would prevent the loss from happening. If these activities are not done

collectively, man will still be lost. You will notice the sūrah does not waste time detailing all those activities that would cause a loss, because such activities are endless in number. Instead it simply points out four desirable activities.

The first activity: The first activity is to believe (*imān*). Everybody believes in one thing or another. Even non-believers believe in some higher power outside of themselves. But the word *imān* implies proper and appropriate belief—as endorsed by the Qur'ān. The word *imān* is not a mere verbal profession, but it entails an intellectual progression towards the realization of Allāh's existence, His propositions, and His creations. *Imān* involves certain practices (*'amal*), some of which are prescribed as rites and others that call for an innate response.

The second activity: The second desirable activity is *'amal swālihāt*, i.e., practice doing good. *'Amal swālihāt* is integral to one's faith; therefore, it is placed immediately after the first activity. Notice again the sūrah does not detail the good deeds. It leaves the decision to an individual and his or her judgment. The list of good deeds is endless. In other places, the Qur'ān mentions various obligatory deeds that qualify as good deeds. The best way of beginning *'amal swālihāt* is to do good to one's own soul (2:110; 41:46; 45:15; 64:16) by striving to improve oneself, followed by doing good to humanity.

The third and fourth activities: The third and fourth desirable activities draw from two virtues: seeking truth (*haqq*) and practicing perseverance (*sabr*). These two virtues are not only to be practiced by the individual, but are also to be exercised through mutual counseling. The Qur'ān recognizes that human beings are not isolated individuals in a society; they have a collective identity, too. Human beings cannot be selfish and self-oriented individuals. They are like one unit in a complex bond of other units, where if one unit suffers or deteriorates, it will have an impact on the others. Therefore, the requirements expected of an individual member of society also become the requirements expected of other members of the society. It is viewed as a collective responsibility of all members, but that collective responsibility must begin with the individual.

There is a practical problem in implementing the third and fourth desirable activities. The problem is that other members of the society may not possess the same faith, and therefore they are not governed by the same ideologies. Furthermore, the Islamic ethos strictly forbids coercing faith upon another; therefore, how can believers exhort one another to Truth, and enjoin one another to perseverance? This can be done by entering into mutual agreements towards honoring certain social activities. The dual mention of *wasaya* (literally, to enjoin, to command) highlights bringing members of the society together to remind and honor each other's obligations toward truth and patience.

Interconnected activities:
In this sūrah, the four independent activities are designed to interconnect with each other. We mentioned earlier that if the four activities are not done collectively and simultaneously, there would still be a loss. For example, faith alone will not suffice if one does not do righteous deeds; and if a person simply does righteous deeds all his life, but does not possess the proper faith, it would not yield desirable results. Similarly, if a person simply enjoins others to good or to persevere, but does not do good deeds or profess faith, it will not be enough.

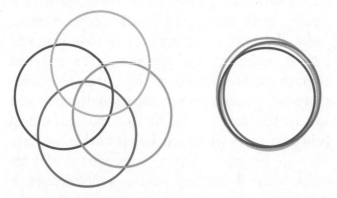

It is like a Venn diagram where four circles, each representing one of the activities, overlap each other. If lifelong deeds do not include any of the desirable activities, man will be at a loss. Notice one or two of the single activities by themselves will have some good outcomes, but it will not be enough. Complete and total success will be achieved only when all four circles overlap fully over one another. (In the diagram all the circles are not shown to overlap completely for ease in understanding and for allowing slight human shortcomings that are natural.)

Mathematical equation:
Another way of looking at the formula of success given in Sūrah Al-'Asr is to put the elements of success in to an equation. These activities cannot be done one at a time, but must be done simultaneously.

Success = Believing + Doing Good + Enjoining Truth + Enjoining Perseverance

If one of the items is missing from the equation, the formula will only partially work. For example, here are some of the possible iterations:

Believing + Doing Good – Enjoining Truth – Enjoining Perseverance = Partial Success

Believing + Enjoining Perseverance – Doing Good – Enjoining Truth = Partial Success

Doing Good – Believing – Enjoining Perseverance – Enjoining Truth = Partial Success

When you look at the lives of famous people from other faiths, you will notice the above formula worked in their lives—but only, partially. But a lifetime of good deeds will be meaningless if one does not have faith. The same formula applies to Muslims, too. They have faith, but if they do not have other elements of the equation in their lives, they will only have partial success.

In light of the sūrah, may Allāh guide all of us toward success by giving us the strength, motivation and inspiration to practice all four elements of the equation.

homework**weekend 5**

1. How many desirable activities does Sūrah Al-ʿAsr prescribe?

    A.   Two activities.
    B.   Three activities.
    C.   Four activities.
    D.   Five activities.
    E.   Ten activities.

2. According to the lesson, when was Sūrah Al-ʿAsr revealed?

    A.   Right before hijrah.
    B.   During hijrah.
    C.   In Madīnah.
    D.   During the later half of Rasūlullāh's (S) life.
    E.   During the early part of Rasūlullāh's (S) career.

3. According to the lesson, how many sūrahs in the Qur'ān use the time of day in its title?

    A.   Two sūrahs.
    B.   Three sūrahs.
    C.   Four sūrahs.
    D.   Five sūrahs.
    E.   Six sūrahs.

4. The opening letter of the sūrah, *waw* (و) is used as a particle. What is the name of this particle used in the sūrah?

    A.   waw al-qasam
    B.   waw al-hafiz
    C.   waw al-mubin
    D.   waw al-sūrah
    E.   waw al-fātihah

5. When the Sūrah Al-ʿAsr was revealed, the Makkan society represented a predominant social system. Write the name of the system and describe some of its features.

    When a small group has power

6. Explain how the annual pilgrimage during pre-Islamic Arabia economically benefitted the Makkan people.

They put their god in the Kabbah.

7. According to the lesson, what does the word *wasaya* encourage people to do?

A. Practice mutual enjoining of activities
B. Practice unilateral activities
C. Practice selfish activities
D. Coerce each other into activities
E. None of the above

8. Which of the following choices is correct about how activities prescribed by Sūrah Al-'Asr should be implemented?

A. All activities should begin during the last part of human life.
B. All activities must be done collectively and simultaneously.
C. All activities should be performed only by Muslims.
D. All activities should be done one at a time.
E. Only (c) and (d).

9. Briefly explain which one or two desirable activities might be missing from the life of an ordinary Christian person. Explain your reasoning.

Believing in one god.

10. In the lesson, the four activities prescribed by Sūrah Al-'Asr are shown using a Venn diagram. Ideally, how should the circles of a Venn diagram look if the four activity requirements are satisfied?

A. All circles should be separated from each other.
B. All circles should merge into each other.
C. All circles should disappear in a person's life.
D. All circles should touch each other superficially.
E. Only one circle should merge with another, while the rest of the circles remain separated.

Qur'ānic Calligraphy

Objective of the Lesson:

This lesson provides a historical background of the rich heritage of Qur'ānic calligraphy, a skill that is still practiced in an age of digital composing.

One of the major contributions of Muslims to the world is the concept of graphic design and page layout, which form the basis of any printed or electronic media. The Qur'ān was carefully recorded at the time of Rasūlullāh (S) and formally codified at the time of the third khalifa 'Uthmān Ibn 'Affān (r). Whenever a āyah was recorded, it was not only done reliably and correctly, but it was also recorded with a great sense of awe and honor. The scribes recorded the very words of Almighty Allāh with utmost care—honoring the correctness and the majesty. Scribing was a counterpart of reciting with tajweed as both required perfect ways of displaying the words of Allāh, whether in written or verbal form. In today's world, almost all of us have acquired printed copies of the Qur'ān. Many of these *mushafs* (i.e., written forms of the Book) were originally hand-calligraphed before printing. Some newer *mushafs* are digitally composed. This lesson provides an historical background of the rich heritage of Qur'ānic calligraphy, a skill that is still practiced in an age of digital composing. Since the advent of the printing press, the practical need for calligraphers has declined.

Earliest copies of the Qur'ān: The earliest copies of the Qur'ān, probably none of which are in existence now, were written in a style called Hijāzi script. The name traces its origin to the Hijāz province of the Arabian Peninsula. As both Makkah and Madinah are located in the Hijāz province, this script was the default way of scribing the Qur'ān. While many ancient texts were written in scroll format, the earliest copies of the

Fig: The Qur'ān written in Hijāzi script.

Qur'ān were in *codex* format (Latin for a book in the shape of a block of wood). Earlier scriptures, such as the ones identified as the Dead Sea Scrolls, or the Hebrew Bible in codex format known as the Aleppo Codex, were written in two columns or more per page. However, the Qur'ān was scribed in a single column per page. More recent copies of the Bible, such as the first printed copy of the Gutenberg Bible, or any copy of the Bible that is printed today, have at least two columns. The style of Qur'ān scribing retains the single column format. The only difference that we may see is a translation of the Qur'ān that is presented in two columns, yet that retains the single column for the Arabic text.

The earliest available copies of the Qur'ān in the Hijāzī script have a distinct right slant of the characters. The characters were thick and mostly

vertically elongated. Many pages in these mushafs also showed a slight inclination of the lines from the right to the left; an unintentional affect of handwriting starting from the left. These mushafs did not contain vowel marks (fathah, kasra, damma, and so forth) and they also did not always contain number of each ayats. Some earliest copies marked every tenth ayats with a circular pattern. Such circular marking denoting the end of an ayat continues even today.

Kufic calligraphy: Within 100 years, the Qur'ānic script slowly incorporated the Kufic style, a style that was formulated in the Southern Iraqi town of al-Kufah. As the writing style progressed, so did the development of the *diatrical* marks. Vowel marks

were written in red and green was used to mark hamzah or a glottal stop. In contrast to the Hijazi scripts, the Kufi scripts were horizontally elongated. Similar to the Hijazi mushafs, the earliest Kufi scripts also depicted extreme care in inscriptions as the scribes were awed to write the very words of the Almighty Allāh. The margins of the earliest mushafs did not contain any geometric or floral patterns, or any textual marks, primarily to avoid contaminating the Words of Allāh with stray ink strokes. These early Kufic style mushafs were in landscape format instead of portrait format. In time, ornamental decorations in the mushaf were introduced. Usually sūrah titles were colored in gold. Markings for sujud āyāt were also introduced. As the Islamic land started to expand, the Kufic style developed into two distinct yet connected styles, eastern and western.

Eastern Kufic style developed in the eastern part of the Islamic land, and is appropriately called *al-kufi al farisi* (Persian Kufic) or *al-kufi al-baghdadi* (Baghdad kufi). Mushafs in this style were in portrait format. The characters were thin and vertically elongated. Many of the letters adopted a distinct triangular shape. A grammarian named al-Khalil ibn Ahmad was instrumental in introducing the vowel designs in the Qur'ānic text, which is still used today. These vowel designs were written in black the mushafs retained the red vowel marks from early Kufic style.

Western Kufic style or *al-kufi al-Maghribi* flourished in the western part of the Islamic land, specifically in North Africa and Morocco. This style developed rounded characters and elongated curves that flowed below the lines. The vowel marks were in red or blue. Over a period of time this style spread to Islamic Spain. The mushafs scribed in Islamic Spain were artistically designed with ornamental sūrah titles written in gold.

Scribing the mushafs remained a noble and respected skill, and the scribes continued to perfect their style to reflect the majesty of the Words of the Qur'ān.

Nakshi calligraphy: Around the 10th century, the art of scribing the Qur'ān saw another development. A cursive script, known as nakshi, was used earlier in non-Qur'ānic documents in the Eastern part of the Islamic land. This script was vertically elongated and was highly legible. The early nakshi script was a simple and plain style that did not seem appropriate for recording the majestic Words of Allāh. This script was improved over the years to a visually appealing refined style. When the elegant nakshi script was introduced in scribing the Qur'ān, it immediately gained popularity. Some of the early nakshi scripted Qur'ān displays a large amount of text on a single page, due to the legibility.

A master calligrapher from the Abbasid court, Ibn Muqlah, developed a mathematical proportion of every letter based on the length of alif. Every letter was measured, which improved the legibility of the text. Another master scribe, Ibn al-Bawwab, further improved this style of proportional writing. As the characters were based on set measurements, many later-generation scribes could easily reproduce similar elegant writing. Many of these later-generation scribes may not have been master calligraphers, but their work appeared almost as equally majestic as the works of Ibn Muqlah and Ibn al-Bawwab. This is one reason for the popularity of the nakshi script. Another reason for the popularity of the nakshi script

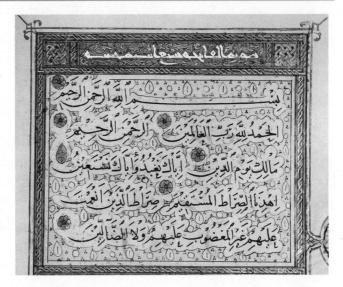

Fig: The word Qur'ān written in nakshi script.

is the condensed yet legible text, which reduced the size of the mushaf so that it could be easily held and carried.

Thuluth script: Some of the modifications of the Nakshi calligraphy established a separate identity. One such script is the Thuluth, which is mostly used in titles rather than lengthy texts. Thuluth literally means third. The patrons of Thuluth script were Mamluks and Ottomans. Mamluk Thuluth scripts were the earlier style, thick and bold, while the newer Ottoman Thuluth script is finer and simpler.

Fig: The word Qur'ān written in calligraphic format.

Fig: The word Muhammad written in calligraphic format.

Thuluth is also mathematically proportioned, the ratio between the curves of the letters and the straight line is one-third (i.e., one-third of each letter has a slope) compared to Nakshi script. The āyāt written on the Kiswah covering the walls of the Ka'bah are in Thuluth script. The Shahada inscribed on the Saudi Arabian flag is also in Thuluth script, while the takbir "Allāhu Akbar" written on the current Iraqi flag is in Kufi script.

Diwani script: This cursive script based on Kufi was developed during the times of the early Ottoman Turks. A variation of the Diwani script, Diwani-al-Jali, was a popular script for the Qur'ān in North Africa.

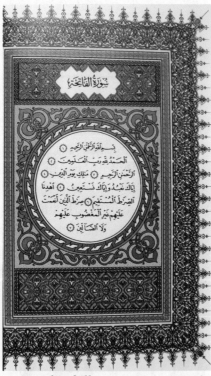

Fig: An example of illumination—Sūrah Al-Fātihah carrying the floral motifs.

Ta'liq/Nasta'liq script: This Persian script, developed in the 14th and 15th centuries, is characterized by rounded forms and elongated horizontal strokes. Persian, Kashmiri, and Urdu script use the Nasta'liq as the preferred style.

A few other elegant scripts were developed, such as Muhaqqaq and Raihan. These scripts are large and cursive. In this style, the curves below the lines are shallow. These scripts were popular with large-format mushafs.

Chinese (Sini) script: A script was developed by the Chinese Muslims in the 14th century that combined the elements of both nakshi and Chinese calligraphy. Many of the Sini calligraphy were found in ceramic items, such as dishes, vases, or rosewater sprinklers. These decorative wares, primarily in blue or red with a white porcelain background, were sought-after items in Arabia, Persia, and India. The Sini artistic forms flourished during the Ming dynasty when the Muslims had connections with the imperial court. The Hui people of eastern and central China influenced this style as they had easier access to Persia and Turkey. The mushafs from the Hui tradition incorporated Chinese motifs such as cloud bands and peonies. The illumination and script style allowed only three to five lines of text per page. The tradition in China was to read one juz every day with the imam in a community gathering. This practical need and the legible style of 3 to 5 lines per page in the mushaf in Sini script led to binding each juz in a separate, thick volume. The complete bound set was a massive collection on a shelf, similar to a set of encyclopedias.

Sections of the mushafs: While the Sini and many other mushafs were in 30 volumes, some mushafs were produced in a single volume, and some in seven volumes and some in 60. Seven-volume sets are now rare. Printed mushafs are mostly in a single volume. Hand-calligraphed 30-volume sets were popular as these allowed ease of recitation—one juz a day, particularly during the month of Ramadan.

Illumination: Illumination is the addition of decoration to the text of a sacred book. The earliest copies of the Qur'ān did not contain any illumination. The illuminations were avoided in fear of contaminating the Words of the Qur'ān. Elaborate illumination of the mushafs started during the ninth or tenth century. These illuminations were incorporated to reflect the majesty of the words of the Qur'ān, and they often showed the skills of the calligrapher and possibly the financial contributions of the patrons. Illuminations were present on almost every page of the Qur'ān, specifically on the front page. Some illumination had arabesque floral motifs, while the sini mushafs contained clouds and peonies as illumination.

'Carpet' pages: The illumination was particularly evident on the 'carpet' pages—the first and last pages of the codex. The carpet page is so named as it resembles the intricate designs of an Oriental carpet. Obviously these pages are not part of the Qur'ān.

Fig: An example of illumination—a carpet page showing intricate designs.

However, the calligraphers provided these pages as an introduction and conclusion to the grand content.

Illumination of Surah al-Fatihah: The first page of the Qur'ān, containing the text of the Sūrah Al-Fātihah, traditionally continued to carry the floral motifs of the 'carpet' page or other kinds of illumination. The page containing Sūrah Al-Fātihah is illuminated not only by being the first chapter of the Qur'ān, but also by being the sūrah that is most recited.

Recording surfaces: Early mushafs were made of cloth, velum (animal skin), or papyrus. As a white reading surface was considered strenuous on the eyes, the page surfaces were dyed with colors, such as tan or brown. The surfaces were also coated to prevent leaching of the ink.

When paper was developed in China, the technology quickly spread over the Middle East.

Many Muslim cities established paper manufacturing factories that could produce papers of high quality. As expected, the Eastern part of the Muslim land, being close to China, adopted paper as the scribing surface of the Qur'ān while the Western part of the Islamic world continued using velum and papyrus.

Writing tools and inks: Most of the Islamic calligraphic pens were created from reeds growing in swamps or water beds. The raw reeds were dried to a firmness suitable for writing. The drying technique employed embedding the reeds in manure for several years. The manure provided a secure place for the slow-drying process in the harsh, dry weather. Once dried to a reddish brown color, the tips of the reeds were sharpened with a knife on a bone or ivory pen rest. One drawback of using the reeds was the subsequent lack of firmness and blunting of the tip after some use. For scribing the Qur'ān, the calligraphers preferred using a wooden pen derived from trees in Java. These hard wooden pens retained their sharp tips even after prolonged use. Bamboo reeds were also used for large writings. Each calligraphic style required its own specific writing instruments.

Most of the black writing was done using soot ink from burning linseed oil and beeswax. Gold was used frequently in many mushafs. Inks were also made from natural substances such as yam and glue.

Some museums and libraries have collections of early mushafs. Some magnificent samples can be viewed on the British Library web site (http://www.bl.uk), the British Museum web site (www.britishmuseum.org) and the website Sheridan Library of Johns Hopkins (http://goldkoran.mse.jhu.edu/). Examples of Islamic art and calligraphy can be viewed on the website of The Metropolitan Museum of Art (http://www.metmuseum.org/).

1. In what format were the earliest copies of the Qur'ān scripted?

    A.   In scroll format.
    B.   In codex format.
    C.   In multiple column format.
    D.   In carpet format.
    E.   In single-volume format.

2. In which script were the earliest copies of the Qur'ān written?

    A.   In Kufic script.
    B.   In Nakshi script.
    C.   In Hijāzi script.
    D.   In Ta'liq script.
    E.   In Sini script.

3. What were the main characteristics of the script that was used in the earliest copies of the Qur'ān?

....

....

4. What were the two main scripting styles that emerged under the Kufic style of calligraphy?

    a. ....

    b. ....

5. Who was instrumental in introducing the vowel signs in the Qur'ānic text which is still used today?

    A.   Khalil Gibran.
    B.   Ibn Muqlah.
    C.   Ibn Al-Bawwab.
    D.   Al-Khalil Ibn Ahmad.
    E.   Imam Razi.

6. Ibn Muqlah developed a unique feature of scripting the Qur'ānic text. Which of the following choices correctly identifies this feature?

    A.   A mass printing technique.
    B.   An engraving technique.
    C.   The mathematical proportion of every letter.
    D.   A cursive style for quick writing.
    E.   A coding and decoding of the script.

7. Which type of scripting style is mostly used in the title of a work, in the Kiswah of the Ka'bah, or in the flags of countries?

....

8. Which two colors were primarily used in Chinese calligraphy on ceramic items?

....

9. Where in the mushaf of the Qur'ān were the "carpet" pages placed?

....

10. Before the invention of fountain pens, most calligraphers made their pens out which three items?

    a. ....

    b. ....

    c. ....

The Bible and the Qur'ān

Objective of the Lesson:

The Bible and the Qur'ān have some similarities and a lot of differences—particularly regarding their text, structure, spirit, and context. Understanding these features of the two books will benefit students living in the West, particularly as they engage in meaningful discussion with people of other faiths. This lesson provides a comparative analysis of the Bible and the Qur'ān in a tabular format.

In our world the human population is increasing daily and, with that, the human dynamics are also changing. About 2.1 billion people in the world are Christian and about 1.3 billion people are Muslim. In many societies, Christians and Muslims live next door to each other, go to the same schools, work at the same places, and socialize together. In the U.S., Christianity is the major religion, practiced by about 224 million people. In the U.S., Islam is the third major religion, practiced by about eight million people. Islam is also one of the fastest growing religions in the U.S. The two main causes of this growth are: immigration and a high birth rate among immigrants. Interestingly, a third cause of the growth of the Muslim population in the U.S. is acceptance of Islam by people from other faiths, particularly from Christianity. In fact, the biggest growth of the Muslim population in the U.S. in the first four decades of the 20th century was the result of people accepting Islam, not simply from the immigration of Muslims.

Clearly there are several reasons why, out of all other religions, people from Christianity readily accept Islam. The Qur'ān says that when it comes to friendship, Christians are closest to Muslims.[5:82] The stories and teachings in the Bible and the Qur'ān have many similarities, making it easy for Christians to relate to the Qur'ānic message. This lesson presents a comparative understanding of two major religions, particularly the texts they follow. Unless we have a conceptual idea about each book and each religion, a meaningful cross-cultural discussion or spiritual discussion may not be fruitful.

Belief in all revealed books: The Bible is the sacred book of Christians. Christians find moral and spiritual guidance in the Bible. The Qur'ān is the sacred book of Muslims. We find moral and spiritual guidance from the Qur'ān. Additionally, Allāh, in the Qur'ān, tells us that the Injīl—the original Bible is a revealed book and makes it mandatory for Muslims to recognize all revealed books. Thus, belief in the Injīl as a revealed book is part of a Muslim's faith. Here are some of the āyāt to illustrate:

... and who believe in what has been revealed to you, and in what was revealed before you, and regarding the Hereafter they firmly believe. (2:4)

He has revealed upon you this Scripture with the Truth, confirming that which was before it; and He revealed the Tawrat and the Injil, (3:3)

And We have revealed to you the Scripture with the truth, confirming what is before it of the scripture, and a guardian over it; (5:48)

And this is a Scripture, We have revealed it blessed, confirming that which is before it, (6:92)

Key difference and similarities:

The Bible and the Qur'ān differ in many ways—structurally, textually, spiritually, and contextually. The following table highlights some of the major differences and similarities. This table is by no means an exhaustive list.

Bible	Qur'ān
Structural:	
The Protestant Bible consists of 66 books. The Catholic Bible has 73 books, the Eastern Orthodox Bible has 78. Other variations exist.	The Qur'ān consists of 114 chapters.
Total number of verses in the Protestant Bible is 31,175. The number varies in other versions.	Total number of āyāt in the Qur'ān is 6,237.
Most of the available copies of the Bible look smaller in size due to smaller fonts.	Most of the available copies of the Qur'ān look larger in size due to larger Arabic fonts.
Divided into two parts: the Old Testament or the Tawrat, with 39 books (Protestant) and the New Testament or Gospel, with 27 books.	No such division exists in the Qur'ān.
The Bible consists of the Tawrāt (Old Testament) revealed to Moses, Zabūr (Psalms) revealed to David. Only certain parts of the New Testament were revealed to Jesus; the rest are interpretations and observations of individual writers.	The Qur'ān was revealed to Messenger Muhammad (S) in its entirety.
It is a collection of writings by different authors.	It is a dictation from one source—Allāh.
The speaker is the individual author. The author describes his findings, experiences and understandings of an event.	Allāh is the speaker. He is talking directly to man, sometimes in the first person, sometimes in the second person and at other times in the third person. The communication is always between Allāh and man.

Bible	Qur'ān
Jesus did not supervise, arrange, or instruct how the individual chapters or books of the Bible should be compiled and presented.	All chapters of the Qur'ān were arranged by Nabi Muhammad (S) under divine guidance.[25:32; 75:17-18] Each year, Rasūlullāh (S) verified the compilation with angel Jibril. In the year Rasūlullāh (S) passed away, he reviewed the Qur'ān twice with Jibril.
Individual chapters of the Bible were not arranged by Jesus. The present-day Christian Bible was compiled and collected under the leadership of Constantine the Great, during the First Council of Nicaea in 325 C.E.	The entire Qur'ān and its chapters were arranged in the present format by Rasūlullāh (S) in his lifetime. It was compiled into one book by Abu Bakr, and later 'Uthmān ibn 'Affan (R) circulated this copy as the authentic version.

Textual:

Bible	Qur'ān
The original Bible was in Hebrew and Aramaic languages. Later it was translated into Greek, Latin and English. All Christians read the English and other language versions. The original version was lost and its remnants are preserved in some libraries.	The language of the Qur'ān is Arabic. The present day Qur'ān is the same version revealed by Allāh. Many English translations are available today, but for all practical purposes, the Arabic Qur'ān is widely read, referred to, and memorized.
Several different versions of the Bible exist—the King James Version was authorized by King James in 1611 C.E. There is a New King James version (NKJ), and a New International Version (NIV). There are at least 100 other versions.	There is only one version of the Qur'ān from the time of revelation. There is no "authorized" version. The Qur'ān we read today is the same Qur'ān revealed to Nabi Muhammad (S).
All books written by different authors were not included in the Bible. The Bible compilers disputed the authenticity of many of the books and excluded them. Some of the 'lost' gospels are saved in churches and museums.	No chapter of the Qur'ān was left out from compilation.
Individual chapters of the Gospel, as available today, were not directly revealed by God. These are human interpretations of what the authors thought was God's revelation.	All chapters of the Qur'ān were directly revealed by Allāh (4:82; 6:91; 20:4,99; 27:6; 39:23;41).
The name 'Bible' is not mentioned inside the Bible. The Bible does not refer to itself.	The name 'Qur'ān' is mentioned inside the Qur'ān many times. It also refers to itself many times.
Textual style is narrative and detailed. It often provides a lengthy genealogy. There is a definite beginning and ending of a story.	Text is concise. Stories are brief. In most cases, the moral of a story is highlighted. Stories are scattered over different chapters. Sometimes different stories appear next to each other.

Bible	Qur'ān
Contextual:	
The main audience of the bible is: 'O Children of Israel.' It never addresses communities outside of Israel. Its message is regional.	The Qur'ān addresses the believers, non-believers and mankind. Regional references are made because the early audiences were Arabs and Jews, but its message is universal.
The Bible does not say it is a "complete" book. Rather it says that Jesus cannot say everything, and that he left many things unsaid, to be completed by someone else who would come later (John 14:16,26; 15:26; 16:7).	The Qur'ān vouches for itself as a complete book of guidance for mankind.[5:3]
Stories and themes connect to the land and its people around ancient Palestine.	Stories and themes connect to the land and its people around ancient Palestine and Arabia. Rare references of people outside of Arabia are made, for example, Luqmān, Dhul Qurnain, Dhul Kifl, Romans and Sleepers of the Cave.
Spiritual:	
Guidance only for the Children of Israel. One has to be Christian to attain salvation.	Guidance for all of mankind. Anyone who believes in One Allāh, Awaking, and does righteous deed has no fear.[2:62; 5:69]
No spiritual worldview is noticed. It is purely regional in scope, addressed to the Children of Israel. Later the book was adopted by the world.	A spiritual worldview is dominant in its message. The message is not regional or ethnical. The God of Muslims is the same God worshipped by Adam, Abraham, Moses, Jesus.
Some of the messengers in the Bible did morally corrupt deeds, for example, Solomon worshiped idols, David desired the wife of his army general, Job beat his wife, and Joseph lied.	All past messengers are depicted as sinless individuals—morally and spiritually upright.
Contains many good moral and spiritual anecdotes and teachings. Guides people to righteousness.	Contains many good moral and spiritual anecdotes and teachings. Guides people to righteousness.
Core faith of Christianity is not endorsed by the Bible. These are later inventions, e.g. the Trinity, atonement, and the celebration of Christmas.	Core faith of Islam is not only specifically mentioned in the Qur'ān, but it is repeated again and again.
Christianity is a religion **about** Jesus rather than a religion **of** Jesus. The religion practiced today was not taught by the Bible.	Islam is not a religion about Muhammad (S). It is the same religion preached by Abraham, Moses, Jesus, and all past messengers.

1. According to the lesson on the Bible and the Qur'ān, how many areas of key differences and similarities between the two books are mentioned?

    A.   Two areas.
    B.   Three areas.
    C.   Four areas.
    D.   Five areas.
    E.   Ten areas.

2. The Bible consists of 66 books, and the Qur'ān has 114 chapters. Under which classification should we place this information?

    A.   Structural.
    B.   Textual.
    C.   Spiritual.
    D.   Contextual.
    E.   Morphological.

3. One of the key differences between the Bible and the Qur'ān is the speaker. Which of the following statements about the speaker is correct?

    A.   The speaker in the Bible is Moses, while the speaker in the Qur'ān is Rasūlullāh (S).
    B.   The speakers in the Bible are individual authors, while in the Qur'ān the speaker is Allāh.
    C.   The speaker in the Bible is Jesus, while in the Qur'ān it is the angel Jibril.
    D.   The speaker in the Bible is a Pastor in a church, while in the Qur'ān it is Rasūlullāh (S).
    E.   The speakers are the readers in both books.

4. Which of the following choices about the Books in the Bible is correct?

    A.   They were not arranged or supervised by Jesus.
    B.   The total number of books in the Protestant Bible is 66.
    C.   The books were collected and arranged under the supervision of Paul.
    D.   All of the above.
    E.   None of the above.

5. Who is the main audience of the Bible? To whom is it mostly addressed?

    A.   O Children of Israel!
    B.   O Mankind!
    C.   O Jesus!
    D.   O Believers!
    E.   O People of the Book!

6. Which of the following choices is correct about "authorized" versions of the Qur'ān and the Bible?

   A. The Qur'ān is authorized by the Saudi government, the Bible is authorized by King James.
   B. The Qur'ān does not have an authorized version, the Bible is authorized by Julius Caesar.
   C. The Qur'ān is authorized by Imams, the Bible is authorized by Martin Luther King, Jr.
   D. The Qur'ān does not have an authorized version, the Bible is authorized by King James.
   E. The Qur'ān does not have an authorized version, but the Bible is authorized by the Queen.

7. The Bible refers to itself as "the Bible" in the Bible.   True / ~~False~~

8. The Qur'ān refers to itself as "the Qur'ān" in the Qur'ān.   ~~True~~ / False

9. Who arranged the individual chapters in the Qur'ān as it exists today?

   A. Mostly Abū Bakr.
   B. Mostly 'Uthmān Ibn 'Affan.
   C. Rasūlullāh (S).
   D. Mostly the scribes of the Qur'ān.
   E. None of the above.

10. The Bible has several versions. What does NKJ mean?

   New King James version

The Ten Commandments and Islam

Objective of the Lesson:

This lesson analyzes the connection between the Ten Commandments and Islam to show that Islam is not a new religion but a continuation of past religions. The Qur'ān endorses many of the moral and ethical commands mentioned in earlier books, particularly, the Ten Commandments of the Bible.

The Ten Commandments, or Decalogue, are a list of ten religious and secular commands recorded in the Judeo-Christian tradition. These commands were authored by Allāh and given to Moses in the form of two tablets. These tablets were given to Moses when he went to Mount Sinai soon after rescuing the Israelites across the sea. In the Qur'ān these two tablets are mentioned in sūrah Al-A'rāf, āyāt 145, 150, and 154.

And We ordained for him on the Tablets admonition of all kinds, and an explanation of everything. "So take hold of them with strength, and command your people to adopt the best of it. I shall soon show you the abode of the evil-livers." (7:145)

Although the term "Ten Commandments" is a widely used term, in the biblical writings these are referred to as "the ten terms." The English name "Decalogue," derived from Greek translation, is sometimes used in place of the Ten Commandments and also stands for "the ten terms." The ten terms are mentioned in the Bible in Exodus[34:28] and Deuteronomy[:4]

Some Bible scholars distinguish between the Ten Commandments and another set of ritual dialogues that appear in the Bible. Chapter 34 in Exodus provides a list of ten commands, whereas the familiar Ten Commandments are generally connected to the commands mentioned in chapter 20 in Exodus and chapter 5 in Deuteronomy. In both of these chapters, 14 or 15 commands are given. However, in common biblical writings the commands are grouped under ten categories. Many Christian denominations divide the commands in different ways, making them conform to the well-known Ten Commandments.

The Ten Commandments: Here is a summarized form of the Ten Commandments:

1. You shall have no other god before God.

2. You shall not make any images of God.

3. You shall not take the name of the Lord in vain.

4. Remember the Sabbath day, and keep it holy.

5. Honor your father and mother.

6. You shall not murder.

7. You shall not commit adultery.

8. You shall not steal.

9. You shall not lie or bear false witness.

10. You shall not desire another man's wives.

Islam and the Ten Commandments: Although the term "Ten Commandments" is intimately associated with Judeo-Christian theories, the message in the commands is so enduring that all religions, including Islam, espouse one way or other, these teachings. It became possible because the Ten Commandments are an excellent ethical system for all religions.

Islam confirms these teachings for many different reasons. First of all, the teachings of the Ten Commandments were sent by none other than Allāh to guide the Israelites. The Qur'ān says that one of the objectives of the Injīl was to confirm the truths in the Tawrāt.[3:50; 5:46] Similarly, one of the objectives of the Qur'ān is to confirm the previous scriptures.[2:41; 5:48] We have to remember that Islam is not a new religion, but a continuation of the same core message sent to other messengers over time. For that reason, it is not unusual to find many of the moral and ethical commands mentioned in the previous scriptures in the Qur'ān.

It is not surprising that every principle of the Ten Commandments can be found in the Qur'ān. However, unlike the Bible, the Qur'ān does not mention these ten religious and secular principles in a single chapter. Instead, these principles are mentioned throughout the Qur'ān.

The table below provides the Ten Commandments and the parallel āyāt from the Qur'ān.

The Ten Commandments	Āyāt from the Qur'ān
You shall have no other god before God.	… you do not worship anyone except Allāh… (11:2)
	And your Lord has commanded that you should not worship anyone except Him. (17:23)
	Surely I am, I am Allāh, there is no deity but I, therefore you worship Me, and keep up the salāt for remembering Me. (20:14)
	And do not call with Allāh any other deity; there is no deity but He. (28:88)
	He is the ever-Living, there is no deity but He. Therefore you call upon Him, making religion exclusively for Him. All praise belongs to Allāh, Lord of all the worlds! (40:65)
You shall not make any images of God.	Nothing is there in His likeness, and He is all-Hearing, the all-Seeing. (42:11)

The Ten Commandments	Āyāt from the Qur'ān
You shall not make any images of God.	Shun the filthiness of idols and shun the words of falsehood, (22:30) And remember! Ibrāhīm said: "My Lord! make this town secure, and save me and my children from worshipping idols." (14:35) What you worship besides Allāh are mere idols, and you formulate a lie. Surely those whom you worship besides Allāh do not control any provision for you; (29:17) When (Ibrāhīm) said to his father and his people, "What are these images to which you are so devoted?" They said, "We found our ancestors worshipping them." He (Ibrāhīm) said, "Surely, you and your ancestors were in clear error." (21:52—54)
You shall not take the name of the Lord in vain.	And do not make Allāh a target for your oaths for doing good or avoiding evil or reconciling people. (2:224) Allāh does not hold you responsible for what is vain in your oaths; but He holds you responsible for what oaths you deliberately make… (5:89)
Remember the Sabbath day, and keep it holy.	Note: The Israelites were instructed to observe the Sabbath: And We said to them: "Do not violate in the Sabbath." And We took from them a firm covenant. (4:154) Note: Muslims were commanded to perform Jumuah salāt. They are asked to postpone all business and other activities and rush to perform the salāt of Jumuah. O you who believe! when call is given for the salāt on the Day of Jumuah, then hasten towards the remembrance of Allāh, and postpone trading. That is better for you if you but knew! (62:9)
Honor your father and mother.	Note: Showing respect to parents and obeying them is such an important duty that it is placed next to worshipping Allāh. And your Lord has commanded that you do not worship anyone except Him alone; and do good to the parents. If one of them or both of them reach old age in your presence, even then do not say to them "Ugh," and do not scold them, and speak to them a generous speech. (17:23)

The Ten Commandments	Āyāt from the Qur'ān
	And doing of good to parents, (6:151)
	And We have enjoined on man goodness towards his parents. (29:8)
	And We have enjoined on people the doing of good to his parents. (46:15)
You shall not murder.	…whoever kills a person without another, or makes mischief in the land, then it is as if he had killed all mankind. And whoever saves him, it is as if he has saved all mankind… (5:32)
	…and that you do not kill any soul which Allāh has forbidden, except with justice… (6:151)
	And do not kill any soul which Allāh has forbidden except for a right cause. (17:33)
You shall not commit adultery.	And do not go near fornication, it is certainly an indecency; and it is an evil way. (17:32)
	…and do not commit fornication… (25:68)
You shall not steal.	And as for the thievish man and the thievish woman, cut off their hands as retribution for what they have earned—an exemplary punishment from Allāh. And Allāh is Mighty, most Wise. (5:38)
	…that they will not associate anything with Allāh, and they will not steal, and they will not commit adultery, and they will not kill their children… (60:12)
You shall not lie or bear false witness.	…condemnation of Allāh be upon him, if he was lying. (24:7)
	…And do not conceal the evidence; for whoever conceals it, then he is indeed wicked at his heart… (2:283)
	And those who do not give false evidence… (25:72)
	…and those people who are upright in their evidence, (70:33)
You shall not desire another man's wives.	And do not covet what Allāh has favored some of you over others. (4:32)
	And do not stretch your eyes towards what We have provided some of them. (15:88)

General observations: As mentioned above, one of the objectives of the Qur'ān is to attest to the previous divine books. The Qur'ān confirms the truth contained in these books. It is also the "mother" of all scriptures in the sense that it oversees them and contains the original core messages in it.

Jealous God: In the Bible, God is often mentioned as a 'Jealous God.' The phrase implies that God does not like to share His divinity with others, not even with His alleged Son, that Christians attribute to Him. We see a similar message in Islam, as Allāh strongly dislikes shirk—i.e., associating with Allāh. In the Qur'ān Allāh says, "Surely, Allāh will not pardon that partners be set up with Him, but besides that He pardons whom He pleases. And whoever associates with Allāh, he then surely has forged a tremendous sin."[4:48]

Sabbath: The principle of the Sabbath was to encourage the Israelites to establish a form of salāt on a very special day. For the Jews, the day of Sabbath is a day of no work. The Jews were asked not to do any activity on the day of Sabbath, such as fishing.[7:163] This was a test for them. Islam mandates performing a very special salāt on Friday, the Jumuah salāt. Muslims were commanded to perform Jumuah salāt. They are asked to postpone all business and other activities and rush to perform the salāt of Jumuah.[62:9] The Qur'ān does not consider the special day of congregational salāt to be a day of inactivity or of no work.

Adultery: The Bible prohibits adultery and illegal relationships. Allāh attempts to eliminate all forms of illegal sexual relationships through a series of mandates applicable to men and women alike. Lowering each other's gaze is the first step towards curbing sexual desires. The Qur'ān also prohibits us from marrying close family relations—mother, sister, aunt, stepmother and so on.[4:22-24] The Qur'ān also asks us to restrain our passions[23:5] and sexual desires until we get married.[4:25]

False evidence: Allāh forbids concealing evidence.[2:140] Giving false evidence is a crime.[25:72] Allāh requires us to maintain honesty and justice during testimony and not to hide evidence even if it implicates ourselves, parents, or near relations.[4:135]

1. What is the other name of the Ten Commandments, which provides ten religious commands?

    A. Decadence.
    B. Decarecord.
    C. Decameter.
    (D) Decalogue.
    E. Decanotes.

2. In which two books of the Bible are the Ten Commandments mentioned?

    A. Genesis and Exodus.
    (B.) Exodus and Deuteronomy.
    C. Deuteronomy and Leviticus.
    D. Genesis and Psalms.
    E. Corinthians and Mark.

3. Which of the following commands are not mentioned in the Ten Commandments?

    A. You shall not murder.
    B. You shall not make images of God.
    C. You shall not commit adultery.
    (D) You shall not withhold charity.
    E. You shall not give false witness.

4. How many of the principles of the Ten Commandments, as mentioned in the Bible, can be found in the Qur'ān?

    (A.) All ten principles.
    B. Nine principles.
    C. Eight principles.
    D. Seven principles.
    E. Six principles.

5. Christians do not follow two of the Ten Commandments. After careful analysis, write down which two commandments they do not follow.

    A. _You shall not have another god before god_

    B. _You shall not make any images of God_

6. Read āyāt 24:30. Which principle(s) of the Ten Commandments is/are covered by this āyah? Explain your answer.

#7 You shall

#10

7. Read āyah 17:32. Which principle(s) of the Ten Commandments is/are covered by this āyah? Explain your answer.

#7

#10

8. Read āyah 2:283. This āyah supports one of the Ten Commandments. Which commandment does it support? Explain your answer.

#9

9. Read āyah 60:12. This āyah states some of the principles of the Ten Commandments. Write down three of the commandments below.

#1

#7

#8

#9

10. Mark ☑ if the sentence is true, mark ☒ if the sentence is false.

A.	Muslims should not believe in the principles of the Ten Commandments.	☒
B.	The Ten Commandments are excellent ethical and moral principles.	☑
C.	The Ten Commandments are abridged form of 14 or 15 commands in the Bible.	☑
D.	All the principles of the Ten Commandments can be found in the Qur'ān.	☑
E.	The Ten Commandments are only for Jews, not for Christians.	☒

Adam and Eve in The Garden

Objective of the Lesson:

This lesson analyzes how Shaitān tempted Ādam (A) by giving him a false impression about life. Ādam (A) was able to correct himself despite a temporary lapse in his judgment. Through the story of Ādam (A), the lesson shows how each one of us can correct lapses in our lives and remain steadfast in our religion.

We learned about Ādam (A) and his wife in two different lessons in the elementary and junior level classes. In this lesson, our purpose is not to narrate the same story, but to explore some of the complex issues mentioned in the Qur'ān about Ādam (A) and his wife. As always, the Qur'ān is not interested in telling a story, but emphasizing the inner meanings and morals of a story. Sometimes we tend to focus on the outward details of a story, overlooking the inner meanings and ignoring the teachings. We tend to rely on the popular legends and fail to see the true message of the Qur'ān. This lesson will illustrate how to go beyond the story and extract the abiding moral conveyed by the story.

Significance of the "names": After Allāh disclosed His intention to place khalīfah on the earth, the angels became apprehensive about human beings. They were afraid the new creation would create disorder and shed each other's blood. In āyah 2:30 the angels expressed their concern: *"Are You going to place therein one who would make mischief in it and shed blood; while we celebrate Your praise, and we glorify Your holiness?"* In the same āyah, Allāh replied: *"I surely know which you do not know."* Obviously Allāh is more knowledgeable. He knows the past, present, and future. He knew what the angels did not know. Subsequently, Allāh created mankind.

After creating human beings, Allāh gave them knowledge. Allāh says in āyah 2:31:

وَعَلَّمَ ءَادَمَ ٱلْأَسْمَآءَ كُلَّهَا

And He taught Ādam the names— all of them.

What did Allāh mean by the word *al-asmā'a* (literally, names)? Did Allāh teach Ādam only the names of everything? Will that complete his knowledge?

The term '*names*' plays a significant role in the Qur'ān. Allāh mentioned: *"And to Allāh belongs all the finest Names."*[7:180] Allāh's names are not mere names, but they are His qualities. If Allāh simply told Ādam (A) the name of a tree, river, plant, apple, animal, fruits, cloud, rain and so forth, he could not have fully understood or remembered the items. It is clear that the word 'names' implied the physical and functional characteristics of these items. Thus, when Ādam was taught the names of all things, he did not simply learn the names, but he also understood the inner qualities and attributes of each item.

It is also reasonable to assume that Allāh also told Ādam (A) about abstract things, e.g., good, bad, right, wrong, repentance, fear, and forgiveness. In other words, he was taught everything that Allāh needed for mankind to live in the Garden. Once Ādam (A) learned about himself and his surroundings, Allāh presented him to the angels and told him to tell them the names of all things. Āyah 2:31 says:

ثُمَّ عَرَضَهُمْ عَلَى ٱلْمَلَـٰئِكَةِ فَقَالَ أَنۢبِـُٔونِي بِأَسْمَآءِ هَـٰٓؤُلَآءِ إِن كُنتُمْ صَـٰدِقِينَ

He presented them to the angels, and said: "Tell Me the names of all these if you are truthful."

The angels admitted they had no knowledge other than what Allāh taught them. When Ādam (A) was asked, he was able to say name everything.[2:33]

Subsequently the angels and Iblīs were asked to bow down to Ādam (A) in recognition of his superiority. The key factor in determining the superiority of human beings was based on their knowledge of 'names', not based on how they were created.

Tree of temptation: After establishing the superiority of mankind over the angels and Iblīs, Allāh told Ādam (A) to dwell in the garden with his wife and eat everything, but not to go near a certain tree. This is mentioned in 2:35 and in 7:19.

And We said: "O Ādam! you and your wife dwell in this garden, and you eat from it plentifully where-and-when you wish; but do not go near this Tree, lest you become of the wrongdoers." (2:35)

The identity of the tree is irrelevant in understanding the moral of the story. It is certainly not an apple tree as the Bible described. Allāh simply used a tree to test if Ādam (A) obeys or defies Him.

It is possible that mention of the tree is symbolic to man's boundaries of right and wrong that he may not cross. Allāh allowed Ādam to dwell freely in the Garden, but asked him not to go 'near' the tree, i.e., not to overstep the boundaries of man's moral and ethical limits.

Shaitān's temptation: When Iblīs refused to bow down to Ādam (A), Allāh condemned him until the end of time. In 15:35 Allāh says: *"and upon you be indeed the condemnation up to the Day of Judgment."* Then Shaitān sought respite from Allāh so that he could prove that man is weak and could succumb to his temptations. He said:

Respite me till the day they are raised up. (7:14)

In response to Shaitān's appeal, Allāh granted him respite until the end of time. However, after receiving respite, Shaitān became more rebellious. He turned out to be an open enemy of mankind.

He said: "Now, as You have adjudged me as gone wrong, I will certainly lie in ambush for them on Your Straight Path, (7:16) "then I will certainly come upon them from their front and from their back, and from their right, and from their left. And You will not find most of them thankful." (7:17)

Allāh could not leave mankind without protection from the evil conspiracy of Shaitān. Allāh promised: *Surely as to My servant you have no authority over them except the misguided ones who follow you.[15:42]*

However, even the exclusive servant of Allāh can sometimes fall in the trap of Shaitān. In the example of Ādam (A), we see that Shaitān sneaked upon him and gave him some false promises. He said:

فَوَسْوَسَ إِلَيْهِ ٱلشَّيْطَانُ قَالَ يَـٰٓـَٔادَمُ هَلْ أَدُلُّكَ عَلَىٰ شَجَرَةِ ٱلْخُلْدِ وَمُلْكٍ لَّا يَبْلَىٰ ۝

Then the Shaitān made an evil suggestion to him; he said: "O Ādam! shall I lead you to the Tree of Eternity and a kingdom which does not decay?" (20:120)

In another āyah Shaitān lied to Ādam (A) about the tree. He told Ādam (A) that the tree was prohibited because it could lead them to become angels or to live forever.[7:20]

The original sin: When Ādam (A) tasted from the tree, he did not become an angel nor did he become immortal. Nothing physically happened to him, but spiritually he committed a sin—the sin of disobeying Allāh. This is clearly the original sin of mankind. It is important to note that the Qur'ān does not blame Eve for the fall of Ādam (A). Therefore, in the viewpoint of the Qur'ān, women are not guilty of causing the downfall of mankind.

Shame of Ādam (A): The Qur'ān says that after Ādam (A) and his wife ate from the tree their 'shame' (*sawātun*) became apparent (*badā*) to both of them.

Casual reading of the translation of the āyāt appears to indicate that first Shaitān wanted to show them their private parts.[7:20] After they ate from the tree, their shame became apparent to them.

فَدَلَّىٰهُمَا بِغُرُورٍ ۚ فَلَمَّا ذَاقَا ٱلشَّجَرَةَ بَدَتْ لَهُمَا سَوْءَٰتُهُمَا وَطَفِقَا يَخْصِفَانِ عَلَيْهِمَا مِن وَرَقِ ٱلْجَنَّةِ ۖ وَنَادَىٰهُمَا رَبُّهُمَآ أَلَمْ أَنْهَكُمَا عَن تِلْكُمَا ٱلشَّجَرَةِ وَأَقُل لَّكُمَآ إِنَّ ٱلشَّيْطَـٰنَ لَكُمَا عَدُوٌّ مُّبِينٌ ۝

Then he made them fall through enticement; then when they tasted of the tree, their shame became disclosed to them and they began to sew together the leaves of the garden over them. And their Rabb called out to them: "Did I not forbid you from this tree, and tell you that the Shaitān is an open enemy to you?" (7:22)

We have to understand the original intention of Allāh and the avowed plan of Shaitān. When Allāh ordered Ādam (A) not to eat from the tree, did He mean Ādam (A) and his wife should never find out about their private parts, and consequently, all their progeny should also never find out? Why is finding one's private parts sinful? It appears that "shame" (*sawa'* meaning evil) becoming clear or manifest (*badat*) to them indicates something different.

Commenting on this, Yusuf Ali wrote: *"Our first parents as created by Allāh were innocent in the matters of material as well as spiritual. They knew no evil. But the faculty of choice which was given to them and which raised them above the angels, also implied that they had the capacity of evil, which by the training of their own will, they were to reject. They were warned of the danger. When they fell, they realized the evil. They were (and we are) still given the chance, in this life on a lower plane, to make good and recover the lost status of innocence and bliss."*

Avowed plan of Shaitān: Shaitān's main plan is not to disclose our private parts, but to destroy us by derailing us from the righteousness and the Straight Path. His promise to lie in ambush and attack us from all directions[7:16-17] is intended to make us evil, abominable, disgraceful and, above all, neglectful of our duties towards Allāh. Yusuf Ali's explanation, as given above, rightly brings out the inner significance of the shame of Ādam (A) becoming disclosed to him.

Clothing of Ādam and Eve: After finding out their 'shame,' Ādam (A) and his wife started to sew together the leaves of the garden to cover them.[7:22] However, in āyah 7:26 Allāh says the clothing of piety (*libāsu at-taqwā*) is the best. After the soul is touched by guilt and soiled by evil, the appropriate remedy comes from righteousness.

يَٰبَنِىٓ ءَادَمَ قَدْ أَنزَلْنَا عَلَيْكُمْ لِبَاسًا يُوَٰرِى سَوْءَٰتِكُمْ وَرِيشًا ۖ وَلِبَاسُ ٱلتَّقْوَىٰ ذَٰلِكَ خَيْرٌ ۚ ذَٰلِكَ مِنْ ءَايَٰتِ ٱللَّهِ لَعَلَّهُمْ يَذَّكَّرُونَ ۝

O Children of Ādam! We have certainly bestowed upon you a clothing that covers your shame, as well as an adornment to you. But the clothing of righteousness,—that is the best. This is out of the Messages of Allāh, that they may receive admonition! (7:26)

Forgetfulness and forgiveness: Why did Ādam (A) and his wife taste from the tree, even after Allāh specifically instructed them not to do so. The answer to this question shows an inherent weakness in the human character. This weakness is "forgetfulness." Ādam (A) did not want to willingly defy Allāh, but he forgot.

And most surely We had already made a covenant with Ādam before, but he forgot, and We did not find on his part any determination. (20:115)

The beauty of Ādam's character is that as soon as he realized his sin, he immediately sought forgiveness from Allāh.

رَبَّنَا ظَلَمْنَآ أَنفُسَنَا وَإِن لَّمْ تَغْفِرْ لَنَا وَتَرْحَمْنَا لَنَكُونَنَّ مِنَ ٱلْخَٰسِرِينَ ۝

They said: "Our Rabb! we have done wrong to ourselves; and if You do not forgive us and have mercy on us, we shall surely become of the losers." (7:23)

1. What is the significance of the word '*name*' when the Qur'ān says, "He taught Adam the names – all of them"?

....

....

2. Which of the following choices is true about the tree Adam was warned not to go near?

    A.   It was an apple tree.
    B.   It was a tree of which the nature and characteristics are not known.
    C.   It was a tree that could make Adam immortal.
    D.   It was a tree that could make Adam equal to angels.
    E.   All of the above.

3. Which of the following choices is correct about the specific temptation Shaitān used to fool Adam?

    A.   He tempted him to be naked.
    B.   He tempted him to taste the delicious apple.
    C.   He tempted him with the promise of becoming an angel or immortal.
    D.   He tempted him with knowledge and wisdom.
    E.   He tempted him to become a friend.

4. Which of the following choices is correct about the "temptation" to which Adam succumbed?

    A.   His wife advised him to eat from the tree, therefore she was the temptress.
    B.   Shaitān told him to eat from the tree, therefore he was the tempter.
    C.   Adam ate from the tree on his own because he liked the look and color of its fruit.
    D.   Angels tempted Adam because they thought he might shed blood.
    E.   None of the above.

5. Read āyah 15:39-40. What will Shaitān be unable to do?

    Cannot tempt servants who are truthful/purified

6. After eating from the tree, what specific thing happened to Adam and his wife?

    A.   They developed skin diseases and covered themselves with leaves.
    B.   They discovered their shame.
    C.   They ran away from each other.
    D.   They had babies born to them.
    E.   They saw Shaitān in the form of a snake.

7. Which of the following choices is a logical conclusion from the story of Adam?

    A.   It is possible for any person to succumb to the temptations of Shaitān.
    B.   It is the moral weaknesses in mankind that causes a fall from righteousness.
    C.   Shaitān tantalizes the improbable things as probable, and lures us towards them.
    D.   Mankind has to remain alert at all times to recognize Shaitān's temptations.
    E.   All of the above.

8. Which of the following choices is a logical conclusion from the story of Adam?

    A.   Shaitān proved he could mislead mankind.
    B.   Shaitān proved he was better than mankind.
    C.   Man's fall results from disobeying or neglecting divine teachings.
    D.   Only (a) and (c).
    E.   Only (a) and (b).

9. Although Adam and his wife started to cover themselves with the leaves of the garden, the Qur'ān says a certain type of clothing is best for mankind. Which is the correct answer?

    A.   Any silk clothing.
    B.   Clothing made of leaves.
    C.   Clothing of taqwā.
    D.   Any clothing man can wear before listening to Shaitān.
    E.   All of the above.

10. Based on the lesson, which of the following choices is correct about the "shame" of Adam and Eve?

    A.   The shame was about physical nakedness, which was unknown to Adam.
    B.   The shame was discovering Adam and Eve could defy God and go against Him.
    C.   The shame was an allegory of mankind's vulnerability and need for guidance.
    D.   Only (a) and (b).
    E.   Only (b) and (c).

Women in the Qur'ān

Objective of the Lesson:

The Qur'ān mentions several women who played significant roles in many events and established several moral stories. Many women shaped the course of history. This lesson lists these women and classifies them based on their involvement in events or the morals they established.

In the Qur'ān we find an impressive number of female characters. Except for Maryam, none of them are mentioned by their actual names. Many of them did not speak a word or perform any actions, but their narrations were included to illustrate a story or moral.

Three groups: For the sake of our study, we can sort these women into three broad groups.

In Group 1, we include those Qur'ānic women who did not speak a word or perform any action. A cursory reference to them was necessary to ensure a smooth flow of the stories.

In Group 2, we include those women who performed an action or spoke.

In Group 3, we include those women who performed significant actions and contributed immensely to set the course of history. In certain cases, the Qur'ān uses several āyāt to discuss these episodes.

Stories of Group 1 women: The women in this group did not speak a word or perform any action. However, their presence in the story helped establish an underlying moral principle.

Zakariyyāh's wife: A reference to her in the Qur'ān appears during a brief mention of Zakariyyāh (A) in sūrah Al-e-'Imrān and sūrah Maryam. Prophet Zakariyyāh (A) prayed to Allāh to give him a child, however, he knew he was old and his wife was barren. He was not sure how he could have a child, but believed that Allāh could always grant a wish. In response to his prayer, Allāh assured him that a boy would be born to him, whose name would be Yahyā. Even after this assurance, Zakariyyāh (A) was not

Group 1	Group 2	Group 3
The wife of Zakariyyāh (A), mentioned in 19:5,8; 21:90.	Wife of Lūt (A), mentioned in 7:83, 29:33, 11:81, 15:60, 27:57, 66:10.	*Zawj* or wife of Adam, known as Eve or Hawwa' 2:35, 4:1, 7:19.
Banāti, or my daughters or girls (of my town), said by Lūt (A) in 11:78.	Wife of Ibrāhīm (A), Sara, mentioned in 11:71, 51:29.	Mary or Maryam, 3:36-37, mother of Jesus.
'Ā'ishah, one of the wives of Rasūlullāh (S), referred to in 24:11.	Zulaikhā', the lady of the house who tempts Yūsuf, mentioned in 12:23.	Hannah, Anna, or Anne, 3:35, woman: *imra'ah* of Imran, mother of Mary.
Zaynab, one of the wives of Rasūlullāh (S), mentioned in 33:37.	Women guests of Zulaikhā', *al-Niswa*, mentioned in 12:30.	'Asiyah, 28:9, 66:11, wife of the Pharaoh.
Banāti, or the girls in his town, Rasūlullāh's (S) daughters, mentioned in 33:59.	Raytah bint Sa'd,' woman who untwists the thread, mentioned in 16:92.	Mother of Mūsā, 20:38–40; 28:7.
Imrāt-Nūh, wife of Nūh (A), mentioned in 66:10 (family mentioned in 21:76).	*Ukht-Mūsā*, 20:40, 28:7, Mūsā's sister.	Bilqīs, *imra'ah* 27:23, Queen of Sheba.
Umm Jamil bint Harb, mentioned as *imra'ah*, i.e., the wife of Abū-Lahab, in 111:4,5.	Two women of Madyan, Imra'atan, 28:23.	
	Azwaj-al-nabi, 33:28, wives of Rasūlullāh (S), also known as Ummahat al-Mu'minin: the mothers of the Faithful.	
	Khawlah bint Tha'labah, al-Mujadilah, 58:1, wife of Aws.	
	al-Muhajirat, 60:10, women refugees.	
	Ba'd-azwaj-hu, one or more of Rasūlullāh's (S) wives, 66:3; in this case it is believed to refer to 'Ā'ishah and Hafsah.	

convinced. Allāh assured him that it is possible for Allāh to remove the obstacles to his wife bearing a child. The child was not born miraculously. In āyah 21:90, Allāh confirmed his wife was cured of her infertility.

Banāti of Lūt (A): The word *banāti* means "my daughters," (11:78). When a group of males desired immoral relationship with other males, Lūt (A) was utterly annoyed with them. His entire prophet mission was largely directed towards correcting the moral wickedness of the community. But the male members of the community would not listen to him. Then Allāh sent some messengers to Lūt (A) to warn the community about impending punishment and to advise him to leave the township before disaster strikes. When the male members saw the messengers, they ran towards them, expecting to do immoral acts. At that point, Lūt (A) frantically tried to stop them from approaching the messengers. He even offered them his 'daughters'—implying that these lustful men should establish formal relationships with women, not men. These daughters could have been his biological daughters or symbolic of all pious unmarried women, whom he affectionately addressed as his daughters.

'Ā'ishah: The Qur'ān mentions an incident involving Rasūlullāh's (S) beloved wife 'Ā'ishah (24:11). After an expedition against Bani Mustaliq, Rasūlullāh (S) was returning to Madīnah. During the return journey, 'Ā'ishah was inadvertently left behind where they had stayed overnight. When Rasūlullāh's (S) caravan was preparing to depart in the pre-dawn darkness, 'Ā'ishah discovered that she lost a necklace near the place where she had gone to wash. As she searched for the necklace, the caravan departed, assuming she was on her camel. In the morning, Safwān bin Mu'attal Sulami, a companion of Rasūlullāh (S), was passing by the area. He discovered 'Ā'ishah, recognized her, and escorted her to Rasūlullāh's (S) caravan. The leader of the hypocrites, Abduallh ibn Ubayy, who was also returning with Rasūlullāh (S), used this incident to spread a slander that 'Ā'ishah spent the night with Safwān. Rasūlullāh (S) investigated the incident thoroughly and found 'Ā'ishah and Safwān innocent. The Qur'ān states that due to this incident, Muslims learned a costly lesson about spreading slander—it kills three people: the speaker, the one spoken to, and the one spoken of. Every person who participates in spreading a slander earns a sin, but the one who plays a major role in spreading it will face grievous punishment. Slander against righteous women should be refuted, suppressed, and prevented from spreading.

Zaynab: Rasūlullāh (S) arranged the marriage of his adopted son, Zayd, with Zaynab. Thus, Zaynab was the daughter-in-law of Rasūlullāh (S). Soon the marriage ended in divorce as the couple could not reconcile their problems. This divorce became the discussion topic at different levels of the society. Because the marriage was conducted at the behest of Rasūlullāh (S), he was divinely instructed to take the divorced Zaynab as his wife (33:37). The significance of the marriage with Zayd, divorce and marriage with Rasūlullāh (S) are discussed in the Level 9 book in this series.

Banāti of Rasūlullāh (S): The daughters of Rasūlullāh (S) are mentioned in āyah 33:59 as well as his wives. The āyah says: *O you Nabi! say to your wives and your daughters and the women of the Believers that they lower upon them their coverings. This is better, so that they will be recognized, and may not be annoyed. And Allāh is ever most Forgiving, most Rewarding.*

Imrāt-Nūh (A): The wife of Nūh (A) is mentioned in āyah 66:10. She was a disbeliever and acted treacherously against her husband. Despite being a prophet's wife, she will suffer punishment in hell. Family ties will not save anyone from Judgment as each person is accountable for his or her own deeds.

The wife of Abū Lahab: Sūrah Masad, also known as sūrah Lahab, mentions the wife of Abū Lahab, the uncle of Rasūlullāh (S). Abū Lahab was bitterly opposed to Rasūlullāh (S) and the religion of Islam. The sūrah refers to her as *imra'ah* i.e., his wife. Her actual name was Umm Jamil bint Harb. She used to taunt Rasūlullāh (S) and compose rhymes to desecrate him and his family. The Qur'ān does not say what she used to do or speak against Rasūlullāh (S), but she was an equal participant in the evils perpetrated against Rasūlullāh (S). The Qur'ān, therefore, condemns her in āyāt 111:4-5.

Stories of Group 2 women: In this group, we include the names of those Qur'ānic women who either spoke or performed some action. Without narrating the stories, we simply mention what these women said or did.

Wife of Lūt (A): References to her can be found in āyāt 7:83, 29:33, 11:81, 15:60, and 27:57. The Qur'ān does not say what she specifically said, but based on these āyāt we know that she refused to be a believer. When Allāh asked Lūt (A) to leave the city before destruction, Lūt (A) asked his wife to accompany him. He wanted to save her, but she refused and chose to stay behind.

Wife of Ibrāhīm (A): Ibrāhīm (A)'s first wife was Sara. References to her can be found in āyāt 11:71 and 51:29. She received a divine prophecy about the birth of a boy. She knew it was impossible for her to bear a child due to her old age and infertility. In response to the prophecy she said: *"Oh woe is me! shall I bear a child while I am an old woman, and this my husband is an old man? This is surely a strange thing."*

Zulaikhā': References to Zulaikhā' can be found in sūrah Yūsuf. She tried to tempt Yūsuf (A) into having a physical relationship with her. When Yūsuf (A) refused to obey her and ran towards to door, she tore his shirt from the back. Later, she falsely testified in front of her husband and accused Yūsuf (A) of advancing towards her. It was her testimony that sent Yūsuf (A) to prison, and after about a decade, it was her testimony that finally absolved Yūsuf (A) from the crime he did not commit.

Women guests of Zulaikhā': The Qur'ān mentions them as *al-Niswa* in 12:30. Zulaikhā' invited these women to her house to seek their compassion for desiring the young servant. When Yūsuf (A) appeared before them during the luncheon, these women were so captivated by his charm that they unwittingly cut their fingers with the food knives.

Raytah bint Sa'd: The Qur'ān does not mention her name but speaks about one of her activities. She is referred to as the woman who untwists the thread, mentioned in 16:92. The āyah says: *And do not become like her who breaks her thread into shreds after spinning it strong.*

Ukht-Mūsā: Her story is mentioned in āyāt 20:40 and 28:7. When Mūsā's mother put the infant Mūsā (A) in a basket and cast him in to the river, she asked her elder daughter to walk by the river to see what happened to the basket. The basket floated down the river and reached a place where the Pharaoh's wife and her attendees noticed it. They picked up the basket to find, to their amazement, an adorable infant in the basket. When infant Mūsā (A) refused to suckle milk, the sister came forward and offered to find them a wet-nurse who might be helpful. This wet-nurse would be none other than Mūsā's own mother.

Two women of Madyan: Their story is briefly mentioned in 28:23. These two women came to fetch water from a well for their goats. But they were unable to access the water as some desert people were vandalizing the source of water. Mūsā (A) intervened and helped the women fetch water. Later these women asked Mūsā (A) to come meet their father, who thanked Mūsā (A) for helping his daughters and offered one of them in marriage.

Wives of Muhammad: They are mentioned as *azwaj-al-nabi*, also known as *Ummahat al-Mu'minin* in 33:28.

Khawlah bint Tha'labah: Her story is mentioned in sūrah al-Mujādilah in 58:1. She complained to Rasūlullāh (A) about her husband who invoked the pre-Islamic practice of zihar. Under this practice, husbands would cut off all marital ties with their wives, but would not divorce them.

Al-Muhajirat: In the Qur'ān, āyah 60:10 discusses women refugees. They are believers who migrate to a Muslim camp to avoid persecution by their unbelieving community.

Ba'd- azwaj-hu: In āyah 66:3, the Qur'ān refers to one or more of Nabi Muhammad (S)'s wives. In this case, it is believed to refer to 'Ā'ishah and Hafsah.

Stories of Group 3 women:
This group of women had significant roles to play and, thus, contributed immensely to set the course of history.

Wife of Adam (A): She is not mentioned by name, but a reference to her can be found in āyāt 2:35, 4:1, and 7:19–23. Allāh advised Adam (A) and his wife to live in the Garden, but not to go near a tree. Shaitān tempted both of them and made them fall from grace. The Qur'ān does not blame Adam's wife for the fall of mankind—the blame is equal. Thereafter, both of them prayed to Allāh for forgiveness and they were forgiven.

Mother of Maryam: The mother of Maryam was instrumental in shaping the life of Maryam. Before the birth of her child, she vowed to dedicate the baby for the service of Allāh.[3:35] She thought the baby would be a boy, but after giving birth to a girl, she did not hesitate to keep her vow. If she had not dedicated Maryam to the service of the temple, the history of Christianity and Islam would have been much different.

Maryam: Detailed accounts of Maryam can be found in two sūrahs in the Qur'ān. These are *Al-e-'Imrān* and *Maryam*. The Qur'ān describes Maryam's life from the time she was in the womb of her mother until she became an adult. Her mother dedicated her to the service of the temple when she was a baby.[3:37] All her life, she was a chaste woman. When she was still a virgin, she received a prophecy about the birth of a child.[3:42] After she conceived, she moved to an eastern land where she gave birth to 'Isa (A).[19:23] Later she returned to her native home with her son. The Qur'ān gave her the unique honor of being the chosen woman of all the nations.[3:42]

'Asiyah: She was the wife of Fir'awn. The Qur'ān describes her as a believer.[66:11] When Fir'awn issued a state order to kill all Israelite newborn boys, it was 'Asiyah who saved Mūsā (A) and adopted him as her son.[28:9] If it was not for her meritorious act, the history of the Israelites would have been different.

Mother of Mūsā (A): Her name is not mentioned in the Qur'ān, however, her brief but important role helped determine the course of history. When she feared that the army of Fir'awn would kill her child, she relied upon Allāh. She received a divine inspiration to put her son Mūsā in a basket and cast him in the river.[20:39] Allāh assured to return baby Mūsā back to her.[28:7] She knew either way there was danger—if she let Mūsā stay with her, Fir'awn would kill him. If she cast the basket into the river, there was the risk of drowning. In the greatest test of her life, she demonstrated the utmost trust in Allāh. The rest is history.

Bilqīs: The Qur'ān does not mention her name but her account is narrated in great detail in sūrah Naml. In the first part of her account, she is shown as a ruler of a country—the Queen of Sheba, where people worship the sun. She is depicted as a woman who has power and command over her people. Her interaction with Sulaimān (A) changed the course of her future and the destiny of her country. She protected her country from possible attack by Sulaimān (A). Instead of provoking Sulaimān (A) to come to her country, she ventured out to meet him. This showed her good sense of judgment, which ultimately saved her country. But it also paved the way for her to become a Muslim. After she met Sulaimān (A) in his palace, she realized that she was chasing false things in life by ignoring the truth. She accepted Islam.

1. Several female characters in the Qur'ān are mentioned by their proper names.   True / False

2. Which of the following choices is/are true about all female characters mentioned in the Qur'ān?

    A.   All of them spoke and performed some action.
    B.   All of them spoke, but did not perform any specific action.
    C.   All of them performed some specific action, but did not speak.
    D.   Not all of them spoke or performed an action.
    E.   None of the above.

3. In our attempt to group female characters in the Qur'ān based on their actions and/or words, which of the following choices about Zainab is/are true?

    A.   She performed an action and spoke in a āyah.
    B.   She spoke in a āyah, but did not perform a specific action.
    C.   She did not perform an action nor speak in a āyah.
    D.   She performed some specific action but did not speak in a āyah.
    E.   None of the above.

4. All of the women mentioned in the Qur'ān were spiritually faithful.   True / False

5. In our attempt to categorize female characters in the Qur'ān, all Group 2 women have something in common. In this regard, which of the following choices is correct?

    A.   All Group 2 women were pious in their lives.
    B.   All Group 2 women performed some action or spoke in a āyah.
    C.   All Group 2 women first rejected faith, then became believers.
    D.   None of the Group 2 women spoke in a āyah.
    E.   All Group 2 women were wives of different messengers.

6. Based on the lesson, which Group 2 woman prayed to Allāh, saying: *"My Lord! I do hereby dedicate to You what is in my womb...."*

    A.   Maryam.
    B.   Mother of Maryam.
    C.   Mother of Ismā'īl and Ishāq.
    D.   'Asiyah.
    E.   Bilqis.

7. In sūrah Mujādilah, which woman's case was presented?

    A.   'Isa Ibn Maryam.
    B.   Wife of Adam (A).
    C.   Bilqis.
    D.   Khawlah bint Tha'labah.
    E.   Wife of Lūt (A).

8. In sūrah Mujādilah, a particular woman's case is presented to denounce a pre-Islamic custom. What is that custom?

    A.   Zihar.
    B.   Zinah.
    C.   The killing of a female child.
    D.   Polygamy.
    E.   All of the above.

9. In sūrah 60, āyah 10, the case of the migrating women is mentioned. Which is the proper action believers are required to take when they receive a migrating women?

    A.   They should examine the woman.
    B.   They should not return the women to unbelievers if the women was a believer.
    C.   They should pay a dower if a believer wants to marry the woman.
    D.   All of the above.
    E.   None of the above.

10. In the lesson about distinctive women in the Qur'ān, two women were unable to bear a child until Allāh cured them to have sons. Who were they?

    A.   Mūsā (A)'s mother and Maryam.
    B.   Maryam and Zulaikhā'.
    C.   Zakariyyāh (A)'s wife and Ibrāhīm (A)'s wife.
    D.   Aziz's wife and Ibrahim's wife.
    E.   Zakariyyāh (A)'s wife and Zulaikhā'.

A Muslim Family

Objective of the Lesson:

In a typical Muslim family, each member has his or her individual and collective role. Each member has certain rights and certain obligations. These rights and obligations are centered around loyalty and commitment towards Allāh. This lesson presents a short summary of the rights and duties of some of the family members.

The definition of the word 'family' can vary. Miriam-Webster defines family as a group of individuals living under one roof and usually under one head of household. Other lexicons define a family as any group of people living together as if they were related by blood. By virtue of such a definition, your friends and roommates in college become your family. Miriam-Webster also defines family is a basic unit in society that traditionally consists of two parents raising their own or adopted children. Other lexicons also define a 'family' as a group made up of a parent or parents and their children.

The core of a true Muslim family is based on two units, whatever the name of these two units. The two units are husband and wife and/or father and mother. The common tie that would qualify them to be considered a Muslim family is the contract of marriage. In Islam, unless a man and a woman marry, they cannot form a family. Therefore, under Islamic precepts, students who live in a dorm are not a family. They may feel like a family, but they are not. In a Muslim family, even if the father dies and the mother lives with her children, it is still a family because the mother and father were once married and started a family.

Twin aspects of marriage: In Islam, a family is a basic unit consisting of two parents who come together through the institution of marriage. The Islamic marriage is an interconnection of two aspects: (a) social and (b) religious. The social aspect of marriage lies in its contractual nature, by which two individuals enter into a marriage relationship through a contract. This contract not only binds two individuals, but it also, socially, binds the bride's and groom's families. The religious aspect of marriage is the spousal agreement. This agreement provides mutual and parental rights, claimed through the practice of faith, loyalty, love, mercy, and above all, staying within the limits ordained by Allāh.

In a Muslim family, both social and religious aspects play equal roles. Whenever these two aspects are ignored or violated, the family, as a unit, suffers. For example, the contractual agreement between two individuals calls for abiding by the spirit of the contract and living to its fulfillment. Putting this agreement to the test will cause tension and conflict in the family. Similarly, the religious aspect of the marriage calls for fulfilling each other's rights and duties. Failure to fulfill these rights or undermine these duties will cause the moral and spiritual degradation of the family.

Parents' rights: In the context of a Muslim family, the Qur'ān explains the rights of the parents in connection to the parent-child relationship. However, in doing so, the Qur'ān clearly states the rights of Allāh are superior to the rights of the parents. It is interesting to note that the Qur'ān does not specifically mention the father's rights separate from the mother's rights. On the other hand, the mother's rights are mentioned clearly, as we will see later in the lesson.

In the context of family structure, the Qur'ān has also defined a few parental duties or roles. The Qur'ān has clearly defined children's duties towards their parents. Among other duties, the primary duty of children is to show kindness to parents, especially during their old age.

وَقَضَىٰ رَبُّكَ أَلَّا تَعْبُدُوٓا۟ إِلَّآ إِيَّاهُ وَبِٱلْوَٰلِدَيْنِ إِحْسَـٰنًا ۚ إِمَّا يَبْلُغَنَّ عِندَكَ ٱلْكِبَرَ أَحَدُهُمَآ أَوْ كِلَاهُمَا فَلَا تَقُل لَّهُمَآ أُفٍّ وَلَا تَنْهَرْهُمَا وَقُل لَّهُمَا قَوْلًا كَرِيمًا ﴿٢٣﴾

And your Lord has commanded that you do not worship anyone except Him alone; and do good to the parents. If one of them or both of them reach old age in your presence, even then do not say to them "Ugh," and do not scold them, and speak to them a generous speech. (17:23)

وَٱخْفِضْ لَهُمَا جَنَاحَ ٱلذُّلِّ مِنَ ٱلرَّحْمَةِ وَقُل رَّبِّ ٱرْحَمْهُمَا كَمَا رَبَّيَانِي صَغِيرًا ﴿٢٤﴾

And lower to them the wings of humility out of tenderness; and say: "My Lord! have mercy on them as they brought me up in childhood." (17:24)

These two āyāt place two rights—that of Allāh and parents—next to each other for several reasons.

First, the rights separate what is owed to Allāh—worship. This is distinctly separate from what is owed to parents—compassion and mildness. Muslim children cannot worship their parents, but obey Allāh and fulfill their duties towards their parents.

Second, the command to honor parents comes directly from Allāh, not from parents.

Third, the āyāt highlight the idea of mutual care, kindness and compassion. Children are required to be kind to their parents because their parents nourished them during their childhood—with love, care, kindness, and compassion.

Fourth, the āyāt reverse the rights of the parent-child relationship. As parents get older, they become more vulnerable and, therefore, more dependant on their children just as the children once were vulnerable and dependant on the parents.

Obedience to Allāh alone: In another place, the Qur'ān positions the rights of Allāh next to the rights of parents. But in doing so, the Qur'ān points out the mother's role in bearing and nursing children.

And We have enjoined on people concerning his parents—his mother bears him in travail upon travail, and his weaning is in two years—saying: "Give thanks to Me and to your parents. Towards Me is the return.

"But if they strive against you that you should associate with Me about which you do not have any knowledge, then do not obey them; yet keep company with them with fairness in this world. And follow the path of him who bends towards Me, and then towards Me is your return, so I shall inform you as to what you used to do." (31:14-15)

The emphasis in the two āyāt above serves to clarify several points as follows:

First, the mother's role in procreation should not elevate her status to equal to or above that of Allāh's status. Mother is instrumental in generating life, but it is Allāh who is the ultimate Creator and to Him is our final return.

Second, obedience is only due to Allāh, and, should there be any conflict between obeying Allāh or obeying parents, the children should obey only Allāh.

Third, the command to disobey parents does not allow children to uphold any unauthorized religious beliefs, but they are still obligated to understand and follow the divine command. This thesis calls for the children, and every new generation of sons and daughters, to respond to the divine call by means of their own reasoning and knowledge and not by blindly accepting the footsteps of their forefathers.

Fourth, despite Allāh's command to disobey parents in specific circumstances, the command is clear as to how they should be treated: with care, love, and compassion.

Children in the family: We mentioned earlier that the Qur'ān has defined a few parental duties towards the children. Parents must pray to have righteous children.[3:38; 21:89; 25:74] After the children are born, it is the duty of the parents to teach them proper Islamic manners, give them a good education and raise them as believers. The whole process of raising righteous children is called *tarbiyah*, which is a separate topic of discussion. The importance of *tarbiyah* is summarized in the following āyah:

O you who believe! save your own selves and your families from a Fire whose fuel is men and stones... (66:6)

The mother is required to take care of newborn babies by breast-feeding them.[2:233] It is a duty from which many modern women are walking away, but divine wisdom has a reason to point out its importance. It is the duty of the father to provide the material needs of the family and the children.

Fathers and daughters: From the Qur'ānic perspective, the relationship between father and daughter in a Muslim family is important. Historically, this relationship is often mired in abuse, oppression, and condemnation of the daughter. The Qur'ān has clearly displayed its utmost dislike for the way some fathers treat their daughters.

In Arabia, it was a common practice to kill newborn girls, by burying them alive in the sand. Such atrocity towards the girls was addressed in many Qur'ānic āyāt, first, because of the nature of atrocity, and, second, because of the hypocrisy associated with such an action. Ironically, same fathers who were guilty of killing their newborn girl children believed Allāh had daughters. The Qur'ān categorically condemns both actions and associated hypocrisy because it supports the notion of God as Father and that too, only of daughters.

And they ascribe to Allāh daughters. Glory be to Him! And for themselves what they desire! (16:57)

Has He taken daughters out of what He has created, and lined up for you the sons? (43:16)

Or are for him the daughters, while for you are the sons? (52:39)

Although the Qur'ān has strictly condemned fathers for killing their daughters, in many societies even today daughters are not treated the same way as sons.

On the Day of Judgment, Allāh will question for what sin was the girl child buried alive.[81:8-9] Allāh will hold the fathers accountable for killing their daughters, and hold them equally responsible if they oppress them in life.

and when the girl-child buried alive is questioned: "For what sin was she killed?" (81:8-9)

Husbands and wives: We mentioned previously that marriage in Islam is a social contract between two individuals of the opposite sex. The purpose of the contract is to give both spouses, particularly the woman, equal rights. In ancient Arabia, and in medieval Europe, women were largely considered a commodity. In Islam, the institution of marriage contract uplifted the position of women for the first time in the society. A woman was no longer perceived as a commodity, but a person with ownership rights and legally binding, enforceable civil liberties. In the marital agreement, the woman can set not only the conditions of marriage but also divorce. Men are duty-bound to fulfill contract that they have made.[2:177]

Women's rights were not only raised to a higher level through the institution of marriage, but the spiritual position of women was made equal to men. The Qur'ān ordains both men and women to live by the same principles and views are equally qualified to enter haven.

that He may cause the believing men and the believing women to enter Gardens beneath which flow the rivers, abiding in them, and He will wipe off their evils from them. And that, in the presence of Allāh, is a great achievement! (48:5)

And do not envy that by which Allāh has made some of you excel above the others. For men there is a share out of what they earn, and for women there is a share of what they earn. And ask Allāh for His grace. Surely Allāh is ever Knower of everything. (4:32)

O you mankind! We have surely created you out of a male and a female, and We have made you into nations and tribes that you may recognize one another. Surely the noblest of you in the presence of Allāh is the most reverential of you. Truly Allāh is all-Knowing, all-Aware. (49:13)

Allāh promises to the believing men and the believing women Gardens beneath which flow the rivers, they will abide in them, and pure dwellings in Gardens of Eden. And the pleasure of Allāh is the greatest. As for this, it is the supreme attainment. (9:72)

The Qur'ān distinguishes men and women solely on the basis of those who have faith and those who do not. Thus, any hierarchy between men and women is not based on their sexual, racial, or economic superiority, but on the level of *taqwa*.

Relatives: A Muslim family is much more than a mere nuclear family consisting of parents and their children. A Muslim family maintains healthy relationship ties with their relatives.

Allāh commands us in the Qur'ān to be kind to our relatives and to maintain our relationship ties with them.

Therefore give to the kinsman his due; and to the needy and the wayfarer. This is better for those who seek the countenance of Allāh. And they are themselves the successful. (30:38)

They ask you as to what they should spend. Say: "Whatever good things you spend, it is then for the parents and the kindred, and the orphans and the needy, and the wayfarer." And whatever good you do, Allāh then is Knower of it indeed. (2:215)

And worship Allāh and do not associate with Him anything, and goodness towards the parents, and to the near relatives, and the orphans, and the poor, and the neighbor who is related, and the neighbor who is alien, and the companion by the side, and the traveler, and what your right hands possess. Surely Allāh does not love him who is proud, boastful. (4:36)

1. In āyah 17:23, Allāh tells us not to say two things to our parents, particularly when they grow older. What two things we are not supposed to say?

  a. ....

  b. ....

2. A beautiful du'ā is mentioned in āyah 46:15. In this du'ā, we ask for three things for three different people. Who are the three people?

  a. .... b. ....

  c. ....

3. Explain what is meant by the metaphor "lowering the wings of humility" as mentioned in āyah 17:24.

  ....

  ....

  ....

4. Under what conditions are we allowed to disobey our parents? Explain.

  ....

  ....

5. Read āyāt 4 to 6 in sūrah Maryam. Then answer the following:

  Who prayed to Allāh for a child? ....

  What would the child inherit? ....

  What are two reasons the person might not receive a child? ....

6. Based on the lesson, what are the social and religious aspects of marriage?

  Social: ....

  Religious: ....

7. What is single-most important right Islam gave to Muslim women through the institution of marriage?

    A.   The right to enter into a marriage relationship.
    B.   Legally binding ownership rights.
    C.   The right to retain her maiden name.
    D.   The right to denounce ill treatment.
    E.   The right to forfeit dowry.

8. What condition does a group of Muslim people need to satisfy before they can be considered a family?

    A.   They must live in the same household and pay a mortgage.
    B.   They must have one male and one female member in the group.
    C.   They must have a child living with them.
    D.   A man and a woman in the group must be married to each other.
    E.   They must have faith in Allāh.

9. Which of the following choices about a Muslim family as mentioned in the Qur'ān is correct?

    A.   Only children have duties to fulfill towards their parents. Parents do not have duties to fulfill towards their children.
    B.   Both parents and children have certain duties towards each other.
    C.   Children must obey their parents under all circumstances.
    D.   Children must treat their parents with kindness only after they become old.
    E.   Children must disobey their parents in matters other than religion.

10. Which of the following choices about the rights a Muslim person has from his or her relatives is correct?

    A.   The right to be taken care of by the relative if he or she has financial difficulties.
    B.   The right to receive a free education from the relative.
    C.   The right to receive money to buy a house.
    D.   The right to negotiate business matters without an intermediary.
    E.   The right to decline a financial guarantee of the relative in a loan transaction.

The Status of Women in Islam

Objective of the Lesson:

The status of women in Islam is often misinterpreted and misrepresented by Muslims and non-Muslims alike. This lesson summarizes the lengthy topic into a few short, critical issues to help students appreciate how Islam envisioned granting women their rightful status in society.

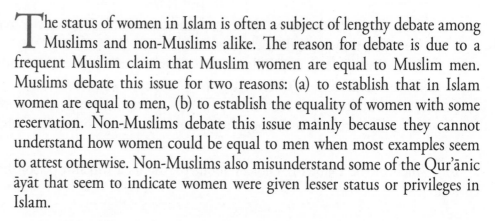

The status of women in Islam is often a subject of lengthy debate among Muslims and non-Muslims alike. The reason for debate is due to a frequent Muslim claim that Muslim women are equal to Muslim men. Muslims debate this issue for two reasons: (a) to establish that in Islam women are equal to men, (b) to establish the equality of women with some reservation. Non-Muslims debate this issue mainly because they cannot understand how women could be equal to men when most examples seem to attest otherwise. Non-Muslims also misunderstand some of the Qur'ānic āyāt that seem to indicate women were given lesser status or privileges in Islam.

Before we begin our study, let us review the status of women in the pre- and post-Islamic era, in Arabia as well as in the rest of the world. This survey will serve as a fair evaluation of how Islam improved the status of women.

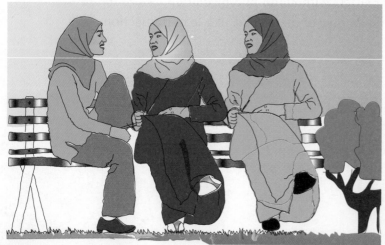

Pre-Islamic period: Before the advent of Islam, the status of women in any of the world civilizations was extremely deplorable. They were treated as if they were not human beings and did not have a soul. They lived under severe subjugation to men. Ancient Greeks viewed women like a poisonous tree and as evil as Shaitān. Women were treated as a commodity and sold in the market as merchandise. Ancient Romans believed women did not have a soul or deserve fair treatment. A woman was considered incapable of doing anything according to her wish. She was forced to live under the control of a male family member.

Ancient Indians kept women under different forms of subjugation, as permitted by the Hindu scriptures. A woman was forever considered impure, therefore, she did not have rights to the scripture. Widows were not allowed to remarry. It was a routine custom in India to burn widows in the pyre of the dead husband. In ancient China, the position of women was no better than women in rest of the contemporary world. Chinese men were allowed to bury their wives alive if things did not go according to their likings. In ancient Persia women were treated inferior to men.

In the past atrocities against women in the Christian world were widespread and well documented. Early Church has many degrading references to the female sex, some of which are so grotesque and mortifying that one would wonder how Christianity could propound these ideas. In the sixth century, the church debated whether women have soul, and if so, whether it was an animal or human soul. The church made Christian women live with the curse that they were the root of all evils and suffering in the world. Women were represented as the door of hell. The church depicted the dress and beauty of women as the root of evil and an instrument of the devil. In the name of religion, the church perpetrated various forms of discrimination against women. In the U.S.A., women did not have voting rights until 60 years ago. In Britain, in the early 19th century, women did not have rights to inheritance and rights to keep their own earnings.

Pre-Islamic Arabia: The story of atrocities in pre-Islamic Arabia is no better than any other story in the rest of the world. Women were at the mercy of men and were treated as mere commodities. Newborn girls were considered to have brought shame and disgrace to the family. Fathers would not hesitate to bury newborn girls alive. Women did not have rights to inherit property. Men would marry as many women as they wanted and ill treat them.

Islam changed the world: With the advent of Islam, a world religion, the position of women in Arabia changed forever. Subsequently, as Islam spread to the rest of the world, it envisioned to uplift the position of women in those parts of the world. Only recently, the modern world reluctantly granted women certain rights that Islam had already granted 1400 years ago. Today's women had to acquire some of her rights through tremendous struggle and sacrifice. Nothing was given to her automatically.

Equality and sameness: In order to investigate how Islam changed the position of women, let us first understand what is meant by equality and sameness. Under an Islamic viewpoint, women and men are equal but they are not the same. While it is well known that two men cannot be the same, it is irrational to think that a man and a woman will be the same. Just as two men cannot be a mirror image of each other, a man and a woman cannot be similar. They are different. Evidently, equality and sameness are two different things.

Created equal: Men and women were not created identically, but they were created equal. In this process, neither men nor women were given an advantage over the other. They were two equal parts of the reproductive equation. Both are needed for the procreation of life. In the Qur'ān Allāh says:

وَٱللَّهُ جَعَلَ لَكُم مِّنْ أَنفُسِكُمْ أَزْوَٰجًا وَجَعَلَ لَكُم مِّنْ أَزْوَٰجِكُم بَنِينَ

And Allāh makes for you mates from among yourselves, and through your mates He gives you children and grandchildren… (16:72)

Several other āyāt carry the same message:

"Originator of the heavens and the earth. He has made for you mates from among yourselves, and mates of the cattle. He multiplies you through it. (42:11)

O you mankind! We have surely created you out of a male and a female, and We have made you into nations and tribes that you may recognize one another. (49:13)

When the Qur'ān describes the process of procreation, the role of both genders is given equal importance. In Arabic usage, *zawj* (زوج) indicates either spouse, male or female. The mates (*zawj*) were created from among yourselves (*anfusikum*), and through the conjugal relations of the mates, Allāh creates the offspring. Thus, from the beginning we see that the Qur'ān did not discriminate between male and female.

Women are not blameworthy: The concept of original sin does not exist in Islam. The original sin, a Christian concept, puts the blame of human's downfall on Eve. In the Bible, she is depicted as the temptress, who caused the moral degradation of Ādam (A) and mankind. The Qur'ān does not indicate that the fall of Ādam (A) was due to his wife.

Equal reward: In the Qur'ān, many of the commandments, rules and regulations are given in masculine terms, although they are equally applicable to men and women. The use of the masculine gender is a writing style in Arabic. However, when it came to addressing many of the issues dealing with women, the Qur'ān used feminine terms. In spiritual matters, she has equal responsibilities to men and has equal claim to receive rewards for her deeds. Her monthly conditions allow her to restrict some of the daily rituals every month, yet her reward is not made inferior to man in any of the messages of the Qur'ān.

فَٱسْتَجَابَ لَهُمْ رَبُّهُمْ أَنِّي لَآ أُضِيعُ عَمَلَ عَٰمِلٍ مِّنكُم مِّن ذَكَرٍ أَوْ أُنثَىٰ ۖ بَعْضُكُم مِّنۢ بَعْضٍ ۖ

So their Lord immediately responds to them— "I shall certainly not leave to waste any deed of any of you, whether a male or a female, you are members, one of another. (3:195)

A similar theme is mentioned in several other āyāt as follows:

And the believing men and the believing women—one party of them are patrons to another. They bid doing good and forbid doing evil, and they keep up the Salāt and pay the Zakat, and they obey Allāh and His Rasul. As for these,— Allāh will soon have mercy on them. Allāh is indeed Exalted in Might, most Wise. (9:71)

Whoever does good, whether male or female,— provided he be a Believer, then We shall certainly cause him to live a happy life, and We shall invariably give them their reward in the best manner for what they used to do. (16:97)

"Whoever does evil, he will not be requited except in the like of it; and whoever does good—out of a male or a female, and he is a Believer—then these will enter the Garden, they will be given sustenance in it without reckoning. (40:40)

Surely as to the Muslim men and the Muslim women, and the Believing men and the Believing women, and the obedient men and the obedient women, and the truthful men and the truthful women, and the persevering men and the persevering women, and the humble men and the humble women, and the charitable men and the charitable women, and the fasting men and the fasting women, and the men guarding their appetites and the guarding women, and the men remembering Allāh much and the remembering women— Allāh has prepared for them forgiveness and a mighty reward. (33:35)

Rights to property: One of the most significant ways Islam elevated the status of women is by providing legal rights in domestic and public affairs. The granting of these rights was a practical demonstration of the Qur'ānic ideology that women were created equal to men. The merit of these rights stands out for two reasons:

First, women did not ask for or struggle to get these rights. The Qur'ān gave the rights in order to cure the social injustice.

Second, the implementation of these rights was revolutionary in light of the fact that these rights were not available to women in the seventh century, and were not available to women in Europe for another 1300 years.

Islam grants women rights to inheritance, wealth, and landed property. She has rights to enter into any contract and business transaction. These rights do not get transferred to her husband when she gets married. While giving her these legal rights, her legal liabilities are equal to man's liabilities. If she commits an offense, her penalty is no less or no more than a man's penalty in a similar case. For the crime of adultery, her punishment is 100 stripes, the same for a man.[24:2]

Rights to dower: In Islam, *Mahr* is the term for a gift given by a man to his wife at the time of his marriage. The amount of *mahr* is included in the nuptial contract. The *mahr* is not a symbolic or actual "price" of the woman getting married. It is a true gift, ordained by Allāh. The Qur'ān has specifically decreed that the wife has full rights to her *mahr*. Ownership of *mahr* does not transfer to her father or husband.

وَءَاتُواْ ٱلنِّسَآءَ صَدُقَٰتِهِنَّ نِحۡلَةً

And give the women their dowers (nihlatan) as a free gift (sadaqa). (4:4)

وَلَا تَحِلُّ لَكُمۡ أَن تَأۡخُذُواْ مِمَّآ ءَاتَيۡتُمُوهُنَّ شَيۡـًٔا

...and it is not lawful for you to take back any part (of the mahr) you have given them... (2:229)

Women in the modern world: Women in the West, particularly in industrialized, developed and developing countries have struggled for and earned many of their rights. During and after World War II, the challenges of war, the pressure of economic needs, the requirement of industrial development coerced women to get out of the home—to work, earn, and survive. As an equal participant with man in the struggle, she demanded equal rights and achieved many of her rights. However, her newly acquired rights also brought her many degrading social and moral challenges that are left unaddressed. The modern Western woman enjoys a plethora of circumstances that her Muslim counterpart does not. Islamic principles not only give her equal rights, but also give her security and protection, and provide much-needed guidance in changing social circumstances. She is entitled to equal reward when Judgment is set up in the Hereafter.

Condition in Muslim countries: In some Muslim countries, women enjoy many of the rights granted by Islam. They can inherit property, get an education, earn their own livelihood, and own property. At the same time, the conditions of women in some Muslim countries are often deplorable. Western media sometimes portrays these conditions out of proportion. They focus on one or two isolated issues from these countries to portray that violence against women in those countries is endorsed by the Qur'ān. In reality, these countries have a system in place that seems to contradict the true teachings of the Qur'ān. Women are treated as second-class citizens. Failure to understand the Qur'ān and to implement its principles is not the Qur'ān's failure, but our own. We are to blame for our deplorable situation. This, by itself, is a topic for a new discussion.

1. Read āyah 4:32. Using your own words explain the equality of women as stated in the āyah.

....

....

....

2. Read āyah 4:7. Which rights of women are discussed in the āyah. Explain.

....

3. Based on the lesson, explain the equality of men and women in terms of how they were created.

....

....

....

4. Which of the choices below about how the Bible and the Qur'ān differ on the status of Eve is correct.

   A.   The Bible depicts Eve as the mother of mankind, the Qur'ān disagreed.
   B.   The Bible described how Adam tasted from the tree on his own, Eve had nothing to do with it. The Qur'ān agrees.
   C.   The Bible blames Eve for tasting from the tree, the Qur'ān does not.
   D.   The Qur'ān puts blame on Eve, but the Bible does not.
   E.   The Qur'ān blames only Adam for tasting from the tree, the Bible blames Satan for it.

5. Which of the choices below is correct about *mahr* given in marriage?

   A.   *Mahr* can be given by a man or a woman, depending on the affluence of the person.
   B.   *Mahr* is the price of a woman getting married.
   C.   If the wife is very rich, she does not deserve *mahr*.
   D.   After *mahr* is given, the bride's father has the right to own it.
   E.   *Mahr* is a gift given by a groom to his bride at the time of marriage.

6. What are two important rights that Islam granted women.

....

....

7. Which of the following choices about the legal liabilities of women in Islam is correct?

  A.   The legal liabilities of women are half that of men.
  B.   The legal liabilities of women are equal to that of men.
  C.   The legal liabilities are reduced for women if they are not educated.
  D.   The legal liabilities of women are doubled in the crime of adultery.
  E.   The legal liabilities of women are minimal since they suffer many other injustices.

8. In Islam, men and women are equal, but they are not the same.   True / False

9. Which of the following choices about the equality of men and women is correct?

  A.   They are equal only in the sight of Allāh.
  B.   They are equal only when rewards for them are considered.
  C.   They are equal only in the court of law.
  D.   They are equal subject to the approval of the law of the land.
  E.   They are equal in all respects.

10. Along with the rights enjoyed by non-Muslim women in the West, sometimes these women also suffer many different subjugation or evils. Mention some of their sufferings.

....

....

....

....

Marriage to Non-Muslims

Objective of the Lesson:

Can a Muslim man marry a non-Muslim woman? Can a Muslim woman marry a non-Muslim man? What about marrying an idol worshipper or a member who belongs to the People of the Book? This lesson analyzes the criteria Islam has established for Muslim men and women to consider before marrying people of other faiths.

Several āyāt in the Qur'ān and authentic teachings of Rasūlullāh (S) encourage Muslims to be married. Celibacy, which means a state of, or a vow of, not getting married, is not recommended for any Muslim. Marriage is considered a religious duty in Islam and enjoined upon all believers who can afford it. Marriage is not only a contract between two persons committed to each other, but it is also a contract with Allāh, insomuch as it fulfills a duty enjoined by Allāh. Marriage provides a legal platform to enter, develop, and sustain relationships with the opposite sex and to extend the family. It also serves as a defense system for many forms of moral downfalls.

In a famous Hadīth mentioned in Mishkat, Messenger Muhammad (S) is reported to have said that when a Muslim marries, he has fulfilled half of his religious duties, so let him fear Allāh regarding the remaining half. In another Hadīth mentioned in Muslim, Rasūlullāh (S) is reported to have said, "Marriage is my Sunnah, he who shuns my Sunnah is not of me."

All the Muslim youths, insha-Allāh, will one day get married. Finding the right life partner has never been easy and it will never be easy. When choosing the right life partner, Muslim youths living in the West will likely face many challenges and experience many conflicting pressures that their elders did not experience. The purpose of the selection process, in the past or present, is to find the right life partner who can help nurture a healthy, loving, and respectful family environment.

Longest phase in life: Ideally, the conjugal period is the longest phase in a person's life. If the average life span of a person is about 70 years, married life easily constitutes about 65% of one's life span, assuming the person was married by age 25. Under the above scenario, it is extremely critical to determine with whom one wants to spend 45 years of one's life. With the right partner, one can have a morally, socially and spiritually fulfilling life experience. On the other hand, with the wrong partner, one could suffer from loss of love and compassion that could potentially lead to mutual distrust, ill feelings, and separation. Keeping this point in mind, choosing the right life partner is even more important.

The social environment: The life partner of a Muslim youth will, in all likelihood, come from the social environment where he or she lives. In the West, this environment is a melting pot of practically every culture, religion, ethnicity and language. The most important element of this melting pot is the existence of people of other faiths. Due to this coexistence with other faiths at all levels of social interaction, it is highly possible that a Muslim youth might believe a person of another faith could be his or her ideal life partner.

The big question is—can a Muslim man marry a woman of another faith? Can a Muslim woman marry a man of another faith?

The Qur'an on the life partner: The Qur'an has clearly laid out the guidelines for marriage. According to the Qur'an, the main criteria that one should look for in a potential mate is similarity in faith. For that reason, the overall tone in the Qur'an and sunnah is against marriage between a Muslim and a non-Muslim.

However, one exception to the rule is allowed: if the marriage is between a Muslim man and a Christian or a Jewish woman.

Let us carefully read two āyāt from the Qur'an—2:221 and 5:5. These two āyāt clearly state the rulings of inter-faith marriages. Let us analyze āyah 2:221 first.

وَلَا تَنكِحُوا۟ ٱلْمُشْرِكَٰتِ حَتَّىٰ يُؤْمِنَّ ۚ وَلَأَمَةٌ مُّؤْمِنَةٌ خَيْرٌ مِّن مُّشْرِكَةٍ وَلَوْ أَعْجَبَتْكُمْ ۗ وَلَا تُنكِحُوا۟ ٱلْمُشْرِكِينَ حَتَّىٰ يُؤْمِنُوا۟ ۚ وَلَعَبْدٌ مُّؤْمِنٌ خَيْرٌ مِّن مُّشْرِكٍ وَلَوْ أَعْجَبَكُمْ ۗ أُو۟لَٰٓئِكَ يَدْعُونَ إِلَى ٱلنَّارِ ۖ وَٱللَّهُ يَدْعُوٓا۟ إِلَى ٱلْجَنَّةِ وَٱلْمَغْفِرَةِ بِإِذْنِهِۦ ۖ وَيُبَيِّنُ ءَايَٰتِهِۦ لِلنَّاسِ لَعَلَّهُمْ يَتَذَكَّرُونَ ﴿٢٢١﴾

Do not marry idolatrous women, until they believe; while a believing maidservant is better than an idolatrous woman, even though she attracts you. And do not give (your girls) in marriage to idolatrous men until they believe, while a believing slave is better than an idolatrous man even though he attracts you. They invite you to the hellfire, while Allāh calls to the Garden of Paradise and forgiveness by His authority. And He makes clear His message for mankind so that they may pay attention. (2:221)

Explanation of āyah 2:221: In this āyah, the word *mushrik* (derived from root *sharika*, meaning 'to be a companion,' 'to be a partner') literally means people who associate partners with Allāh. Those who ascribe partners with Allāh are the idol worshippers and polytheists.

The āyah clearly instructs men not to marry idolatrous women. One of the reasons for this prohibition is to avoid conflicts of interest in a relationship where the faiths and objectives of two individuals are not only poles apart, but also fundamentally incompatible. Children born within such households would experience contradictory faiths that could result in apostasy or other forms of spiritual downfalls.

The āyah further states that idolatrous men or women invite believers to hellfire while Allāh invites them to the Garden of Paradise. Evidently, marriage with idolatrous men or women has the potential for disaster for believers. We have to keep in mind that despite many good teachings available in other religions, the path of Islam is the only accepted and valid one in the sight of Allāh.[3:19; 3:85] Only Islam can help one achieve success in the Hereafter.

The term *amah* (literally, maidservant) primarily means slave-girls, but its use is to contrast an otherwise attractive idolatrous woman with a humble, believing woman. The āyah teaches us that a humble, believing woman is more preferable, because she would not invite us to hellfire.

Interestingly, in the first part of the āyah, the believing man is directly prohibited from marrying an idolatrous woman. However, when it comes to the marriage of a believing woman to an idolatrous man, the āyah continues addressing male readers. The āyah says: *and do not give (your girls) in marriage to idolatrous men…*, thus the āyah is speaking to the male members of the family. This is because the male members of a family typically broker the marriages of women; therefore, the āyah prohibits 'them,' i.e. male family members, from offering their female offspring to polytheistic or idolatrous males.

Explanation of āyah 5:5: The second of the two āyāt to clearly state the rulings of inter-faith marriages is 5:5.

ٱلْيَوْمَ أُحِلَّ لَكُمُ ٱلطَّيِّبَٰتُ ۖ وَطَعَامُ ٱلَّذِينَ أُوتُوا۟ ٱلْكِتَٰبَ حِلٌّ لَّكُمْ وَطَعَامُكُمْ حِلٌّ لَّهُمْ ۖ وَٱلْمُحْصَنَٰتُ مِنَ ٱلْمُؤْمِنَٰتِ وَٱلْمُحْصَنَٰتُ مِنَ ٱلَّذِينَ أُوتُوا۟ ٱلْكِتَٰبَ مِن قَبْلِكُمْ إِذَآ ءَاتَيْتُمُوهُنَّ أُجُورَهُنَّ مُحْصِنِينَ غَيْرَ مُسَٰفِحِينَ وَلَا مُتَّخِذِىٓ أَخْدَانٍ ۗ وَمَن يَكْفُرْ بِٱلْإِيمَٰنِ فَقَدْ حَبِطَ عَمَلُهُۥ وَهُوَ فِى ٱلْءَاخِرَةِ مِنَ ٱلْخَٰسِرِينَ ۝

This day the good things have been made lawful for you. And the food of those who have been given scripture is lawful for you, and your food is lawful for them; and the chaste women out of the believing women and the chaste women out of those whom scripture has been given before you,

when you give them their dower money, seeking to preserve their chastity, not to prostitute them and not taking (them as) illicit lovers. And if anyone repudiates faith, his work gets nullified, and he will be a loser in the Hereafter. (5:5)

The second half of this long āyah states that marriage between Muslim men and some non-Muslim women are allowed, provided that certain restrictions are observed. Before discussing the āyah, we should remember that despite the restrictions and reservations, Islam embraces a broad outlook on marriage, unlike those seen in Judaism or Christianity.

Neither shalt thou make marriages with them; thy daughter thou shalt not give unto his son, nor his daughter shalt thou take unto thy son. [Deut. 7:3]

For they will turn away thy son from following me, that they may serve other gods: so will the anger of the LORD be kindled against you, and destroy thee suddenly. [Deut. 7:3]

The word *hasanat* used in āyah 5:5 means 'chastity', not 'virginity'. Muslim men are permitted to marry *muhsanāt* or chaste and virtuous women from the People of the Book, i.e., primarily Jews and Christians, provided that they believe in one God and they are not idol worshippers.

Under the restrictions mentioned above, Islam allows a Muslim man to marry a Jewish or Christian woman because the difference in beliefs between them is minor compared to other faiths. All three religions are known as the Abrahamic faiths, and they have many commonalities among them. Therefore, the fear and risk of a woman corrupting the faith of a Muslim man is less. Now the question is: does the rule not apply to women? We will discuss the issue later in the lesson.

Āyah 5:5 gives permission to a Muslim man to marry a woman of the People of the Book. It also makes it clear that the man must fulfill the obligation of a legal marriage: paying her the dower. After he pays the dower, the women are recognized as family members and are given property rights from the very first day.[4:4] Furthermore, relations with such women must be maintained in the true spirit of Islam—without fornicating (4:24-25) and without taking them as paramours.

Marrying non-Muslim men: While reading āyah 5:5, we see that the Qur'ān does not allow Muslim women to marry non-Muslim men. Why not?

In most modern societies, the husband is the head of the family. A wife often accepts the nationality, culture, and status of her husband. A Muslim woman, living in the household of a non-Muslim husband, may find it difficult to carry out her religious obligations. She may constantly be under the influence of her husband's viewpoint and may fear opposing his beliefs and opinions. At many social gatherings, she will be surrounded by her husband's friends and family, who profess a non-Islamic faith. She runs the risk of religious suppression, which might lead to possible apostasy. Islam encourages non-compulsion in the matter of faith and advocates religious freedom, but in a non-Muslim household, Muslim women may not enjoy the same rights. Islam granted social dignity, rights, and honor to women, but these rights may not be honored in an alien household. For this reason, Islam has prohibited Muslim women from marrying non-Muslim men.

Under all circumstances, we should follow the Qur'ānic guidelines. When it comes to marriage with a non-Muslim person, let the messages of āyāt 2:221 and 5:5 be our guiding principles. We do not want to be in relationships that will lead us to hellfire. We want to be in relationships whereby we can receive forgiveness from Allāh and qualify to enter the Garden of Paradise.

1. Explain the significance of the following Qur'ānic statement: a believing maid or slave is better than an extremely charming non-believing woman or man.

....

....

....

2. According to the Qur'ān, to what consequence do an idolatrous person invite a Muslim person through the marriage?

....

3. According to āyah 5:5 marriages between Muslim men and some non-Muslim women are allowed, provided that certain restrictions are observed. What are these restrictions.

....

....

....

4. According to the Qur'ān, what criteria should a person look for in his or her potential spouse before getting married?

    A.   Speaking the same language.
    B.   Fitting his or her list of requirements.
    C.   The husband should be older than the wife.
    D.   Similarity in faith.
    E.   Social status and compatibility of the two families.

5. A Muslim man wants to marry a non-Muslim woman. She has not accepted Islam yet, but she will in about a year after she finishes her studies. Which of the following choices explains the Qur'ānic ruling about them getting married?

    A.   There is no problem if the man marries her now.
    B.   The man can marry her provided that he gives her *mahr*.
    C.   The man cannot marry her until she accepts Islam.
    D.   The man can marry her but they cannot live together.
    E.   The man can marry her provided that an Imam officiates the marriage.

Marrying Four Women

Objective of the Lesson:

While Islamic ethos advocates strict monogamy, Islam has allowed a Muslim man to marry up to four women. However, a Muslim man can have multiple wives only if he is under certain obligations, and provided that he meets certain conditions. This lesson analyzes the divine wisdom behind granting the approval to have plural wives.

Islam allowes a Muslim man to marry up to four women. The women can be married while the man's other wife or wives are still alive and living in marital relationship with the same man. This provision to allow a Muslim man to marry up to four women caused a lot of debate over the past 1,400 years. Both Muslims and non-Muslims sometimes confused by the teaching and, thus, misinterpret the true purpose behind this provision. Many Muslims misuse the provision. It is common in developing countries to find elderly and socially powerful men taking advantage of the provision to marry young girls with total disrespect of the conditions stated in the āyah that allows multiple marriages. In social circles, the issue of marrying four women is often treated as a joke. Many times non-Muslim critics refer to the provision with derision to undermine Islamic social values. A simple Google search using the phrase "marrying four women" results into more than three million hits!

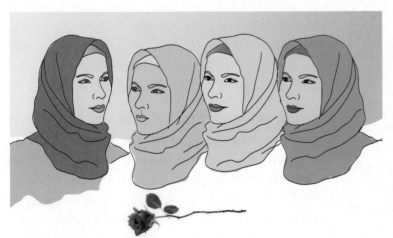

Polygamy and polygyny: Strictly speaking, polygamy and polygyny are two different things. Polygamy is a marriage in which a spouse of either sex may have more than one mate at the same time. Thus, by definition, polygamy is a marriage in which a man can marry multiple women, or a woman can marry multiple men at the same time. Polygyny is a marriage in which a man marries more than one woman. Yet another term, polyandry, is a marriage in which a woman marries more than one man at the same time. Strictly speaking, Islam has allowed polygyny, not polygamy or polyandry, with a limit of four wives. Although in common usage the word polygamy is used to mean a man marrying more than one woman, in order to distinguish one form of poly-marriage with the other, we should use the proper term.

Let us discuss the issue of polygyny in Islam to get a better understanding of the spiritual and social aspects of the provision.

Āyah in sūrah An-Nisā': Sūrah An-Nisā' is the only sūrah in the Qur'ān where the provision to marry two, three, or four women (*mathnā wa thulātha wa rubā'ā*) is clearly stated. We must remember that the permission of polygyny is not a mandatory duty, but only a provision. The āyah reads as follows:

وَإِنْ خِفْتُمْ أَلَّا تُقْسِطُوا۟ فِى ٱلْيَتَـٰمَىٰ فَٱنكِحُوا۟ مَا طَابَ لَكُم مِّنَ ٱلنِّسَآءِ مَثْنَىٰ وَثُلَـٰثَ وَرُبَـٰعَ فَإِنْ خِفْتُمْ أَلَّا تَعْدِلُوا۟ فَوَٰحِدَةً أَوْ مَا مَلَكَتْ أَيْمَـٰنُكُمْ ۚ ذَٰلِكَ أَدْنَىٰٓ أَلَّا تَعُولُوا۟ ۝

And if you fear that you cannot do justice to the orphans then marry who seem good to you from among women —two or three or four. But if you fear that you cannot deal justly, then only one; or whom your right hands possessed. This is more proper so that you may not deviate. (4:3)

This āyah has several key elements, all of which need to be carefully analyzed and understood. The historical context under which the āyah was revealed cannot be ignored.

Issues of the orphans: The issue of taking care of orphans is the main reason behind granting the permission of polygyny in Islam. Before granting the permission of polygyny in āyah 3 of sūrah An-Nisā', āyah 2 begins with the theme of orphans. In fact, the entire passage in the sūrah is devoted to the issues of orphans. For example:

Āyah 2: Deals with the property of orphans. Do not substitute inferior things with the good things of the orphans.

Āyah 5: Take due care of the orphans.

Āyah 6: The age when orphan's property can be handed over to them and its procedure.

Āyah 8: The fair division of property. Orphans and the poor should be considered during the division.

Āyah 10: The consequence of usurping the property of orphans—punishment of fire.

It is important to note that it is an "obligation" to deal properly and fairly with orphans. However, in order to look after their interests, it is not an obligation but only an "option" to marry up to four women. And, if multiple women are married, it is an "obligation" to deal justly with these wives. Such obligations apply to providing them housing, food, clothing, support, and treating them kindly. If a husband is not sure whether he will be able to deal justly with multiple wives, he is commanded to marry only one.

Who seem good to you: Scholars of Islam have provided possible explanations as to who could be married (*fānkihu*, literally, then marry, *nikaha*, literally, marry). The question is whether the orphan girls themselves, the mothers of the orphan girls, or any other women can be married. This question is answered in the āyah itself as *mā tāba lakum* or "those who seem good to you." These additional wives could be the mothers of such orphans, the orphan girls themselves or another woman who could devote time to the welfare of the orphans.

Mathnā wa thulātha wa rubā'ā: This phrase means two, three or four. The question is: why does the provision of such a marriage start with two women, then three and then four women. In order to understand this issue, we have to realize that āyah 4:3 has two sets of "if… then…" constructions.

The first "if… then…" (*wa in….fā…*) construction states that "if" a man fears that he cannot do justice to the orphans, "then" he can marry two, three, or four women. Therefore, the instruction is not to an unmarried man, who apparently may not have much of a responsibility compared to a married man. A married man, who has one wife, is now allowed to marry multiple women, provided that he encountered two issues: (a) he is afraid, concerned, or anxious (*khiftum*), and (b) he is afraid of not doing justice to the orphans (*tuqsitū*, derived from *qasata*, literally, to act justly). If the husband feels that with two wives he can ensure justice, there is no need to take additional wives. Under no circumstances can the number exceed four.

Fear of injustice: The married man is first afraid (*khawfa*, literally, to fear, to be anxious) of a duty that has fallen upon him. This duty is to take care of the orphans who are, presumably, under his care. If they were not under his care, his worry is unjustified. He is worried because āyah 4:2 has imposed a serious duty upon him. He is commanded to:

(a) give the orphans their property,

(b) not substitute his worthless goods with the good things of the orphans,

(c) not consume the orphan's property.

If this married man has his own children, he will have the obligation to give due attention to them. However, in doing so, he might not be able to give due attention to the orphans and might not do justice to them. Therefore, he is now allowed to marry another woman, thus, starting with *mathnā* or two women, then proceeding to *thulātha wa rubā'ā*, if necessary.

Some scholars clarify that this provision is equally applicable to an unmarried man as well. If an unmarried man is imposed with the responsibility of orphans, he can marry two women at a time, because the āyah states *mathnā* or two women, and he, too, can proceed to *thulātha wa rubā'ā*, if necessary.

Equal treatment of the wives: Of the two "if… then…" constructions in āyah 4:3, the second "if… then…" construction bases the conditions on the similar fear (*khafa*) and sense of justice (*qasata*) in the mind of the man. Earlier, this man was fearful of not doing justice to the orphans, which necessitated the provision of plural marriage. Now this man is again fearful of not doing justice—this time to his plural wives. If he is afraid, concerned, or anxious (*khiftum*) about not doing justice (*tuqsitū*), he is commanded to stay with one wife.

The same āyah that gives permission for plural marriages also protects the rights of the women involved. None of the women involved in such a marriage should be exploited or taken advantage of—by the man or by the women involved. Each of the additional three marriages has to be equally legally binding, with the same rights, responsibilities, and obligations as the first marriage. The children born from these wives have the same rights of inheritance. The first wife is not in any way superior in rank, honor, or responsibility, nor is the youngest wife unduly pampered at the expense of the other wives.

Plural marriage is not a law: We have to understand that the provision to marry plural women is not a law. It is only an avenue to address a necessity. However, to stay with a single woman is a law and it is proper so that the man may not deviate, as mentioned at the end of the āyah: *dhālika adnā allā ta'ūlū*.

Law of the land to be followed: Since the Qur'ānic ruling in āyah 4:3 is only a provision, all Muslim men must follow the laws of the land. If the law of the country prohibits multiple marriages, that law should be followed. Following the laws of the land will not violate the Qur'ānic teaching on multiple marriages.

Sharing the husband: No woman would like to share her husband with another woman. It is very likely that multiple marriages will give rise to jealousy and tension in the family. However, in general Islamic laws give precedence to the overall welfare of the society over personal gains and pleasure. Therefore, multiple marriages should not have a devastating emotional impact upon a Muslim woman. The most important factor in a good Islamic marriage is the piety of the partners involved.[2:221] This point is beautifully illustrated in the following hadīth :

> *"A woman may be married for four reasons: for her property (wealth), her rank (lineage), her beauty and her religion. However, you should marry the one who is religious and you will be satisfied." (Narrated in Sahih Al-Bukhārī).*

The provision of plural marriage in Islam also has the provision of addressing the physical and emotional needs of marriageable females in many societies. Instead of pushing the marriageable women to the vices of society or to become mistresses, they could be given equal rights through legal marriage. In this respect, we should understand that love, as understood in Western culture, is not a prerequisite in Islamic marriage. Love usually follows after marriage.

Why not polyandry: Islam gives tremendous importance to the identification of both the father and the mother of a child. If a man has multiple wives, the parents of all the children born to the wives could be easily identified without the need for DNA analysis. But if a woman marries more than one husband, the identity of the father of the child cannot be determined without DNA analysis. Even then, social tension and emotional trauma cannot be averted. However, DNA analysis is a fairly new technology. We have to realize that before DNA technology was available, it would not have been possible for parents and society to determine the identity of the father. By disallowing polyandry, Islam provided a lasting solution for all time periods.

Monogamy is the preferred norm: The nature of human being is such that no matter how much man tries, it is practically impossible to treat all wives equally. This is clearly stated in another āyah in the Qur'ān:

> *And you have no capability that you will treat equitably between the wives even though you wish. (4:129)*

Based on this declaration, and based on the requirement to treat all wives equally (4:3), in general, the Qur'ān is directing Muslims to practice strict monogamy. Therefore, what shall a man do if he took multiple wives? Men were prohibited from discarding multiple wives already taken into marriage prior to the promulgation of the ruling. They were required to make peace with the wives taken prior to the promulgation of the ruling, by honoring all of them equally. However, if they must divorce one of them, it must be done in an honorable manner. If this approach is adopted, Allāh is ever more Forgiving of the past faults and most Rewarding for good deeds.

1. In which sūrah can the āyah allowing a Muslim man to marry multiple women be found?

    A.   In sūrah Baqarah and An-Nisā'.
    B.   In sūrah Baqarah.
    C.   In sūrah A-e-'Imrān.
    D.   In sūrah An-Nisā'.
    E.   In sūrah Al-Ahzāb.

2. Explain the difference between polygamy and polyandry.

    ....

    ....

3. In the āyah allowing multiple marriages, what is the significance of the phrase *mathnā wa thulātha wa rubā'ā*?

    A.   Whenever multiple marriages are needed, the man must start with two wives.
    B.   Multiple marriages must start with one wife and gradually progress until four wives are taken.
    C.   The instruction is to a man, who is already married, to take a second wife if needed.
    D.   Two, three and four wives must be married one by one.
    E.   Experiment with two wives; if does not work, divorce them and marry the third and fourth.

4. Explain the reasons for the word *khiftum* (fear) is mentioned twice in āyah 4:3.

    ....

    ....

    ....

    ....

5. Which of the following statements is correct regarding multiple marriages allowed in the Qur'ān?

    A.   Multiple marriages are allowed only when the issue of orphans exist.
    B.   Multiple marriages are allowed as long as a person can maintain four wives.
    C.   Multiple marriages are allowed when a person is afraid.
    D.   Multiple marriages are allowed to establish social justice.
    E.   Multiple marriages are allowed so that all women can get married.

6. Multiple marriages is a provision, not a law mandatory upon all Muslim men.   True / False

7. Explain the significance of the phrase *mā tāba lakum* (who seem good to you) in āyah 4:3.

....

....

....

8. Which of the following statements about multiple marriage with reference to orphans is correct?

   A.   It is an obligation to marry multiple women, but it is an option to take care of the orphans.
   B.   It is an obligation to take care of the orphans, but it is an option to marry multiple wives.
   C.   It is an obligation to marry multiple women and to take care of the orphans.
   D.   It is an obligation to marry multiple women, whether or not the issue of orphans exists.
   E.   Multiple marriages are allowed as long as the orphan girls are married.

9. Which of the following statement about multiple marriage and state law is correct?

   A.   Multiple marriages are an Islamic law, therefore they must be observed in all countries.
   B.   Multiple marriages are not a law, therefore the law of the land must be followed.
   C.   Multiple marriages must be performed in states where they are allowed by law.
   D.   All Muslims should attempt to change state law to accommodate multiple marriages.
   E.   One must relocate to a state where multiple marriages are allowed.

10. With respect to multiple marriages, explain why Islam does not permit polyandry.

....

....

....

Difficult Questions on Marriage

Objective of the Lesson:

In this lesson students will analyze several difficult real life questions on marriage to find a reasonable answer based on the Qur'ān and Sunnah of Rasūlullāh (S). The purpose of this lesson is not to issue fatawa, but to engage in critical discussion and gain knowledge on the subject matter.

The following questions were compiled based on several real-life situations and a few hypothetical ones. The purpose of the compilation is to understand how Islam would address these issues. The lessons are not intended to issue fatawa on the issues, but merely to shed light. Our knowledge about marriage acquired from previous four lessons should help us in this exercise.

Q. What conditions must be fulfilled to solemnize a marriage?

Nikah (نكاح), or marriage in Islam, requires that some conditions are met before a man and a woman can marry. These conditions should be met primarily by the man and the woman who are getting married rather than their families. These conditions are as follows:

The man and the woman intending to get married should not have a *mahram* relationship between them. A *mahram* is a near relative with whom it is unlawful to establish a marriage, for example brother–sister, mother–son. The forbidden relationships with whom a marriage cannot be consummated is mentioned in āyah 4:23.

A *nikah* involves agreeing to a marriage contract. Both the man and woman who do not have a *mahram* relationship between them take the vow of contract. This contract is called *'aqd* (عقد).

The man and the woman getting married must express their consent to marry each other. The consent must be made or expressed in an understandable manner.

At least two witnesses must be present when the man and the woman express their consent.

A gift, *mahr* (مهر), must be given at the time of the marriage by the man to his would-be wife. In Islam, *mahr* is considered as a *sadaqah* or *ajr* (اجر, reward). *Mahr* can be cash, gold, silver, a car, a house or any tangible item of value. After the marriage ceremony, the wife becomes the sole owner of the asset. This gift must not be confused with a dowry, commonly called *jahaz* (جهز) or *dahez*.

Q. Should a person pay *mahr* at the time of marriage or at a later time?

Mahr should be given at the time of marriage. The gift given as *mahr* should be mentioned and specified. A man should give *mahr* according to his means. It is not an amount to be given to the wife should they sever the ties of marriage. The compensation given to the wife upon divorce is not *mahr*.

Q. What if a man cannot pay *mahr* at the time of marriage, but wants to pay it later?

According to all madhāhib, *mahr* should be given at the time of marriage. However, they also agree that a second option of giving *mahr* at a later time is available. Under this option, the future date of payment must be specified; it cannot be indefinite, and it must be agreed to by the wife. This arrangement must be settled at the time of marriage and witnessed by others.

This second method of payment, known as *mahr muwajjal*, should not be used as an excuse to willfully postpone the payment.

Q. A marriage was solemnized, but before the bride and groom had sexual relations, it ended in divorce. What shall be done with the *mahr*?

According to āyah 2:237, in an unconsummated marriage that ended in divorce, the *mahr* can be reduced to half the amount. The husband is required to pay half the *mahr* unless the divorced woman forgoes her share. At the same time, the husband is also advised to forego his share, i.e., half of the original *mahr* that he is now entitled to keep. In other words, the āyah encourages the husband to relinquish the entire *mahr* in favor of the woman. The āyah encourages the importance of benevolence even when two parties agreed not to pursue the relationship any further due to incompatibility or unhealthy circumstances.

Q. Is it harām to have Mehendi, Henna, or a similar party before marriage?

Allāh instructed us not to arbitrarily declare something as lawful or unlawful.

And do not say—because your tongues are given to telling lies: "This is lawful and that is unlawful,"— so that you forge a lie against Allāh. Surely those who forge a lie against Allāh do not prosper. (16:116)

While all activities in life should be based on the principles of halāl and harām, we should be careful not to say something is harām if it is not specifically mentioned. Islam has declared most items and activities as permissible and only a few as prohibited. Items and activities that can benefit people morally, socially, and spiritually are halāl for Muslims. Items and activities that can harm people in this world and in the Hereafter are declared as harām.

Mehendi or Henna are more a cultural matter than religious. As long as the celebration does not violate Islamic etiquette and codes of conduct, it is permissible for women to participate in such celebration.

Q. Is it harām to attend a bridal shower?

The bridal shower is more of a Western cultural event. It is not endorsed by the Bible or the Torah. Many of the customs of Christian weddings, including the engagement, bachelor party, and bridal shower are not dictated by religion, but date back to Roman times. Islam has neither endorsed the bridal shower nor declared it as harām.

In a famous hadīth, it is reported that Rasūlullāh (S) said, "*He is not one of us, he who imitates others. Do not imitate either the Jews or the Christians.*"(Reported by Abū Dawūd and Tirmidhī).

According to many scholars, this hadīth refers to imitating Christians and Jews in the matter of their faith, not in non-religious matters. For example, should every Muslim man stop wearing shirt, suit and neck tie because it is not specifically Islamic attire? Christians wear these clothes, but it is not biblical attire either. Muslim men in many Muslim majority countries wear cultural attire, not "The Muslim" clothing endorsed by the Qur'ān or the Sunnah.

The bridal shower is an event of Western culture. It is acceptable for Muslim women to participate in this event as long as Islamic manners, etiquette, and codes of conduct are not violated.

Q. Can a person marry his or her cousin?

Under Islam, a person can marry any of his or her relatives except those mentioned in sūrah An-Nisā, āyah 4:23. In this āyah, we find a long list of relatives whom a man cannot marry. He can marry any of the relatives, not mentioned on this list. Therefore, we can conclude that a man can marry his first cousin, a relationship not mentioned on the list.

We can also find an example from the life of Rasūlullāh (S). He married his own daughter, Fātimah (r), to his nephew, 'Ali (r). Fātimah (r) and 'Ali (r) were first cousins. When this marriage was solemnized, Muhammad (S) was already a Messenger. If marriage between first cousins was not allowed, this marriage would not have taken place.

Furthermore, in sūrah Al-Ahzāb, āyah 33:50, Allāh permitted Rasūlullāh (S) to marry the daughters of his uncles and aunts from his father's and his mother's side. Islamic jurists agree that this permission was given to Rasūlullāh (S) in the first place, and through him, to the rest of the believers.

Whether marriages between cousins can lead to hereditary problem is a separate issue. If there are reasons to believe such marriages in a family could aggravate a hereditary issue or give rise to a medical problem, one should seek expert advice.

Q. Should a woman adopt the family name of her husband after her marriage?

It is not necessary for the wife to change her last name or add the family name of her husband to her own. If the laws of the land make it easier the couple to have the same last name, it is advisable, but it is not a requirement under Islam.

1. Read āyah 24:33. What is the significance of the word "restrain" in this āyah? At what point can a person get married?

....

....

....

2. Read āyah 4:19. The āyah advises men not to do two things with respect to women. What two things are mentioned in the āyah?

....

....

3. Read āyah 2:237. What item can be divided in half? Under what circumstances would one consider giving or taking half?

....

....

....

4. Which of the following choices is correct about giving *mahr*?

    A.   It should be paid in cash, but the timing of the payment is not specified.
    B.   It should be paid at the time of marriage.
    C.   If the man cannot pay it, he can forego it.
    D.   If the man cannot pay it, the wife is obligated to pay it.
    E.   If *mahr* is not paid, the marriage is still valid.

5. Read the āyah which forbids marrying certain relatives. Then circle the correct choices below.

    A.   A man can marry a daughter of his sister.
    B.   A man can marry his foster sister.
    C.   A man can marry a stepdaughter of his paternal aunt.
    D.   A man can marry a stepdaughter of his former wife.
    E.   A man can marry a wife of his own biological son.

Who are the Khalīfah on Earth?

Objective of the Lesson:

When Allāh intended to create human beings, He mentioned them as khalīfah. Evidently, the role of human beings as khalīfah requires them to live up to the status of being true representatives of Allāh. However, sometimes we fail and sometimes we violate our status. This lesson analyzes the importance of being true khalīfah on earth.

When Allāh decided to place human beings on the earth, He did not use the word *insān* on *an-nās*, both of which mean human being or mankind. Instead, Allāh used the word *khalīfah*. Evidently it was a divine plan to indicate, from the very beginning, the purpose of placing these new creatures on earth. These new creatures would play the role of being *khalīfah* and fulfill the truest meaning of the word.

What, then, is the meaning of the word *khalīfah* (plural, *khulafa*)? It means 'to leave behind', 'a successor', 'a lieutenant', 'a vicegerent', or 'a deputy'. The role of a human being is to act as an administrative deputy, a magistrate, or a successor of someone. Since Allāh is the creator, clearly Allāh wanted these new creations to be His administrative deputies. In fact, in the Qur'ān the word *khalīfah* is used in the sense of one who judges or rules in accordance with the command of God. In āyah 2:30, the word *khalīfah* is used to mean the children of Ādam (A) as well as all of mankind. In āyah 6:165 the word *khalīfah* is applied to include all of mankind.

The administrative deputy: As an administrative deputy of Allāh, these new creations, to be known as human beings, would follow the directives and uphold the interests of their Creator. Human beings have the overwhelming responsibility of being Allāh's representative.[35:39] They take the place of Allāh on earth, and their primary task is to act and rule on behalf of Allāh. They were given power over the subjects they would rule. These subjects are be the living and non-living creatures of the universe. How would human beings accomplish this overwhelming job? They would do it by manifesting Allāh's attributes at all times. They would do this by embodying Allāh's qualities in their conduct.

A political system: In many Islamic writings, the word khalīfah is understood as a political system. The title khalīfah is used for the leader of the Islamic world. The leader has the right to adopt the divine rules, protect the religion, and rule the Islamic world. The khalīfah is also responsible for spreading the message of Islam to the world. Thus, all the leaders after Rasūl Muhammad (S) were political successors to Rasūlullāh (S), therefore, known as khalīfah. The English word Caliph was coined from khalīfah. A Caliph or Khalīfah is recognized as the *Amīr al-Mu'minīn,* or the Commander of the Faithful.

This meaning of the term does not override the original sense applied during the creation of Ādam (A). However, our purpose here is to see how the concept of the term applies to all of us and how each of us can be khalīfah on earth.

Angels' apprehension: When Allāh told the angels about His plan to create human beings, their response was surprising. In contrast to their dutiful obedience to everything that Allāh tells them, in this instance the angels were apprehensive. The angels were able to foresee certain elements in the 'new creation' that did not make them happy. They mentioned two things that these creations would do: (a) they would create trouble (*fasad*) on the earth, and (b) they would shed each other's blood.[2:30]

Apprehension resolved: The doubt and apprehension of the angels were resolved when Allāh taught Ādam the names of all things on earth.[2:31] The term 'names' plays a significant role in the Qur'ān. Allāh mentioned, "*and to Allāh belong all the finest names…*"[7:180] Allāh's names are not merely names; they are His qualities. Similarly, when Ādam was taught the names of all things, he did not simply learn the names, but also understood the inner qualities and attributes of each name.

By teaching the names, Allāh gave Ādam power over the things he learned.[22:65; 31:20] All other creations only know the 'names' of certain things—i.e., they know the qualities of things that matter to them. Even angels only know the names of few things. Allāh gave human beings power over creation by making them understand the qualities and attributes of everything. This responsibility is enormous. This responsibility qualifies them to be the khalīfah on earth. Because of this responsibility given to human beings, angels were asked to bow down to human beings. We have to ask ourselves this question: do we always fulfill our responsibilities? Do we embody Allāh's qualities in our conduct?

The role of Khalīfah: We mentioned previously that a khalīfah is a representative of another being. The representative is required to follow the directives and uphold the interests of the one who is being represented—in this case Allāh. Human beings have the awesome responsibility of being Allāh's representative.[35:39] In other words, human beings take the place of Allāh on earth, and their primary task is to act on behalf of Allāh.

This awesome responsibility was offered to the heavens, earth, and mountains, but they dreaded the responsibility. Then human beings came forward to accept it, as stated in the following āyah:

$$\text{إِنَّا عَرَضْنَا ٱلْأَمَانَةَ عَلَى ٱلسَّمَٰوَٰتِ وَٱلْأَرْضِ وَٱلْجِبَالِ فَأَبَيْنَ أَن يَحْمِلْنَهَا وَأَشْفَقْنَ مِنْهَا وَحَمَلَهَا ٱلْإِنسَٰنُ إِنَّهُۥ كَانَ ظَلُومًا جَهُولًا ۝}$$

We indeed offered the trust to the heavens and the earth and the mountains, but they shrank from bearing it and dreaded from it; but man bore it. Surely he is ever unjust, very ignorant. (33:72)

Obviously this is an awesome responsibility for human beings; however, we are qualified to do the job. How do we do it? We do it by manifesting

Allāh's attributes in our actions. We can do it by embodying Allāh's qualities in our conduct.

Failing to be khalīfah:
If we fail to manifest Allāh's qualities in our conduct, we will cease to be khalīfah on earth. When we fail to obey Allāh's command, we cease to be khalīfah on earth. Instead of making a list of all the activities that would disqualify us from being khalīfah on the earth, let us sum them up in a few broad categories. These are: neglecting duties, abusing power, and inventing falsehood,

Neglecting duties:
In reality, many of us fail to manifest Allāh's qualities even though we have faith and follow the Islamic rituals. This is because we become heedless or commit *ghafla*. The word *ghafla* means to be heedless—to be neglectful, inattentive, and unmindful. A *ghafilun* (singular) is one who is heedless or neglectful.

Being heedless is not the same as being forgetful. When we are heedless, it indicates that we remember out duties, but neglect them. Thus, it is intentional conduct. To forget something is involuntary, but to neglect something is voluntary. The moment we intentionally disobey our God-given duties, we cease to be true *khalīfah* on earth.

We may sometimes become forgetful of our duties. This is not the same as being neglectful of our duties. Ādam (A) forgot (*nasiya*, literally, to forget) Allāh's instruction not to go near a tree. He forgot to remain alert to Shaitān's evil prompting.[20:115] Allāh did not use the word *gafla* in the case of Ādam (A), because he was not heedless; he simply forgot.

In the story of Ādam (A), we find an important lesson. The moment Ādam (A) realized his mistake, he immediately repented and sought the forgiveness of Allāh. By expressing repentance and seeking forgiveness, Ādam reinstituted his status as *khalīfah* on earth.

Contrary to the example of Ādam (A), when we intentionally neglect our God-given duties, including the primary duties of making salāt and giving zakāt, we no longer remain *khalīfah* on earth.

Abuse of the power:
In the seventh century, Islam provided mankind the ideal code of human rights. These rights conferred honor and dignity to mankind and eliminated oppression, exploitation, intimidation, coercion, and injustice. Allāh is the ultimate provider of law and He is the source of all human rights. Establishing and upholding human rights is integral to overall Islamic order. Thus, it is obligatory for Muslim government and rulers to implement human rights in true Islamic spirit. Therefore, no ruler, government, or king should curtail or violate the human rights conferred by Allāh.

In reality, many community leaders, local administrations, and governments violate human rights and abuse their power. When we abuse our power, we cease to be khalīfah on earth. Human history is full of examples of presidents, prime ministers, kings, rulers, leaders, judges, scholars, teachers, pastors, and imams abused their power for their own gain. Many times, they abuse their power without realizing the error.

وَإِذَا قِيلَ لَهُمْ لَا تُفْسِدُوا۟ فِى ٱلْأَرْضِ قَالُوٓا۟ إِنَّمَا نَحْنُ مُصْلِحُونَ ⑪ أَلَآ إِنَّهُمْ هُمُ ٱلْمُفْسِدُونَ وَلَٰكِن لَّا يَشْعُرُونَ ⑫

And when it is said to them: "Do not make mischief in the earth," they say: "Surely we are indeed peacemakers." Is it not that they themselves are the mischief-makers? But they do not perceive. (2:11-12)

Inventing falsehood:
Human beings have the unique ability to speak and write. The ability to express ideas and thoughts in coherent, complete sentences, together with the ability to translate ideas and thoughts into writing, is exclusive to human beings. This ability, indeed, makes us superior to other creatures. However, this also gives human beings the ability to express their thoughts in two different ways—truthfully and dishonestly.

On the other hand, animals cannot use language like human beings and they cannot write. Therefore, animals cannot express their thoughts in a duplicitous or misleading manner. Whatever sounds they produce, it is only truthful expression of their feelings. There is no falsehood in their expression. A dog will not wag its tail if it is going to bite. A tiger will not hide and lurch if it is not going to attack. A snake will not wield its fangs if it is not going to bite. However, sometimes human beings talk nicely face to face, but they may be ready to harm. Sometimes humans speak to instill confidence and earn trust, but they intend to deceive. Sometimes they speak and write to propagate falsehood, half-truths, rumors, and defamation. Sometimes they mislead others and express pride.

Every time we, as human beings, express our thoughts in words and writing to propagate falsehood and mislead others, we degrade ourselves as human beings, or more precisely, khalīfah on earth.

Inventing false gods:
Animals can be creative, but they are not inventive. Many animals are creative in their search for food, shelter, and survival. But animals cannot invent new things that nature did not already provide. A gorilla today lives the same way a gorilla lived 5,000 or 50,000 years ago. Over time, they did not invent new things to make their survival easier. On the other hand, human beings continue to invent new things. They invented and fabricated idols and began worshipping them. The ability to invent new things made human being superior creation, but the same ability also degraded them because they invented false gods.

Fard al-ayn:
According to many scholars of Islam, to establish the institution of khalīfah is *fard al-ayn*. It is a legal obligation that must be performed by each individual Muslim. Just as performing salāt, paying zakāt, fasting, and pilgrimage are individual obligations, upholding the duties of true khalīfah is also an individual obligation. According to some scholars, to establish the institution of khalīfah is a *fard kifayah,* or communal obligation. Although it is a duty for each individual, as long as a sufficient number of community members perform it, the duty is fulfilled.

To be the true Khalīfah:
We should exert our best efforts to live up to the expectations of Allāh. We can be true khalīfah and successfully represent Allāh by obeying His commands and following the teachings of Rasūl Muhammad (S).

1. When Allāh decided to place human beings on earth, what term did He use to describe them?

    A.   *An-nās.*
    B.   *Khalīfah.*
    C.   *Malaika.*
    D.   *Fard al-ayn.*
    E.   *Insān.*

2. When Allāh told the angels about His plan to create human beings, what was their initial response?

    A.   They thought these creations would rule the earth.
    B.   They thought these creations would turn into angels.
    C.   They thought these creations would turn into *Amīr al-Mu'minīn.*
    D.   They thought these creations would create trouble and bloodshed.
    E.   They thought these creations would learn the names of all things.

3. Read āyah 33:72. To how many things did Allāh offer trusteeship? List them.

....

....

4. What would disqualify human beings from being *khalīfah* on earth?

....

....

....

5. How is heedlessness different from forgetfulness? Explain in light of Ādam's (A) example.

....

....

....

6. Is the following statement true or false? Be ready to explain your answer.

Based on the opinion of many scholars, establishing the   True / False
duties of *khalīfah* is both *fard al-ayn* and *fard kifayah.*

7. Which of the following actions disqualifies human beings from being *khalīfah* on the earth?

    A.   When human beings talk nicely with others.
    B.   When human beings invent images of God.
    C.   When human beings talk about false gods.
    D.   When human beings draw pictures of nature.
    E.   When human beings want to assume power to rule a country.

8. After a person abuses the status of *khalīfah* on earth, how can he or she reinstitute his or her status? Explain in light of the experience of Ādam (A).

....

....

....

9. The differences and/or similarities between human beings and animals in terms of their capabilities is:

    A.   Human beings can falsify, animals never falsify.
    B.   Animals do not have a sense of acting truthfully, but human beings do.
    C.   Both human beings and animals can invent new things to make their lives better.
    D.   Human beings can act under false pretext, but animals cannot.
    E.   Both human beings and animals can be creative and inventive.

10. Which of the following choices about the nature of human beings is correct?

    A.   Human beings can commit moral errors.
    B.   Human beings have the ability to ask for forgiveness.
    C.   Human beings can go against the divine.
    D.   All of the above.
    E.   Only B. and C. are correct.

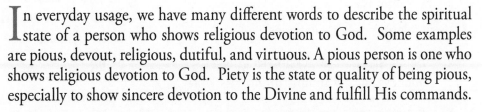

False Piety

Objective of the Lesson:

Depending upon how and with what intention we perform some of the prescribed religious duties, we may be showing only false piety. We thereby nullify the rewards that would otherwise have come with these duties. This lesson analyzes how believers can identify, be alert for, and avoid any show of false piety.

In everyday usage, we have many different words to describe the spiritual state of a person who shows religious devotion to God. Some examples are pious, devout, religious, dutiful, and virtuous. A pious person is one who shows religious devotion to God. Piety is the state or quality of being pious, especially to show sincere devotion to the Divine and fulfill His commands.

Piety is, therefore, a way to win the approval, mercy, favor, blessings, guidance, and forgiveness of God. In order to win these favors, as well as many other rewards from God, one has to perform both observable and non-observable religious duties to God. The observable duties include those rites and rituals, as well as conducts that can be seen by others. Non-observable piety includes the spiritual conditioning of one's mind that is not clearly visible to others. For example: sincere trust in God, focus on the Hereafter, maintaining spiritual devotion.

These ideas are beautifully illustrated in the following āyah. We will discuss this āyah further later in this lesson.

لَّيۡسَ ٱلۡبِرَّ أَن تُوَلُّواْ وُجُوهَكُمۡ قِبَلَ ٱلۡمَشۡرِقِ وَٱلۡمَغۡرِبِ وَلَٰكِنَّ ٱلۡبِرَّ مَنۡ ءَامَنَ بِٱللَّهِ وَٱلۡيَوۡمِ ٱلۡأَخِرِ وَٱلۡمَلَٰٓئِكَةِ وَٱلۡكِتَٰبِ وَٱلنَّبِيِّـۧنَ وَءَاتَى ٱلۡمَالَ عَلَىٰ حُبِّهِۦ ذَوِى ٱلۡقُرۡبَىٰ وَٱلۡيَتَٰمَىٰ وَٱلۡمَسَٰكِينَ وَٱبۡنَ ٱلسَّبِيلِ وَٱلسَّآئِلِينَ وَفِى ٱلرِّقَابِ وَأَقَامَ ٱلصَّلَوٰةَ وَءَاتَى ٱلزَّكَوٰةَ وَٱلۡمُوفُونَ بِعَهۡدِهِمۡ إِذَا عَٰهَدُواْ وَٱلصَّٰبِرِينَ فِى ٱلۡبَأۡسَآءِ وَٱلضَّرَّآءِ وَحِينَ ٱلۡبَأۡسِ أُوْلَٰٓئِكَ ٱلَّذِينَ صَدَقُواْ وَأُوْلَٰٓئِكَ هُمُ ٱلۡمُتَّقُونَ ۝

There is no virtue in that you turn your faces towards the East and the West, but virtue is in him whoever believes in Allāh and the Last Day, and the angels, and the books, and the messengers; and who gives wealth out of love for Him to the near of kin, and to the orphans, and the needy, and the travelers, and the beggars, and to those in captivity; and who establishes the salāt, and pays the zakāt; and the fulfillers of their contracts when they make a contract; and those who persevere in hardship and injury, and during the panic. These are those who have verified the truth; and these are themselves the pious. (2:177)

Broad categories of piety: The previous āyah divides piety into two broad categories: (a) pertaining to matters of faith, (b) translating faith into certain prescribed actions.

Piety relating to faith includes:

a. Belief in Allāh by acknowledging His oneness and by submitting to His will,

b. Belief in the Hereafter,

c. Belief in angels,

d. Belief in the divine books, primarily the Qur'ān, but in principle, in the divine origin of all earlier revealed books, and

e. Belief in all the messengers of the world, whether or not they are mentioned by name in the Qur'ān.

Translating faith into action includes:

i. Spending wealth on charity,

ii. Establishing salāt,

iii. Paying zakāh,

iv. Honoring contracts, and

v. Persevering during hardships, and anxiety.

The spending of wealth does not entail gratifying personal desires by means of extravagance. Instead, spending must directly benefit the following persons, in order of preference:

a. needy near relatives,

b. orphans,

c. needy people,

d. travelers,

e. beggars and

f. prisoners.

What is false piety: Using the previous definition of piety, then, piety that is genuine pleases Allāh. Piety that is false is only a show done in order to gain public esteem or approval. If an act of worship is performed, not with the intention to please Allāh, but as a public show of devotion, it is false piety. Intention, therefore, is a very important aspect of piety. Lack of sincerity and commitment renders all pious acts fruitless. In addition, insincere acts of worship earn the disapproval and condemnation of Allāh. It is like pretending to exercise to lose weight, but gaining weight.

The Qur'ān has several āyāt that caution believers to identify, be alert for, and avoid any show of false piety.

Riyā: The simple meaning of the word *riyā* is 'to show.' In Islamic Sharī'ah, the word *riyā* describes an action that was supposed to please Allāh, but was performed with the intention of pleasing someone else. Riyā is, therefore, a form of shirk (*shirk-e-asghar,* or the lesser shirk) because devotion to Allāh is compromised.

Next we will discuss the performance of salāt as an act that amounts to false piety. Such salāt compromises devotion to Allāh with the onlooker's praise or commendation. If there is a division in the purpose of salāt—seeking pleasure of Allāh along with the approval of onlookers—a minor shirk was committed.

A profound example of *riyā* can be seen in a hadīth of Nabi Muhammad (S). This particular hadīth implies that the Antichrist or Dajjal is less of a threat to a believer than a virtuous act performed only as an act of show.

Turning towards the East or West: One of the classic examples of disassociating true piety from false piety is mentioned in āyah 2:177. During the first two years after Messenger Muhammad (S) migrated to Madīnah, Muslims faced Jerusalem as their qiblah for prayer. In 624 CE, during one prayer, a revelation was sent, changing the qiblah to the Ka'bah. Switching the qiblah created a lot of controversy among the people of that time. A new revelation was sent to caution Muslims not to get embroiled in arbitrary acts, but to focus on the aspects that reflect true piety.

This āyah points out that turning east and west is only an outward action of devotion. Such outward rituals should not take priority over actual piety and they should not obstruct the spirit of Islam.

False piety and zakāt: Charitable giving is one of the major pious acts. In Islam, two forms of charitable giving are prescribed: compulsory giving is zakāt, and voluntary giving is sadaqah, or simple charity. All major religions, not only Islam, emphasize the importance of charitable giving. Before Messenger Muhammad (S), past messengers taught their people to give zakāt. Messenger 'Isa (A) was commanded by Allāh to give zakāt.[19:31]

Zakāt, a pillar of Islam, constitutes a fundamental duty of all well-to-do Muslims. Allāh tells us that zakāt wipes away our evil.[2:271] The importance of charitable giving is highlighted in innumerable āyāt in the Qur'ān.

لَن تَنَالُوا۟ ٱلْبِرَّ حَتَّىٰ تُنفِقُوا۟ مِمَّا تُحِبُّونَ ۚ وَمَا تُنفِقُوا۟ مِن شَىْءٍ فَإِنَّ ٱللَّهَ بِهِۦ عَلِيمٌ ۝

You will never attain virtue (birra) unless you spend out of what you love. And whatever thing you spend, then Allāh indeed knows about it. (3:92)

However, often what we give and how we give neutralizes the piety that would have come with the charity.

Those who spend their wealth in the way of Allāh, then do not follow up what they have spent with obligation, nor injury; for them is their reward with their Lord, and there is no fear on them nor will they grieve. (2:262)

The phrase "do not follow up what they have spent with obligation, nor injury" implies we should not remind others of their generosity, and should not expect favor from the beneficiary in return for our generosity. Similar caution can be noted in the following āyah.

O you who believe! do not render void your charity by obligation and injury, like him who spends his wealth for show of mankind, while he does not believe in Allāh and the Last Day. So his likeness is as the parable of a smooth rock with soil on it, then a heavy rain falls on it, and it leaves it barren! They are not able to gain anything out of what they have earned; because Allāh does not guide the unbelieving people. (2:264)

Giving worthless or inferior things to charity defeats the spirit of giving.

O you who believe! spend of the good things which you earn, and out of what We produce for you from the earth; and do not aim at the bad things thereof to spend, while you would not accept it yourselves unless you connive at it. And know that Allāh is self-Sufficient, Praiseworthy. (2:267)

And those who spend their wealth for show of people, while they do not believe in Allāh nor in the Last Day. And for whom the Shaitān has become his companion, then he is a bad companion! (4:38)

False piety and salāt: Salāt is a direct form of worshipping Allāh. It is one of the most virtuous acts a person can undertake. However, how, where and why a person performs salāt can indicate false piety rather than true piety. For example, a person who lengthens his salāt for show or for praise because someone is watching him; someone who unduly advertises an urgency to perform a salāt; or someone who advertises performing salātul Tahajjud so people will think he is pious, is falsely pious. Such piety for the sake of praise or show, and not for the sake of Allāh, amounts to false piety. Let us read some of the relevant āyāt from the Qur'ān:

Surely the hypocrites strive to deceive Allāh, and He sends back such deceit to them. And when they stand up for salāt, they stand up unmindfully— to make a show to men; and they do not remember Allāh except a little; (4:142)

Call upon your Lord with humility and in secret. Surely He does not love the transgressors. (7:55)

So woe be to those performers of salāt, those who are themselves unmindful of their salāt, those who are themselves showy, and refrain from the acts of kindness. (107:4-7)

We must take particular note of the āyāt in sūrah al-Mā'ūn. Salāt is a very important duty for all Muslims. Yet in this sūrah, the performers of salāt are rebuked because they are guilty of showing false piety. Their outward demonstrations of piety through the performance of salāt do not make them good Muslims. They deny the teachings of the religion and refuse to help the poor. Above all, they perform salāt carelessly.

All of us must avoid false piety and refrain from any act that would compromise our worship of Allāh. Acts of false piety will undermine our righteous deeds, and divine blessings will be curtailed. These points are amply illustrated and confirmed in the Qur'ān and the authentic sayings of Rasūlullāh (S).

1. All of the following are examples of piety. Which of these choices correctly represent piety translated into action?

    A.   Belief in angels.
    B.   Trusting the importance of the Hereafter.
    C.   Paying zakāh.
    D.   Belief in the five pillars of Islam.
    E.   Belief in the revelation of the books of Allāh.

2. Read āyah 4:142. Knowing that a hypocrite stands up in salāh in a particular manner, how can we correct ourselves so as to not become like him?

....

....

....

3. Which of the following points was established with the change of qiblah from Jerusalem to the Ka'bah?

    A.   Jerusalem ceases to have any significance in Islam.
    B.   The Ka'bah has a better right to become the qiblah since it is located in the Arabia.
    C.   To make the Jews in Madīnah regret.
    D.   To fulfill a prophecy in the Torah about changing the qiblah.
    E.   To prove that piety is not about turning one's face toward the East or West.

4. Based on āyah 2:177, the lesson divides piety into how many categories?

    A.   10 categories, five relating to faith and five relating to translating faith into action.
    B.   10 categories, six relating to faith and four relating to translating faith into action.
    C.   12 categories, five relating to faith and seven relating to translating faith into action.
    D.   14 categories, seven relating to faith and seven relating to translating faith into action.
    E.   15 categories, ten relating to faith and five relating to translating faith into action.

5. What action will neutralize the reward of giving zakāh?

    A.   If zakāh is given once every year.
    B.   If zakāh is given to a traveler to alleviate his problem.
    C.   If zakāh is given secretly without the person's knowledge.
    D.   If zakāh is given by putting the recipient under some obligation.
    E.   If zakāh is given openly to a person.

6. Using your own words, explain the meaning of the word *riyā*.

....

....

7. Read āyah 7:55. What two things should we demonstrate when we call upon Allāh in our duʿā as well as when we stand up in salāh?

....

8. Read āyah 2:267. Then answer the following two questions.

What two things should we spend? ....

What criteria should we apply when we decide to give something to charity? ....

....

9. In a hadīth narrated in the lesson, what is stated to be more of a threat to a believer than Dajjāl?

    A.   Giving zakāh by putting the recipient under some obligation.
    B.   Making salāh in a manner to impress people who are watching.
    C.   Making salāh in an unmindful manner.
    D.   Giving zakāh without wanting to purify one's wealth.
    E.   Making salāh irregularly.

Superstition

Objective of the Lesson:

Islam is not a superstitious religion, yet Muslims sometimes believe or propagate harmless as well as harmful superstitious practices. This lesson sheds some light on the origin and practice of superstitions. The lesson also guides students to identify possible superstitious practices and actions in order to avoid them.

A simple definition of superstition is 'a belief or notion not supported by reasoning and knowledge.' Another definition of superstition is an irrational, unfounded, or ignorant attitude of mind towards the supernatural. We can also say superstition is a false notion about the cause of something, despite a lack of evidence or evidence to the contrary. Usually superstition is firmly grounded in a belief system that allows a state of ignorance to continue. Quite often, the sources of superstition are firmly grounded in a religious belief or cult mentality. The religious beliefs of a person, therefore, support and propagate superstition.

In the medieval period, superstition was generally applied to any belief or practice outside, and in opposition to one's faith. Christianity considered all faiths that were not rooted in the Bible to be superstitious. During the formative years of Islam, many pagan practices, which were not supported by Islam, were considered superstitious. The root of all superstition is falsehood. Islam vehemently opposed all falsehood and abolished all practices of superstition.

Superstition in pre-Islamic Arabia: In pre-Islamic Arabia, the entire society was heavily influenced by a variety of superstitious beliefs. Any activity, whether social, economical, political, or religious, was based on one or more superstitious practices. Over the course of time, belief in superstitions created a value system in the society that nobody dared to defy. The reason for such beliefs was due to fear, suspicion, power struggles and enmity in society. Any disease, epidemic, calamity, accident, or loss was attributed to some sort of evil force. Similarly, most gains, successes, benefits or good times were also attributed to superstitious practice.

The Qur'ān condemns superstition: When the Qur'ān, was revealed, Arabs were as superstitious as any other culture or nation. If superstitions were allowed, no matter how harmless, they would undermine the spirit of true Islam. Therefore, one of the objectives of the Qur'ān was to shatter all forms of superstition at at their root.

This point is beautifully illustrated in the following āyāt:

And you say: "The Truth has come, and falsehood has vanished. Surely the falsehood does ever vanish away." (17:81)

In fact, We cast the Truth against the falsehood, so that it knocks out its brains, and lo! it vanishes. And woe be to you on account of what you attribute. (21:18)

Pre-Islamic superstitious belief

- Set free special animals to appease idols.
- Shoot arrows to decide important matters.
- Observe the movements of the planets to predict the future.
- Believe in the power of astrology.
- The birth of daughters was a bad sign.
- Newborn daughters should be buried alive to prevent bad luck in family.
- Travel during the month of Safar brought bad luck.
- The first 13 days of Safar were specially bad.
- Charms and omens were true.

In order to abolish superstition, the truth must be established and falsehood must vanish. The truth of Islam attacks falsehood and 'knocks out its brain' (*dimagh*), the center that originates and propagates falsehood and superstition.

Pre-Islamic superstition: Pre-Islamic Arabs believed in the power of soothsayers or *Kahin*. Soothsayers were people who claimed to know about the future through contact with evil spirits. People trusted them and solicited their services to know about their future. The Qur'ān says nobody except Allāh knows the future.

And with Him are the keys of the unseen—no one knows them except Him. (6:59)

Say: "No one in the heavens and the earth knows the unseen except Allāh." (27:65)

People in Arabia believed unseen evil spirits caused every sickness, disease and calamity. In order to appease the evil spirits, people used to worship them and make sacrifices to pacify them. Even today, people from many societies believe evil spirits cause sickness, mental disease, and calamities. They adopt different precautionary measures to prevent bad things from happening to them. All calamities and setbacks in life happen according to the Plan of Allāh. There is no power other than Allāh that can cause setbacks and also alleviate them. The Qur'ān says:

No calamity falls on the earth or in your own selves, but is in a book before We bring it into operation. Surely this is easy for Allāh. (57:22).

He calls upon besides Allāh that which does not harm him nor does it benefit him. This is itself the far-off straying. (22:12)

The pagan Arabs used to rely upon divination by shooting arrows. Before a marriage, journey, war or other important social event, people would go to the temple and shoot arrows to ascertain whether to proceed or stop. The Qur'ān says:

O you who believe! surely the intoxicants and gambling, and setting up of stones, and divining by arrows are unclean things—among the handiwork of Shaitān; therefore avoid this that you may attain success. (5:90)

Such divination in the past is equivalent to present-day palm readings, horoscopes, astrology, and psychic readings and so forth—all of which are the handiwork of Shaitān. We should, therefore, avoid them.

Weak faith leads to superstition: One of the main reasons for the endless rise and propagation of superstition is weak faith or lack of faith. In ancient times, people lacked faith or had weak faith and nearly every strange event was explained using superstition. People invented new gods out of their superstitious beliefs. When people saw the power of nature, out of ignorance, they failed to realize these events were caused by Allāh. As a result, they erroneously attributed these particular aspects of nature as a god, e.g., wind god, rain god, earth god, fire god, and sea god to name a few. Some people started creating images and idols of their gods to worship One God. Over the course of time, they forgot about their One God and began showing more devotion to the idols.

In an ancient religion like Hinduism, for example, the role of superstition is extremely important. Many practices, customs, and devotions are based on one or several superstitions. For example: wiping the floors with cow dung is believed to sanctify the house. Planet Saturn is supposed to cause all evil, therefore, to thwart evil, one should wear a ring with an amethyst gem, the symbol of Saturn. Widows are considered to bring bad luck, therefore, it is bad sign to see a widow when a person is going out for important work. In marriages and social functions, widows are unwelcome because they bring bad luck.

Superstition in advanced nations: It is true that superstition arises out of ignorance. Ironically, most advanced nations, in terms of science, education and technology, are equally prone to superstition. Halloween, for example, is a traditional annual event to keeps evil spirits and demons at bay.

In the U.S. and many other advanced countries, many people still believe that bad omens can predict our destiny and cause misfortune. Some superstitions

Present-day superstitious beliefs

- Breaking a mirror will bring you seven years of bad luck.
- Garlic is a protection from evil spirits and vampires.
- Finding a horseshoe brings good luck.
- If a black cat crosses your path, you will have bad luck.
- Finding a four-leaf clover brings good luck
- An itchy palm means money will come your way.
- A lock of hair from a baby's first haircut should be kept for good luck.
- Knock on wood to keep good luck coming your way.
- A cat has nine lives.
- Wearing your birthstone will bring you good luck.
- Crossing your fingers helps to avoid bad luck and helps a wish come true.
- Friday the 13th is an unlucky day.
- When a dog howls, someone will die soon.
- If you hiccup, someone remembered you.
- A cricket in the house brings good luck.
- A house lizard in the house brings good luck.
- Opening an umbrella in the house brings bad luck.

are attached to bad luck and some are attached to good luck. Black cats, broken mirrors, walking beneath a ladder, owls, the number 13, and so forth are commonly attached to bad luck and omens. Horseshoes, four-leaf clovers, rabbit's feet, knocking on wood and so forth are attached to good luck.

While some superstitions may be fun, there are several that may deeply affect our lives due to the unwarranted values we attach to them. It is unfortunate that sometimes the choices we make in our lives are based on superstitious notions. In fact, no superstition is based on truth, but they have deep roots in our traditions and history.

Muslims and superstition: If we think that because Muslims do not worship idols, therefore they are not prone to superstition, we would be wrong. Many different forms of superstitions prevail among Muslims. Many of the superstitious practices among Muslims are borrowed from other religions. These practices came to Islam from two sources: (a) they remained with people as they converted to Islam and (b) the influence of mingling of different faiths.

For centuries, Muslims in Southeast Asian countries lived in close proximity with Hindus, Buddhists and people of other religions. People of different religions spoke the same language, which made it conducive for one culture to influence another. In these regions, Hinduism, being the predominant religion, contributed to more superstitious practices among Muslims.

Angels and superstitions: Angels obey Allāh and praise His glory. They never disobey Allāh.[66:6] The Qur'ān has mentioned two angels, Hārūt and Mārūt, who are commonly believed to be the fallen angels who propagated superstitions.[2:102] The story of Hārūt and Mārūt as fallen angels, itself, is based on superstitions and folklore. In the Qur'ān, three things are mentioned about Hārūt and Mārūt: (a) they were angels; (b) nothing was revealed to them about witchcraft; and (c) they were trials and they did not teach anyone anything except to believe. Since these two angels did not know about witchcraft and did not teach to disbelieve, it is absurd to accuse them of teaching witchcraft.

Sulaimān (A) and superstition: According to the Bible, Sulaimān (A) became a polytheist in his old age, a theory rejected by the Qur'ān.[2:102] Additionally the Jews claimed that Sulaimān (A) knew sorcery and the book of sorcery was concealed under his throne. However, āyah 2:102 of the Qur'ān shows it was the devilish human beings who indulged in the character assassination of Sulaimān (A). The term *shayātin* (plural, devil, Satan), in this context, refers to rebellious and disobedient men who follow illusions (*awham*) and their own imaginations (*khayalat*).

Superstitious beliefs and occult practices became so rampant among the Israelites that at one point the entire community succumbed to superstition.

Horoscope, astrology, omen, charms: To believe in any form of horoscopes, astrology, omens, or charms is a sin in Islam. We should not indulge in them, even if it is for fun. Can anyone say, "I am committing this sin for fun?" It does not make sense. It is the duty of all Muslims to advise our friends and family to stay away from these types of practices. Many Muslims believe in the power of amulets or drinking water on which some "religious" person blows charms from some āyāt of the Qur'ān. Drinking such "holy" water or passing it on is not only a sin, but it amounts to a form of shirk.

What about the Zamzam water that people drink and bring back after Hajj or umrah? First of all, we should remember that Zamzam water by itself has no healing power. We drink Zamzam water as a show of respect and acknowledgement of the divine gift that Allāh once sent to Ismā'īl (A) and his mother. By drinking Zamzam water, we recognize that Allāh is the source of all *rizk* (provisions) and He is the ultimate Provider. Mother Hajar was searching for water desperately, but could not find it. Her efforts were great, but it was Allāh who ultimately provided.

Is Islam superstitious? Islam is not a superstitious religion. Superstition and Islam cannot go hand-in-hand. Islam is a rational religion. It does not promote unfounded, baseless notions that are not supported by reasoning and knowledge. Islam teaches us to turn to Allāh and rely on Him for the good in our lives and seek refuge in Him during the bad times.

In summary, as good Muslims, we should stay away from believing or propagating in any forms of superstition.

1. What are four conditions that are likely to originate and propagate a superstition?

....

....

....

....

2. Read āyah 17:13. Which creature that pre-Islamic Arabs relied upon for foretelling the future is mentioned in the āyah?

....

3. Relate the message in āyah 17:13 to āyah 36:19. Which creature that assured pre-Islamic Arabs about their future is mentioned in the āyah?

....

4. What four categories of animals did the pre-Islamic Arabs let loose in honor of their idols? Read āyah 5:103 to learn their Arabic names and their meanings.

Arabic Name	Meaning
....	....
....	....
....	....
....	....

5. During the pre-Islamic period, when a person stepped out of his house for Hajj, but needed to go back to his home for some reason, he would enter the house in a peculiar way. It was a superstition. Read āyah 2:189. What mode of entry is mentioned in the āyah? How is the person advised to enter the house?

....

6. Read āyah 6:138. Which two things did pre-Islamic Arabs prohibit due to superstition? Whose 'backs' did they forbid?

(a) ....   (b) ....

....

7. Many Muslims believe in superstitions despite the Qur'ān condemning these practice and beliefs. What are some of the reasons Muslims believe in superstitions?

....

....

8. Explain why fortune telling, reading horoscopes, palm reading, astrology or other means of predicting the future are sins.

....

....

9. Which two key factors indicate that Islam is not a superstitious religion?

....

10. The disobedient and rebellious people at the time of Sulaimān (A) (or for that matter at any other time), believe two things that propagate superstition. What are the two things mentioned in the lesson?

....

....

Do Not Transgress Limits

Objective of the Lesson:

We, human beings by nature, transgress because we think we are self-sufficient. We transgress in our dealings with people, diet habits, and worship, to name a few. Allāh has cautioned us not to transgress, but to stay within the limits. This lesson provides an overview of the topic and suggests ways to guard ourselves and avoid being transgressors.

In the Qur'ān, instructions about prohibited and forbidden acts are very clear and straightforward. Different interpretations of these instructions do not exist. In addition to the Qur'ān, the sunnah of Rasūlullāh (S) gave further injunctions against the prohibited and forbidden things, again in clear terms. While giving these injunctions, Allāh intends ease, not hardship for man. Therefore, in Islam, necessity overrides the laws of prohibitions. If one is driven by dire necessity, even things that are expressly disallowed become allowed for him. For example, the meat of a naturally dead animal, blood, and the flesh of swine is prohibited. However, if a person is stricken with extreme hunger, he is allowed to eat without exceeding the limit.

He has forbidden you only what dies of itself, and the blood, and the flesh of swine, and that over which any other than Allāh has been invoked. But whoever is constrained, without being disobedient nor transgressing the limit, no sin will be upon him. Allāh is certainly most Forgiving, most Rewarding. (2:173)

In the above āyah, the word for transgress is *'adawa* (ع د و). Allāh has allowed us many things, but cautions us about transgression. To transgress means to do wrong, to violate a command or law, or to go beyond or over the limit. Typically the question of transgression arises in an act that is otherwise allowed, but when one exceeds the boundary of the permissible domain, it constitutes transgression. In the example above, under dire necessity, a person is allowed to eat the prohibited meat. The meat is allowed in a quantity to save a life,

Boundary that man may not cross.

but to go beyond that limit would be a transgression. If we compare āyah 2:173 to 16:115, we will find similar messages and the use of the same root word, 'adawa, to indicate transgression.

In another example, Muslims are allowed to fight (قتال, to fight) back if others fight against them.[2:190] Again, we notice that defensive fighting is a permissible act, however, to exceed the rules of engagement—excessive aggression, unwarranted destruction, disproportionate violence —would be a sin.

The examples above illustrate one shade of the meaning of transgression: 'going beyond or over.' Transgression also means to do something wrong or to violate a command.

In order to understand this shade of meaning, let us look at a simple example. When parents tell their children to wash their hands before touching food, this is a rule set by the parents. But if children touch food without washing their hands, it is not evil or a sin. They only transgressed—violated the parents' rule—but they did not sin. At that point, the parents may ignore the matter altogether, or talk with the children, correct them, reprimand them, or take other steps. Similarly, when a person transgresses divine rules, depending on the severity of the issue, he or she is liable to face some reprimand and corrections. Unlike not washing one's hands, which may not have any serious consequencea, violating the Qur'ānic rules have serious moral and spiritual consequences upon the person. Therefore, this amounts to committing sin.

In the Qur'ān, a large number of āyāt discusses transgression, the transgressor and the limits of transgression. Before we discuss some of these āyāt, we should understand the concept of sin and crime.

Sin and crime: A sin is a deliberate action, inaction, or thought that contradicts the commands of Allāh. It is an offense that has its basis in one's faith. Because not everyone has the same faith, the interpretation of what constitutes a sin varies from person to person,

and religion to religion. For example, not performing salāt is a sin in Islam, but not in the eyes of an atheist or a Christian. Worshipping an idol is not considered a sin in Hinduism, but it is a grave sin in Islam.

On the other hand, a crime means breaking the law set by a country or local authority. If a laws is broken, a criminal act is performed; therefore, a penalty has to be paid. The faith of a person has no bearing on a penalty imposed for a crime. In many cases, a crime defined by man-made laws also qualifies to be a crime under the divine laws. For example, killing an innocent person is a crime defined by the laws of man. It is also a crime under the divine laws of Allāh.

If a person commits a sin, it may or may not constitute a crime. For example, if a person misses his salāt, he has committed a sin, not a crime. But if a person commits a crime, he has also committed a sin. For example, killing a person is both a crime and a sin.

In the human court of law, a person will be punished for a crime only if he gets caught and his guilt is conclusively established. It is possible that after committing a crime, a person may escape punishment through legal loopholes.

Under Qur'ānic principles, transgression can be a sin as well as a crime, depending upon how and against whom the crime is committed.

Arabic word: In Arabic, the root word 'adā (ع د ا) or 'adawa (ع د و) means to overlook, to transgress, to pass by. This root word and its derivatives have been used in the Qur'ān in over 100 āyāt. Such widespread usage indicates that issues of transgression are, indeed, seriously dealt with in the Qur'ān. Some of the derivative words are: t'adau (تعدو) means 'to transgress,' mu'tadīn (معتدين) means 'transgressor,' 'adwān (عدوان) means 'transgressing,' and 'aduwwun (عدو) means 'enemy.' Similarly Ya'dūna means 'they transgressed,' Ta'tadū means 'you transgress,' I'tadan means 'they transgressed,' I'tadina means 'we have transgressed.' La t'dū means 'do not transgress' or 'do not overlook.'

Another word, *tagha* (طغى) means 'exceeding the limits,' 'to be tyrannical,' 'inordinate.' Two derivatives of this word are: *tāghūt* (طاغوت) means 'to be inordinate' (a name of Shaitān) and *atgha* (اطغى) means 'most rebellious.'

Another word, *ghalā* (غلا) means 'to exceed the proper limits,' 'to be excessive.' This word is also used in the Qur'ān to prohibit transgression.

Hudūd: The word *hudūd* refers to Islamic laws that state the limits ordained by Allāh, including deterrent punishments for violating the limits. One main focus of the laws relating to *hudūd* is the sins of adultery and its punishment. These laws are commonly known as *hudūd* laws.

The word *hudūd* is derived from the root word *hadda*, which means 'to define a limit.' It also means 'to punish a culprit' or 'to prevent.' In a wider sense, the word "limit" indicates a line or boundary where two contrasting things meet. In Islamic law, one side of the boundary are all the permissible activities, and on the other side are all the illegal activities. Overstepping the boundary is an extreme step, therefore, under Islamic law it calls for severe punishment.

We will not study the *hudūd* laws in this lesson. Our purpose here is to try to understand why human beings overstep the boundaries, what are some of the boundaries, and how, as youths, we can protect ourselves from transgressing the limits.

Human nature is to transgress: In sūrah al-'Alaq, āyah 6 states that human beings, by nature, are transgressors.

$$كَلَّآ إِنَّ ٱلْإِنسَـٰنَ لَيَطْغَىٰٓ ۝$$

No, verily man does transgress. (96:6)

The word *inna* (literally, surely, certainly) adds emphasis to the sentence. Notice the use of the word *tagha* in this āyah. The reason for their transgression is summarized in the following āyah:

$$أَن رَّءَاهُ ٱسْتَغْنَىٰٓ ۝$$

because he looks upon himself as self-sufficient. (96:7)

The belief that man is self-sufficient causes him to refuse to submit to the Creator and worship Him. Man often thinks that he is in control of his own health, wealth, wellbeing, livelihood, and destiny. He fails to realize that he has no control over any of these things. He forgets that everything is dependent upon Allāh; nobody and nothing in the universe is self-sufficient. Only Allāh is self-sufficient.[2:263; 35:15]

One of Allāh's fines names is *Al-Ghani*, which means 'The Rich.' Because of this quality of Allāh, Muslims declare all that is in the heavens and all that is on earth belongs to Him. He alone is self-sufficient. He is the One to whom all praise is due.[22:64]

If we realize our utter dependence upon Allāh, for anything and everything, we can prevent ourselves from being transgressors.

Dietary habits and transgression: In the matter of dietary habits, conditions of necessity override the laws of prohibition. We have previously discussed that if a person is stricken with extreme hunger, he is allowed to eat prohibited food as long as he does not exceed the limit. A routine or casual visit to a restaurant that serves prohibited meat does not allow us to override the prohibition. We should remember not to abuse the divine permission.

Below is a summary of several āyāt where Allāh cautions us about our dietary habits:

We are allowed to eat only good things that Allāh provided us, but we may not transgress.[20:81]

We are cautioned not to declare things unlawful that Allāh has made lawful for us, because it is transgression.[5:87]

We are cautioned not to arbitrarily declare that something is lawful and something else is unlawful.[16:116]

We are cautioned not to eat the meat of an animal that is slaughtered with a name other than Allāh during the process of slaughtering.[16:115]

Hypocrisy is transgression: In the matter of faith, the Qur'ān identifies three types of people: believers, non-believers and hypocrites. A hypocrite is a person who outwardly declares faith in Islam, but his actions are contrary to his faith. In a large number of āyāt, the Qur'ān has criticized the hypocrites in the strongest terms. They are labeled as transgressors in the following āyah:

The hypocrite men and the hypocrite women— some of them are among the other. They enjoin evil, and forbid good; and they withhold their hands. They have neglected Allāh, so He neglects them. Surely, the hypocrites are themselves the transgressors. (9:67)

After labeling the hypocrites as transgressors, in another āyah, the Qur'ān states their refuge is in hellfire.

But as to those who transgress, their refuge is then the Fire. Every time they wish to get away from it, they will be returned into it; and it will be said to them: "You taste the chastisement of the Fire which you used to belie." (32:20)

Communities destroyed for transgression: In the past, many communities were severely punished and some were destroyed simply because they transgressed.[30:47] The Qur'ān has abundant examples of transgressors and their painful punishments. Fir'awn was destroyed because he transgressed.[20:43] The people of Nūh (A) were transgressors[51:46] and we know the consequence was severe. The people of Lūt (A) were transgressors[21:74] and we know their end was disastrous. The tribe of Thamūd transgressed[91:11] and their end was equally disastrous.

Consequence transgression: We mentioned previously that under Qur'ānic principles, transgression can both be a sin and crime. Many of us will probably never commit a crime, but it is highly possible that we will commit a transgression every now and then. Any form of transgression could have a disastrous effect on us.[32:20] Allāh says:

And whoever disobeys Allāh and His Messenger, and transgresses His limits, He will make him enter the Fire, abiding in it; and for him is a degrading chastisement. (4:14)

This is a serious warning and we must not take it lightly. The best way to avoid transgression is to surrender wholeheartedly to Allāh and seek His guidance in every matter of our lives. If we sincerely have faith in Allāh and act upon His teachings, we will save ourselves from committing transgressions. Allāh says believers and transgressors are not equal.

Will then he who is a Believer be like one who is a transgressor? They are not equal. (32:18)

Keeping this idea in our minds, we should call upon Allāh with humility and utmost sincerity of heart by avoiding any show of vanity. We should remember that Allāh does not love the transgressors.

Call upon your Lord with humility and privacy. Surely He does not love the transgressors. (7:55)

1. Which of the following choices about the principles of harām and halāl in Islam is correct?

    A.   Any of the harām food can be consumed by saying 'Bismillah.'
    B.   Islam allows declaring some of the harām things as halāl in the West.
    C.   In Islam, if one is compelled in day-to-day living, he can eat harām food.
    D.   In Islam, necessity overrides the laws of prohibition.
    E.   In Islam even if a person is about to die from hunger, he cannot eat harām food.

2. Imagine a scenario where Muslims are engaged in a battle with non-Muslims. During the battle, what actions by Muslims would be treated as an act of transgression?

    A.   During the battle, anything is allowed—nothing is transgression
    B.   Showing any type of valor at the time of death.
    C.   Carrying more than the required amount of arsenals.
    D.   Undue aggression, unwarranted destructions, and disproportionate violence.
    E.   Working on a battle strategy.

3. Based on the lesson, is it a crime when a person misses salāt? Explain

....

....

4. What is one of the main focuses of *hudūd* laws?

....

5. Based on sūrah al-'Alaq, what is the main reason human beings transgress?

    A.   They transgress because they forget.
    B.   They transgress because they think they are dependent.
    C.   They transgress because they are mindful of small matters.
    D.   They transgress because they think they are not accountable.
    E.   They transgress because they think they are self-sufficient.

6. All of the following actions are transgressions, except for one. Which one is not a transgression?

    A.   Declaring lawful things as unlawful.
    B.   Using an arbitrary approach to declare lawful things as unlawful.
    C.   Calling upon Lord with humility.
    D.   Resorting to hypocrisy.
    E.   Exceeding the limit with respect to prohibited food when one is starving.

7. Which punishment is in store for one who disobeys Allāh, His Messenger, and transgresses His limits?

A. No punishment will be given as transgressions will be overlooked.
B. Degrading punishment in fire.
C. Humiliation.
D. Mild reproach and correction.
E. He will be denied justice.

8. In āyah 5:77, Allāh says *lā taghlū* (do not exaggerate, do not go beyond the limits). To whom was this caution issued?

....

9. Read āyah 5:77 and the supporting commentary. Provide an example of how these people went beyond the limits.

....

....

10. Compare the message of āyah 5:77 with āyah 4:171. Both āyāt address the same group of people who transgressed. What is the most serious example of their transgression as mentioned in āyah 4:171?

....

....

Secular and Religious Duties

Objective of the Lesson:

Scholars of Islam debate whether Islam is a secular religion. Is it possible for a person to balance his duties toward Allāh with his duties toward the society and government? Where is the conflict and what are the challenges? This lesson provides an overview of secularism as well as secular and religious duties.

The question often arises as to how one can balance one's duties toward Allāh and duties toward the society and government. Broadly speaking, societal and governmental duties can be termed secular duties. Do the two types of duties, secular and religious, go hand in hand or is there conflict between them? Under normal circumstances, a person may not see a conflict between his or her secular and religious duties. However, in the history of human civilization, there are instances when these two types of duties clashed and resulted in bloodshed.

Before we discuss this issue further, let us try to understand the meaning of the term 'secular.' The word 'secular' means separate from religion—something that is worldly and not specifically religious, or something that is not dictated by religious orders. Even this definition has its limitations, as we will see later in this lesson.

Examples of secular activities are eating, bathing, and studying. These activities, by themselves, do not have religious dictates. Nonetheless, many

religious traditions do attach religious importance to these activities; therefore, they can be regarded as religious activities. In Islam, eating the meat of a slaughtered animal after Eid al-Adha is a religious activity. Bathing can be considered a religious activity, because two āyāt in the Qur'ān specifically call for bathing under certain circumstances.[4:43; 5:6] Likewise, studying to gain Islamic knowledge, in particular, memorizing the Qur'ān, can have religious attachments.

Origin of secularism: Secularism means the belief in the doctrine of non-religious ideas that reject religion and religious considerations. The doctrine of secularism is a product of Christian society. The objective of secularism was to deny God and eliminate religion, or to restrict it to one's private world. Before and during the Renaissance, the term 'secular' was used to describe any activity that was outside of strict religious domain. It was a belief that God had no say in people's worldly or secular affairs. For example, marriage was considered a worldly affair, therefore, the Church required its clergy to remain celibate, or unmarried, in order to render duties toward God.

In the 19th century, secularism described a movement in Europe that originated to improve the human standard of living through material means alone, without any reference to God or the Afterlife. In the course of time, secularism intermingled with atheism. In the 19th century, the intellectual works of Freud, Marx, and Nietzsche advocated atheistic thoughts that further delineated 'secular' concepts as devoid of God.

Misunderstanding the duties: As a result of such intellectual thoughts and movements in Europe, the dialogue today between Islam and secularism is often misunderstood. Many Muslim thinkers believe that Islam and secularism are poles apart, and there is no possibility of arriving at a minimum consensus between the two.

One of the main reasons for the sharp increase in religious violence and intolerance in Muslim societies is due to the misperception and mis-interpretation of secular and religious duties. Sometimes secularism is incorrectly viewed as synonymous with *atheism*, i.e., disbelief in the existence of the Deity, and *agnosticism*, i.e., disbelief in either the existence or the nonexistence of God. As a result of such misunderstandings, many Muslim societies are experiencing tremendous turmoil. Societies that want to practice religious duties perceive all or most forms of secular duties as un-Islamic.

Prophetic example: In a hadīth, Ibn ʿUmar reported that Rasūlullāh (S) said: "It is obligatory for one to obey (the orders of rulers) unless these orders involve one's disobedience (to God); but if an act of disobedience (to God) is imposed, he should not listen to or obey it." (Bukhārī, Book 4, #203)

This hadīth shows that it is important to follow the orders of the rulers as long as the orders do not conflict with one's duties toward God.

Qur'ānic example: In one āyah in the Qur'ān, Allāh clearly describes this issue by using another example.

And We have prescribed for man goodness towards his parents. But if they strive to make you associate with Me what you have no knowledge of, then do not obey them. Towards Me is your return, then I shall inform you what you were doing. (29:8)

A similar message also appears in āyah 31:15. Both these āyāt call for secular and religious duties at the same time. However, if one's secular duties sharply conflict with one's religious duties, only then do the religious duties prevail.

"But if they strive against you that you should associate with Me about which you do not have any knowledge, then do not obey them; yet keep company with them with fairness in this world. And follow the path of him who bends towards Me, and then towards Me is your return, so I shall inform you as to what you used to do." (31:15)

However, in order to promote religious duties, secular duties need not be suppressed, as indicated in āyah 31:15. The āyah requires one to disobey one's parents if they encourage shirk, yet the āyah calls for showing fair treatment to the parents.

Biblical example: In the Bible, there is a beautiful illustration of the same message. Some of the people in the temple attempted to trap Jesus (A) into giving an anti-government answer to a question about whether they should pay taxes to Rome. In response,

Jesus (A) asked to see a coin and then asked whose image appeared on the coin. They replied that it was the image of the Roman Emperor. Jesus (A) replied, *"Give therefore, to the emperor the things that are the emperor's and to God the things that are God's."* (Matthew 22:21; Mark 12:13–17; Luke 20:20–25)

This distinction between religious and secular duties was notable during the time of Khalīfah 'Umar Ibn Al-Khattāb. He instituted an extensive tax system and financial reforms, all of which can be classified as secular duties.

Secular duties: The best example of a secular duty that also has a religious bearing is the obligatory zakat. This obligatory duty is part of the five Pillars of Islam. Treating parents with kindness and compassion is both a religious and secular duty. Similarly, taking care of the orphans, the destitute, and the oppressed are religious as well as secular duties. Helping a debtor or a destitute traveler are also secular and religious duties.

Under Islam, secular and religious duties are never viewed as contradictory responsibilities. Islam prohibits excess in religious matters.[4:171] Islam prohibits monasticism[57:27] because religion is not the 'only' affair in man's life—he has secular responsibilities as well.

Huqūq Allāh: With respect to man's secular and religious duties, two terms are often mentioned. Both terms relate to the rights or *huqūq*. One of the rights is the Rights of Allāh, or *Huqūq Allāh* and the other is the Rights of People, or *Huqūq 'Ibad*. A good Muslim is required to fulfill both of these rights. If a person observes only the rights and obligations that are due to Allāh, but neglects his or her duties toward family and community, this is not the best form of piety. In fact, Allāh condemns such a biased approach to life, as noted in sūrah al-Ma'un:

1. *Have you seen him who belies the Religion?*
2. *That is the one who drives away the orphan,*
3. *and does not urge upon feeding the poor.*
4. *So woe be to those performers of Salāt,—*
5. *those who are themselves unmindful of their Salāt,—*
6. *those who are themselves showy,*
7. *and refrain from the acts of kindness.*

Salāt is extremely important. Yet in this sūrah, performers of salāt are condemned because they drive away the orphans, neglect to feed the poor, and refrain from the smallest forms of kindness to others. See the lesson 'False Piety' in this book for additional reading).

We may continue to ask, which huqūq is more important? There is no right answer. However, consider this: Muslim men or women, who observe all the rites and duties that are due to Allāh, but neglect their families, neighbors, and children, oppress people, backbite, lie, take and give bribes, or commit other unethical practices—how does such good piety help these Muslim men or women?

Interpretation of secular duties: The non-religious duties of an individual are often equated with secularism. In the Muslim world, secularism is frequently viewed as an ideology directly opposed to religion. It is equated with Westernization or modernization. Secularism is viewed as a product of the West. Western ideas of liberty, freedom, and emancipation became the universal standard by which Muslim societies began to understand and interpret their secular duties. Those who espouse strong secular viewpoints sometimes marginalize and degrade religion to the point that traditional Muslims become infuriated. The word "secular" was used as a weapon by both parties to attack and counterattack one another.

Islam survived and will continue to survive by interacting with other cultures. We should maintain our religious duties alongside our secular ones. By all means, Islam is a secular religion. However, Islam does not support the Western definition of secularism that abandons God to make life easier. We should remain cautious of Western ideas of secular principles.

1. Which of the following duties are both secular and religious duties?

    A.   Treating parents with kindness and compassion.
    B.   Taking care of the orphans.
    C.   Rescuing a debtor from his debt.
    D.   Helping a traveler who is stranded.
    E.   All of the above.

2. Between *Huqūq Allāh* and *Huqūq 'Ibad*, which one should a good Muslim follow?

    A.   A good Muslim should follow only *Huqūq Allāh*.
    B.   A good Muslim should follow only *Huqūq 'Ibad*.
    C.   A good Muslim should follow both *Huqūq Allāh* and *Huqūq 'Ibad*.
    D.   A good Muslim should follow neither, but only his conscience.
    E.   A good Muslim should follow his Imam.

3. What changed the understanding of secularism in the early 19th century? Explain.

....

....

....

4. Based on the hadīth quoted in the lesson, what do you think the opinion was of Rasūlullāh (S) about the secular duties of Muslims?

....

....

5. As Muslims, how should we differentiate between secularism and the secular duties of a person?

....

....

....

6. The lesson mentions that Islam prohibits monasticism. See āyah 57:27 for reference. This āyah indicates that religion is not about seclusion—it has a secular responsibility as well. Discuss this point below. Use additional space as needed.

....

....

....

....

Islamic Views on Racism

Objective of the Lesson:

Islam is not a racist religion. It does not preach, practice, or support racism in any manner. The teachings of the Qur'ān and the sunnah of Rasūlullāh (S) clearly and conclusively prove that Islam is not a racist religion. This lesson provides an overview of how Rasūlullāh (S) was instrumental in fighting racism and how the Qur'ān directed mankind to overcome racial prejudice.

Anthropologists and socio-biologists define the word "race" as a group of family members, people, tribe, or nation unified by shared interests, habits, and characteristics as these features distinguish them from others. Sometimes we loosely mention human beings as a race, however, in the true sense, we are a species, *Homo sapiens*. Among human species, a race is an inbred group, having certain distinctive physical traits, beliefs, dispositions and an inherited temperament. The differences between human races are very slight, although outwardly they might appear to be different. For example, white people look different than blacks people.

Most anthropologists recognize three or four basic human races today. They are Austroloid, or the Australian Aborigine, Caucasoid, Mongoloid, and American Indian.

These races are sometimes further divided into as many as 30 sub-groups. The key differences between these sub-groups are: language, hair color, facial features, and skin color.

Racism: The Miriam Webster's dictionary defines racism as a belief that race is the primary determinant of human traits and capacities and racial differences produce an inherent superiority for particular races. Racism is a prejudice that affects mankind at all levels, and all periods of time. The history of human civilization shows that mankind was never able to overcome the prejudice of racism. Even Arabia, before and during the lifetime of Rasūlullāh (S), was not immune to racism, as we will see later.

BANU QURAISH

Banu Asad   Banu Nawfal

Banu Hashim   Banu Makhzum

Banu Muttalib   Banu Taim

Banu Zuhra   Banu Adi

Banu Shams

Earliest example of racism: The earliest example of racism surfaced after Ādam (A) was created. When Allāh asked the angels to bow down to Ādam (A), all the angels bowed down except Iblīs, a member of Jinn,[18:50] who refused based on racial prejudice.

He (Allāh) said: "What prevented you that you did not bow down when I commanded you?" He (Iblīs) said: "I am better than he; You have created me of fire, while You created him of clay." (7:12)

In another place, in response to the same question, Iblīs answered:

He (Iblīs) said: "It is not for me to bow down before a human being whom You have created out of sounding clay, out of black mud molded into shape." (15:33)

Allāh never said that fire was a better ingredient than clay, therefore, to assume that creation from fire made one better than the other appears racially motivated and totally unjustified.

Racism in Arabia: Racism in Arabia existed in many different forms before, during, and after the lifetime of Rasūlullāh (S). Some of the visible forms of racism were based on tribalism, the color of skin, and gender. Tribalism means tribal consciousness and loyalty; particularly, exaltation of the tribe above other groups. However, Rasūl Muhammad (S) was able to diminish all forms of racial prejudice through the dictates of the Qur'ān and his sunnah. Long before he was appointed as the Rasūl, Muhammad (S) had the wisdom to attack the very root of color-based racism in an unparalleled manner.

Challenging racial prejudice: After her marriage to Muhammad (S), Khadījah (ra) gave him a black slave as a gift. The slave was Zaid ibn Harith. Muhammad (S) liberated Zaid from slavery and adopted him as his son. Zaid did not do any meritorious work to warrant his freedom, nor did he or anyone buy his freedom. However, on the part of Muhammad (S), the act of freeing a slave

in itself was very meritorious, but to adopt him as his son was unparalleled. By adopting Zaid as his son, Muhammad (S) not only rejected the racial prejudice against people of a different color, but he also challenged tribalism, which is another form of racial prejudice.

The Arabs used to think they were superior to all other people in the world, and the Quraish people, in particular, used to think they were superior among the Arabs. Zaid, who was, until then, an outcast among the Quraish, suddenly found himself after adoption among the elite group of Quraish. Many Quraish found it difficult to accept Zaid as a member of the Quraish, but they had no choice.

Much later, during the Farewell Pilgrimage, in his famous sermon, Rasūlullāh (S) reaffirmed and restated the unity and equality of Muslim brotherhood.

Tribalism: As mentioned above, one of the most visible forms of racism in Arabia was tribalism. A tribe is a social group largely based on kinship that is characterized by a strong sense of identity and loyalty to the group. Preserving the integrity and cohesiveness in the tribe was as important as taking pride in their heritage and ancestry. A tribe would always exalt them over others. Much of the warfare and bloodshed in Arabia was due to inter-tribal rivalry and asserting dominance.

Challenging tribalism: Rasūlullāh (S) dealt with the Arab sense of tribalism in a unique manner. He not only dissolved the tribal mentality of the Arabs, but he also shattered the racial divide that was prevalent. His call to Islam ushered the Muslims to give up their tribal allegiances and become unite as an *ummah* under the common bond of Islam. A new nation was formed that went above and beyond the tribal mentality and ethnic divide. The Makkan Quraish refused to see their tribal heritage disintegrate under the influence of Islam. They launched attack after attack against the Muslims; one purpose for these attacks was to preserve tribal integrity.

Rasūl Muhammad (S) further dissolved the racial divide among different tribes as he married prominent women from different tribes. Marriages with Juwairiyah, a woman of Banu Mustaliq; Saffiya, a widow of Kinānah; and Maimunah, a woman of the Quraish, helped different tribes dissolve their racial divide and unify under the umbrella of Islam.

Marriage of Zaid: Zaid Ibn Harith was a black slave freed by Rasūl Muhammad (S) and adopted as his son. After Muhammad (S) became a Rasūl of Allāh, he arranged the marriage of Zaid to his cousin Zainab (See Lesson 15, Level 9 for the details). The marriage of a black man, a former slave, to an elite Quraish woman was another brilliant example of how Rasūlullāh (S) sought to challenge racial divides among the Arabs and help them recognize the ties of brotherhood enjoined by Islam.

Racism against other religion: Racism also exists in all religions. Often the more fundamentally insecure, unstable, and narrow the religion, the more prominent is prejudice against other religions. The question is: is Islam is a racist religion? The following Qur'ānic āyāt explain the position of Islam.

Surely as to those who believe, and those Jewish, and the Christians, and the Sabians—whoever believes in Allāh and the Last Day, and does good,—for them, then, their reward is in the presence of their Lord; and there is no fear on them, nor will they grieve. (2:62)

You say: "We believe in Allāh and that has been revealed to us, and what was revealed to Ibrāhīm and Ismā'īl and Ishāq and Ya'qūb and to the tribes, and what was given to Mūsā and 'Isā, and to the prophets from their Lord. We make no distinction between any of them and to Him we are submissive." (3:84)

And of His Signs is the creation of the heavens and the earth, and the diversity of your tongues and your colors. Certainly in this there are indeed Signs for the learned. (30:22)

All these āyāt recognize the existence of other people, faiths, languages and colors. The diversity in mankind is considered a sign of Allāh. In āyah 2:62, the Muslim worldview is beautifully illustrated by clarifying that as long as people of other faiths maintain some of the core principles of Islam, they have no fear.

Unity of Mankind: Islam is the only religion to attest to the unity of mankind. The following Qur'ānic āyāt support this idea:

Mankind is but a single nation. (2:213)

Mankind is none but a single nation, then they differed. (10:19)

وَإِنَّ هَٰذِهِۦ أُمَّتُكُمْ أُمَّةً وَٰحِدَةً وَأَنَا۠ رَبُّكُمْ فَاتَّقُونِ ۝

Surely this your community is one single community, and I am your Lord. Therefore worship me. (21:92; 23:52)

These āyāt indicate that Allāh created mankind to be one single nation. The concepts of racial prejudice and inherent differences were created by people themselves.

Essence of āyah 49:13: In order to understand Islamic brotherhood, āyah 49:13 from sūrah Hujurāt is often quoted. Let us read the āyah and understand its essence.

يَٰٓأَيُّهَا ٱلنَّاسُ إِنَّا خَلَقْنَٰكُم مِّن ذَكَرٍ وَأُنثَىٰ وَجَعَلْنَٰكُمْ شُعُوبًا وَقَبَآئِلَ لِتَعَارَفُوٓاْ إِنَّ أَكْرَمَكُمْ عِندَ ٱللَّهِ أَتْقَىٰكُمْ إِنَّ ٱللَّهَ عَلِيمٌ خَبِيرٌ ۝

O you mankind! We have surely created you out of a male and a female, and We have made you into nations and tribes that you may recognize one another. Surely the noblest of you in the presence of Allāh is one who is most righteous of you. Truly Allāh is all-Knowing, all-Aware. (49:13)

Several key ideas are deeply embedded in this āyah. Let us identify these ideas:

1. This āyah and other āyāt in the Qur'ān do not have any ideas equivalent to racial superiority and race-related prejudice.

2. This āyah is addressed to all of mankind; therefore, the message applies to everybody.

3. Creation from a single male and a single female indicates equality in the offspring and uniformity in the process of creation.

4. Allāh created mankind into different groups. However, these groups were not created to propagate racial prejudice, but to provide a sense of belonging.

5. The different tribes and nations of mankind break the monotony and create diversity—the purpose is not to discriminate, but to know one another.

6. These differences are signs of Allāh and His creativity.[30:22]

7. The sole criteria of greatness or preference among human beings lies at the level of individual righteousness, not at national or race level.

8. Therefore, an individual, regardless of his or her nationality, caste, color, or sex, can only be better in the sight of Allāh on the basis of his or her level of righteousness.

9. One's level of righteousness is a yardstick that can only be measured by Allāh, therefore, we, human beings cannot determine who is better or worse.

Last Sermon on brotherhood: During the Farewell Pilgrimage in the year 10 A.H. / 632 C.E., Rasūlullāh (S) delivered a sermon to the pilgrims (see Lesson 21, Level 8 for details). This sermon was the final sermon delivered by Rasūlullāh (S). The details of the sermon are mentioned in almost all the books of Hadīth. In it, Rasūlullāh (S) re-affirmed the principles of equality and brotherhood in Islam, thus making it a sacred legacy for generations to come. In his sermon, he stated the following:

All mankind is from Adam and Eve, an Arab has no superiority over a non-Arab nor does a non-Arab have any superiority over an Arab; also a white has no superiority over a black, nor does a black have any superiority over a white—except by piety and good action. Learn that every Muslim is a brother to every Muslim and that the Muslims constitute one brotherhood. Nothing shall be legitimate to a Muslim, which belongs to a fellow Muslim, unless it was given freely and willingly. Do not, therefore, do injustice to yourselves.

Islam is not a racist religion. It does not preach, practice, or support racism in any manner. The teachings of the Qur'ān and the sunnah clearly and conclusively prove that Islam is not racist. During different periods of Islamic rule, people from other faiths enjoyed religious tolerance. During the time of the Crusades, when the Jews were persecuted in Europe, they found freedom and sanctity in Muslim Spain. Even Jewish scholars acknowledge the period of Jewish settlement in Muslim Spain was one of the golden eras in their history. If Islam was a racist religion, history would have proven the case.

1. In the history of mankind, what was the earliest recorded example of racism?

    A.   The Roman belief that they were superior race.
    B.   The Quraish belief that they were the best among the Arabs.
    C.   Iblīs claiming that his race was superior to the human race.
    D.   Ādam (A) claiming that Iblīs was not better than him.
    E.   Ādam (A) claiming that human race is the best.

2. Which of the following choices are examples of racism in Arabia? Circle all the correct answers.

    A.   The belief that one's own tribe is better than others.
    B.   The belief that one's own clan is better than others.
    C.   The belief that men are superior to women.
    D.   The belief that the color of the skin determines superiority of race.
    E.   The belief that female children are inferior to male children.

3. Explain how Rasūlullāh's (S) relationship with Zaid ibn Harith helped remove racial prejudices.

4. Explain why tribalism was a form of racism in Arabia.

5. Explain how Rasūlullāh (S) challenged and successfully changed tribal racism.

6. Explain why smaller, regional religions often have more prejudices against other religions.

....

....

7. Based on the lesson on racism, which of the following choices is correct?

    A.   Allāh encouraged racism by creating different nations and tribes.

    B.   Allāh created mankind as a single nation. The concept of racial prejudice was created by human beings.

    C.   Different nations and tribes were created so that these groups would not recognize each other.

    D.   The color of the skin determines racial superiority.

    E.   In the Last Sermon of Rasūlullāh (S), he did not say anything about racism.

8. In āyah 49:13 several reasons for making mankind into nations and tribes are given. Which of the following reasons is not given?

    A.   Allāh created diversity by creating different nations and tribes.

    B.   The diversity of mankind is a sign of Allāh.

    C.   The purpose of creating mankind into nations and tribes is not to discriminate, but to help them know one another.

    D.   The diversity of mankind does not to propagate racial divide, but fosters belonging.

    E.   Creating different nations and tribes defeated the spirit of unity of mankind.

9. In the Last Sermon, Rasūlullāh (S) mentioned four different universal truths to refute the sense of artificial superiority that gave rise to racial prejudice. What are these four truths?

    A.   ....

    B.   ....

    C.   ....

    D.   ....

Principles of an Islamic Economy

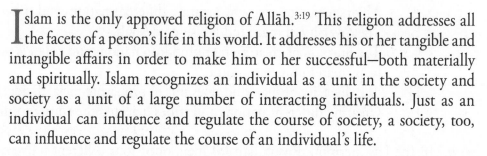

Objective of the Lesson:

This lesson presents a brief introduction to the principles that made the Islamic economic system stand out in comparison to capitalistic and socialistic economic systems. Students will learn some of the key features of the system that help people as they strive to achieve good in this life and good in the Hereafter.

Islam is the only approved religion of Allāh.[3:19] This religion addresses all the facets of a person's life in this world. It addresses his or her tangible and intangible affairs in order to make him or her successful—both materially and spiritually. Islam recognizes an individual as a unit in the society and society as a unit of a large number of interacting individuals. Just as an individual can influence and regulate the course of society, a society, too, can influence and regulate the course of an individual's life.

Islam is not merely concerned with life in this world. Its prime focus is to make people successful in the Hereafter. To this effect, the religion not only thoroughly addresses the belief system of a person, but also thoroughly addresses personal, familial, political, environmental, financial, and international affairs. In the matter of faith, a person is required to completely obey the commands of Allāh. Similarly, in the matter of financial affairs and business transactions, a person is required to completely obey the commands of Allāh.

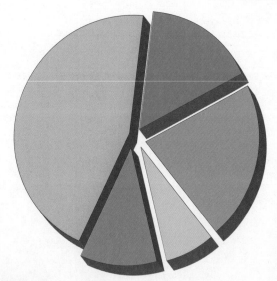

In order to balance the personal and societal life of an individual, Islam has instituted proper methodologies so that nothing in this life becomes asymmetrical. To ensure that financial and business transactions are balanced, Islam has instituted the norms of harām and halāl. To ensure that the poor and deprived are not left unattended, Islam has instituted the norms of zakāt. In order to prevent economic imbalance and subjugation, Islam has instituted laws relating to oppression, persecution, usury, financial transactions, gambling, lotteries, hoarding, wills, inheritances, charity and so on. As students of

Islam, it is our duty to understand and appreciate how Islam envisages equality and justice for all members in the society. In this lesson, we will concentrate on the economic and financial paradigm envisaged in Islam.

Current economic systems: None of the prevailing world economic systems can provide a true path to success, betterment, and satisfaction in this life or in the Hereafter. All of the available economic systems have some kind of polarity. Therefore, there are limitations to their effectiveness.

For example, a capitalistic economy is founded on the premise of the right to own unlimited personal wealth. A person can control his wealth, decide where and how it can be spent. He decides the means that will increase his wealth. He decides what item should be produced, and what item will bring him personal gain. He decides where to invest his wealth and where not to invest. All financial enterprise is driven by the motive of economic gain. Capitalism encourages unrestrained competition in the accumulation of wealth. The government is not allowed to interfere in the economic transactions and earnings of an individual. Instead, the government allows everybody to earn unlimited resources according to one's means. As such, interest, usury, gambling, and speculating are the bases of a capitalistic economy.

When the capitalistic economy was first instituted, mainly in the Western world, it seemed to benefit many and it appeared to provide the best solution. However, its inherent problems and negative impacts soon began to emerge.

In order to counter the capitalistic economic system, a socialist economic system developed. This system advocated that the root cause of all evil in the world was the capitalistic economy. If the capitalistic system could be eradicated, the world would become a better place. Under the socialist system, personal ownership of wealth was restricted. The government would own all the assets and ensure production, equal distribution, and the welfare of the society. In 1917 Russia adopted this economic system after emerging from a drawn-out gruesome revolution. However, instead of social and economic improvement at all levels of society, a horrific system evolved, where personal freedom was severely curtailed. Human beings were rendered into tools of production. They were used like machines without emotion, compassion, and minds of their own.

In short, neither the capitalistic nor the socialist economic system can deliver the desired benefits to society. On the contrary, Islam provide a balanced approach to the economic system. Islam allows personal ownership of capital, however, on the condition that wealth is used for the welfare of the society. Thus, on one hand, Islam regulates personal income and balances it with personal expenses, ensuring that both income and expenses are managed properly. Under the Islamic economic system, there was no provision for unequal wealth distribution, and there is no provision for loss of "human" factors and personal freedom.

Absolute owner: Under an Islamic economic system, the absolute owner of all wealth is Allāh. In more than 30 āyāt in the Qur'ān, Allāh attests to His absolute ownership.

$$ وَلِلَّهِ مَا فِي ٱلسَّمَـٰوَٰتِ وَمَا فِي ٱلْأَرْضِ ۚ وَكَانَ ٱللَّهُ بِكُلِّ شَىْءٍ مُّحِيطًا ۞ $$

And to Allāh belongs all that is in the heavens and all that is in the earth. And Allāh is ever Encircling everything. (4:126)

$$ لَّهُۥ مَا فِي ٱلسَّمَـٰوَٰتِ وَمَا فِي ٱلْأَرْضِ وَمَا بَيْنَهُمَا وَمَا تَحْتَ ٱلثَّرَىٰ ۞ $$

To Him belongs whatever is in the heavens and whatever is in the earth, and whatever is between the two, and whatever is beneath the soil. (20:6)

We are not the owners of the wealth that we possess; we are only its caretaker, a trustee. As a trustee, we hold or manage the assets for our own benefit as well as for the benefit of others. As a trustee, we have certain obligations to the Owner of the trust, Allāh. We need to follow the instructions of the owner as to how the wealth should be spent.

Ultimate provider: Since Allāh is the absolute owner of all the wealth, He is also the ultimate provider. It is Allāh's responsibility to provide the *rizq* (sustenance) to everybody and it is our duty to search for it.

وَمَا مِن دَآبَّةٍ فِى ٱلْأَرْضِ إِلَّا عَلَى ٱللَّهِ رِزْقُهَا وَيَعْلَمُ مُسْتَقَرَّهَا وَمُسْتَوْدَعَهَا ۚ كُلٌّ فِى كِتَٰبٍ مُّبِينٍ ٦

And there is no terrestrial in the earth but upon Allāh is the sustenance of it. And He knows its resting place and its residence. Everything is in a clear Book. (11:6)

In another āyah, Allāh instructs us to search for the provisions.

...therefore seek provision from Allāh and worship Him, and give thanks to Him, towards Him you are going to be returned. (29:17)

Measured distribution: Each one of us has equal rights to earn our livelihood, however, not all of us have the same qualifications to earn it. While it is necessary that the means of survival should be available for each one of us, it is not necessary that these means should be identical. Just as human beings are different in terms of their language, color, ethnicity, and nationality, there are differences in terms of the capability to earn a livelihood. However, they are required to share their wealth with the less fortunate, but they are mostly unwilling to do so.

And Allāh has favored some of you above the others in livelihood; then those who are favored are unwilling to give back their livelihood to those whom their right hands possess, so that they might become equal in it. Will they then deny the favor of Allāh? (16:71)

It is part of a divine principle to favor some over others in the matter of livelihood. One of the reasons for such favor is explained in the following āyah:

Do they divide the mercy of your Lord? We distribute their livelihood among them in the present life; and We have raised some of them above others in ranks, so that some of them may command work from others. And the mercy of your Lord is better than what they amass. (43:32)

Not everybody will end up with the same amount of provisions. Allāh has the wisdom to grant the provisions in a manner that is under His best judgment.

ٱللَّهُ يَبْسُطُ ٱلرِّزْقَ لِمَن يَشَآءُ وَيَقْدِرُ

Allāh widens the provision for whomsoever He pleases, and He measures out. (13:26)

ٱللَّهُ يَبْسُطُ ٱلرِّزْقَ لِمَن يَشَآءُ مِنْ عِبَادِهِ وَيَقْدِرُ لَهُۥ ۚ إِنَّ ٱللَّهَ بِكُلِّ شَىْءٍ عَلِيمٌ ٦٢

Allāh spreads out the provision for whom He pleases of His servants, and He measures it for him. Surely Allāh is aware of all things. (29:62)

Redistribution of wealth: It is practically impossible for each person in the world to have an equal amount of wealth. Unequal amounts of wealth not only creates diversity, but it also brings about social interaction, promotes business, supports enterprise, and advances civilization.

Allāh gives the wealth selectively to some people on the condition that they will not hoard the wealth, but spend it for a good cause. Allāh does not want the wealth to be circulated only among the rich.

كَىْ لَا يَكُونَ دُولَةًۢ بَيْنَ ٱلْأَغْنِيَآءِ مِنكُمْ

...in order that it [wealth] may not be circulating among the rich amongst you. (59:7)

In many āyāt, the Qur'ān strongly discourages the hoarding of wealth.

...And those who hoard gold and silver and do not spend it in Allāh's way—give them then the tidings of a painful punishment—on a day when it will be heated in the Fire of Hell, then with that their foreheads and their sides and their backs will be branded. "This is what you hoarded for yourselves; taste then what you used to hoard!" (9:34–35)

Under the principle of the redistribution of wealth, Islam has made zakāt mandatory for all Muslims who have an annual surplus from any economic activity. A large number of āyāt in the Qur'ān emphasize the importance of zakāt.

And in their wealth is a share for the beggar, and the abstainer. (51:19)

وَٱلَّذِينَ فِىٓ أَمْوَٰلِهِمْ حَقٌّ مَّعْلُومٌ ۝ لِّلسَّآئِلِ وَٱلْمَحْرُومِ ۝

and in whose wealth there is a recognized right, for the beggar and the abstainer. (70:24–25)

Earning emphasized: In order to survive in this world, human beings have to earn their livelihood. When the question of earning is considered, the question of making a profit arises. Along with this comes the issues of ethical balance, fairness, and restrain.

Islam has discouraged self-denial, self-mortification and monasticism.[57:27] Human beings have a duty toward their own soul[64:16] and toward the society in which we live.

And seek by means of what Allāh has given you the Abode of the Hereafter, and do not forget your share of this world, and do good as Allāh has done good to you, and do not seek making mischief in the land. Surely Allāh does not love the mischief-makers (28:77)

Under Islamic economic principles, all earthly resources are treated as blessings from Allāh. People are encouraged to earn the blessings and enjoy them in the prescribed manner. In return, they should express gratitude for these resources. While Islam encourages enjoying the earthly blessings, it prohibits extravagance and waste.

O Children of Adam! take to your adornments at every occasion of prostration; and eat and drink, and do not waste. Surely He does not love the extravagant. (7:31)

And those who when they spend do not spend extravagantly, nor do they act niggardly, but always standing between these. (25:67)

Every person is required to make an effort to ensure a good living. As mentioned above, Allāh is the ultimate provider; however, each one of us is responsible to earn our livelihood based on our means and capability. Here is another āyah to illustrate this idea:

فَإِذَا قُضِيَتِ ٱلصَّلَوٰةُ فَٱنتَشِرُوا۟ فِى ٱلْأَرْضِ وَٱبْتَغُوا۟ مِن فَضْلِ ٱللَّهِ وَٱذْكُرُوا۟ ٱللَّهَ كَثِيرًا لَّعَلَّكُمْ تُفْلِحُونَ ۝

Then when the Salāt is completed, then disperse in the land and seek of Allāh's grace, and remember Allāh much, that you may be made successful. (62:10)

Wealth and pleasure: Without a doubt, wealth brings some degree of comfort and pleasure in life. However, under the principles of an Islamic economy, pleasure is not the objective of earning wealth. The main objective of life should be success in the Afterlife. Therefore, a Muslim should use his or her wealth in a manner that will ensure success in the Hereafter. If this principle is followed in its best spirit, it will not only benefit the person, but it will also benefit society.

Importance of Halāl earning: One of the greatest principles of the Islamic economic system is to encourage and ensure that all economic activities are done in a permissible, or halāl manner. This includes not only the economic activity itself, but also all activities in life, which should be based on the principle of halāl and harām. Islam has declared most of these activities permissible while some as prohibited. Activities that can benefit people morally, socially and spiritually, are halāl for Muslims. Activities that can harm people in this world and in the Hereafter are declared harām. For this reason, Islamic economic principles leave no room for usury, bribery, alcohol, gambling, speculation, cheating, embezzling, and all other forms of monetary misappropriations.

O you who believe! eat of the good things that We have provided you with; and give thanks to Allāh, if it is Him alone Whom you use to worship. (2:172)

O you messengers! eat of the pure things and do good. Surely I am aware of what you do. (23:51)

O you mankind! eat of what is on the earth, lawful, pure; and do not follow the footsteps of Shaitān. Surely he is to you an open enemy. (2:168)

The Qur'ān has provided the key guidelines which Rasūlullāh (S) and his followers used to formulate well thought-out Islamic economic principles. In the next lesson, we will study how these principles took concrete shape during the first 100 years of Islam.

In summary, we can say that Islam provides a balanced economic system that benefits everyone in society. Islamic economic principles are neither fully capitalistic in nature, nor exclusively socialist in spirit. This system recognizes individual wealth, supports fair earnings, takes care of the poor and destitute in society, balances earnings and expenses, directs the fair distribution of wealth, promotes enterprise, and prevents the destruction and waste of resources. Islamic economic principles guide people toward what is ultimately good in this life and in the Hereafter.

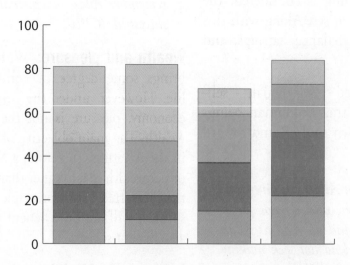

1. Which of the following choices is/are true about the Islamic economic system? Circle all the correct answers.

    A.   Islamic economic principles balance the personal and social life of an individual.
    B.   Islamic economic principles reflect both capitalistic and socialist ideas.
    C.   Under Islamic economic principles, an individual is the absolute owner of his wealth.
    D.   Islamic economic principles have their root only in the Sunnah of Rasūlullāh (S).
    E.   Islamic economic principles encourage earning.

2. One of the Islamic economic principles is to give zakāt. Which of the following statements is correct about zakāt?

    A.   The principles of zakāt are found only in the Qur'ān.
    B.   All able bodied Muslim men must pay zakāt once a year.
    C.   Zakāt is paid based on the annual income of a person.
    D.   Zakāt is obligatory for all Muslims who have an annual surplus from any economic activity.
    E.   Since spending is encouraged, a Muslim can spend all his wealth to have a good life.

3. A Muslim is required to do three things after the Jumuah prayer to achieve success. What are the three things mentioned in āyah 62:10?

    A. ....

    B. ....

    C. ....

4. Write three good features and three bad features of the capitalistic economic system.

    Good: ....

    Good: ....

    Good: ....

    Bad: ....

    Bad: ....

    Bad: ....

5. Based on your response to Q. 4 above, explain how the Islamic economic system corrected the bad features of the capitalistic economic system.

....

....

....

....

6. Under Islamic economic principles, Allāh is the absolute owner of all wealth. How does Allāh want us to handle the wealth under our possession?

....

....

....

Public Finance in Early Islam

Objective of the Lesson:

During the early periods of Islam, an efficient public finance system evolved, based on the Qur'ān and the Sunnah, that strengthened the society and administration and paved the way for the successful spread of Islam. This lesson provides an interesting overview of the emergence and success of an efficient public finance system in the early Islamic period.

Every country and every government must have a sound public finance system. Without this system, the government cannot operate efficiently. In the history of human civilization, it can be seen that the underlying cause why many nations that did not endure was their inability to establish a functional public finance system. Similarly, the nations that prospered in the past had a well-structured public finance system in operation. Public finance is another term for government finance or the fiscal policy of government. It covers the field of economics that deals with balancing the income and expenses of the government to achieve desired economic goals. For ease of understanding, the government can be viewed as a company that earns money, takes out loans, invests money and spends on necessary items, e.g., infrastructure development, salary and wages, health care, research, education, and so forth—all of which are for the benefit of the company and its employees.

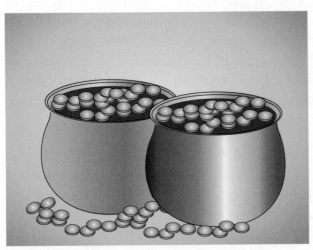

During the seventh century, Muslims emerged as a major nation in the world. The Muslim nation continued to influence regional geo-political systems in the arenas of power, culture, religion, civilization, science, and government. The concept of an Islamic state originated on the Arabian peninsula, but within the first 100 years of Islam, it extended its boundaries to Europe, North Africa, and Central Asia. It is natural that for such a vast empire to last for a long time and rule such a vast territory spanning three continents, it must have developed a consistent and functional public finance system. Some of the elements of a public finance system include:

- Areas of revenue collection,
- A tax system,
- A tax rate,
- The collection of taxes in accordance with Islamic laws,
- The disbursement of revenue for the welfare of the people,
- Use of the revenue for the benefit of the state,
- Use of the revenue to develop military power.

Muslim contributions to the development of a public finance system were ignored by many historians for a long time, and Europe did not recognize Muslim contributions for hundreds of years. Only recently has interest in this subject been

Map showing the approximate areas ruled by Rasūlullāh (S) and other Khalifas.

growing. In this chapter, we will provide an overview of public finance during the early Islamic era.

Nature of public finance in Islam: As always, the source of all Islamic rules and regulations stem from the Qur'ān, followed by the sunnah of Rasūlullāh (S). Interestingly, the Qur'ān does not provide details of fiscal policy. It simply provides the basic financial guidelines and economic principles on which the

fiscal policies would be formulated. The necessary details were provided by Rasūlullāh (S), but even some of his explanations were mostly guidelines rather than detailed procedures. The reason for the lack of details is that during the time of revelation of the Qur'ān, a formal Islamic state was far from being established. Therefore, the need for complex details of a public finance system was not warranted.

Rasūlullāh (S) lived in Madīnah, which was, in a way, the first "Muslim state" ever established. However, the territory of Madīnah was small and its public finance responsibilities were simple. After the death of Rasūlullāh (S), additional details of the policy were left for future jurists to develop based on Qur'ānic guidelines and the teachings of Rasūlullāh (S).

The role of the sunnah in formulating public finance details can be best illustrated by the institution of zakāh. The Qur'ān asked the believers to give zakāh. The Qur'ān also asked Rasūlullāh (S) to collect zakāh as a levy on the wealthy Muslims. But it did not state how much to collect, from whom to collect, and when to collect. The necessary details of the zakāh were formulated by Rasūlullāh (S).

You take for charity out of their wealth, that you may purify them and sanctify them with it, and you bless them. Your blessing is indeed a happiness to them. And Allāh is all-Hearing, all-Knowing. (9:103)

Sources of public finance policy: For the sake of simplicity, we can identify four sources from which public finance policy in Islam derive: (a) the Qur'ān; (b) the sunnah of Rasūlullāh (S); (c) the consensus (*Ijmā'*) of opinion, particularly of Islamic jurists; and (d) analogical reasoning of experts on Islamic law and jurisprudence.

Key words on sources of public revenue: The Qur'ān specifically mentions many different sources of public revenue. These are voluntary contributions of the wealthy (anfāl), zakāh, khumus, sadaqah, jizya, fai', and ghanimah.

Anfāl: During the early periods in Madīnah, a formal state treasury was not established and there were no fixed and regular sources of income. At that time the voluntary contributions of wealthy Muslims were the main sources of income. The word anfāl means 'voluntary gift.'

Zakāh: This is a religious obligation rather than an ordinary tax or alms. It served as the primary source of revenue in the early years of Islam.

Khumus: This is one-fifth share from the government of the war profit. The term is derived from the Arabic number *khamsa*, meaning five. In the Qur'ān, āyah 8:41 stipulates five categories upon which the profit should be distributed.

Sadaqah: These are alms given by anybody—rich or poor. Unlike zakāh, it is not obligatory but strongly encouraged.

Jizya: A type of tax imposed upon non-Muslim subjects in a Muslim nation. They are required to pay this tax in lieu of receiving military protection.

Fai': It denotes property received from the enemy that is not the result of actual fighting.

Ghanimah: It denotes property received from the enemy as a result of actual fighting.

The Qur'ān on social security: The initial purpose behind all public finance policies in Islam was to provide social security to all of its citizens, particularly those who volunteered for the cause of Islam. The system treated public finance as a trust in the hands of the ruler. A trust is a legal relationship between two parties whereby the second party has the responsibility of handling property for the benefit of the first party. In the Islamic system, public money is collected and held as a trust by the ruler, and he spends the money for the benefit of the weaker members of the society in order to ensure social security, general welfare, and equitable distribution of income.

Whatever Allāh has given as Fai' to His Messenger from the people of the townships, it is then for Allāh, and His Messenger, and the near relations, and the orphans, and the needy, and the wayfarer, in order that it may not be circulating among the rich amongst you. And whatever the Messenger gives you take it then, and whatever he forbids you then abstain. And revere Allāh, for Allāh is Severe in retribution. (59:7)

The Qur'ān teaches that the wealth of rich and affluent persons are given to them as a blessing from Allāh. They do not have exclusive rights to spend this wealth. The poor have a right to share a part of their wealth.

and in whose wealth there is a recognized right— (70:24)

for the beggar and the abstainer, (70:25)

During the early days of Islam, the objective of social security was to meet the immediate needs of the poor. Due to a lack of funds, Rasūlullāh (S) or the first khalīfah Abū Bakr (R) could not arrange monthly grants for the poor. The financial situation changed during the time of khalīfah 'Umar ibn Khattāb (R) when the Muslims extended their territory into Iraq and Syria.

Public finance during khalīfah 'Umar: Khalīfah 'Umar (R) was the first Muslim ruler to make revolutionary changes in public finance policies, in accordance with the guidance of the Qur'ān and the sunnah. Some of his decisions were far-reaching in shaping Muslim history.

The conquest of Iraq and Syria brought Muslims substantial amounts of wealth in the form of cash and property. For the first time, the government treasury was full. 'Umar (R) was the first to introduce monthly rations and grants, particularly to benefit those who were involved in the war with the other nations. 'Umar (R) realized the state was morally responsible to provide for those who fought to defend or extend its territory. Many of these warriors became incapacitated in the war. Many died, leaving behind wives and families. Many sacrificed their professions to enroll as soldiers. While instituting state grants to these soldiers, khalīfah 'Umar (R) primarily considered inhabitants of townships more than the villagers. He believed that the inhabitants of townships participated in many active wars or supported a war, whereas villagers were mostly confined to agricultural works. Thus, towns people were given a higher pension and ration than villagers. Also, 'Umar (R) did not grant pensions to the Makkans because he exempted them from military services.

'Umar (R) made another significant policy-related decision. The conquered lands in Iraq were not distributed to the poor or to the army, but he left them in a trust. He imposed *kharāj* (land tax) on the land and a poll tax on the *ahlul dhimmi* (non-Muslim inhabitants of an Islamic state). Thus, he was able to ensure recurring sources of revenue for the Muslim soldiers and their families.

'Umar (R) did not confine himself to assisting the army alone. He granted financial assistance to needy people who did not participate in a war, but suffered in famine or had a bad harvest. He realized the children are the future of a nation, thus, he instituted financial assistance to the newborn children.

He also instituted old-age pensions to those who were unable to earn their livelihood. But the greatest thing about him was that he did not exclude the non-Muslim citizens in the state. He not only exempted the elderly from other faiths (*ahlul dhimmi*) from paying jizya, but he also granted them pensions.

Overall, the reign of 'Umar (R) was marked by an efficient and just administration—firm in its matters of policy and compassionate with the citizens. While addressing one of the governors, 'Umar (R) described one of the qualities of a good governor:

I am appointing you administrators to lead and guide the Muslims in the ways of righteousness and not as rulers and tyrants. Do not appropriate public amenities exclusively to yourselves to the detriment of the subjects. I am appointing you administrators to teach the people their religion, to collect the taxes due and to serve as judges in disputes. The success of an administrator depends on firmness without tyranny and leniency without weakness.

The tax collector: The viability of a government depends upon the ability of the government to collect taxes. In ancient times, there were no tax returns to file. The tax collector had to go door-to-door to assess and collect taxes. This was a tedious and often risky job. The Qur'ān fully recognized the liability for tax collectors and specifically allocated a share of state revenue to be expended upon the tax collector as his salary or pension.

Charities are only for— the poor, and the needy, and the workers upon it, and those whose hearts are made to incline, and for the captives, and those in debt, and in the way of Allāh, and the wayfarer: an ordinance from Allāh. And Allāh is all-Knowing, most Wise. (9:60)

All tax collectors were required to show strong moral standing, keen judgment, and sense of responsibility.

State as a medium for economic development: The responsibility of an Islamic state is not only toward the economic and social welfare of its citizens, but also the requirements of Islamic shari'ah. The social obligation (*fard kifāyah*) of the state is the fulfillment of the needs of the people. It really does not matter who fulfills it—the state, the ruler, or the administrator—it is a duty that must be fulfilled. Thus, everybody is equally responsible to ensure it is accomplished.

The institution of a public finance system alone will not serve the overall good of the society. Early Islamic thinkers realized that the state must play an active role in the economic welfare of the people by providing them with a minimum standard of living. The minimum standard would ensure that resources are properly utilized for infrastructure development, for making favorable markets, for maintaining law and order, and for access to justice for all. Fulfilling basic needs such as food, clothing, shelter, and education etc. are also the primary duties of the state. Since these services benefit the general public, they can be considered *fard kifāyah*.

The basic needs of a community or nation do not remain the same from period to period. They are bound to change, and along with these changes, Islamic thinkers periodically updated the list of state duties. The emphasis and importance of these duties depends upon the depth of the state's revenue.

For example, 'Umar (R) initiated a steady supply of food grain to the needy inhabitants in Madīnah. He also emphasized educating the illiterate persons. But his emphasis upon the social security of the armed forces and their families was more prominent. 'Umar II, also known as 'Umar b. Abdul Aziz, appointed teachers for villagers and established fixed salaries for them. Al-Mawardi believed providing clean water to the city, the construction of protective walls around a city, and bearing the wedding expenses of orphan girls were an obligatory duties of the ruler.

'Umar II ordered the cultivation of the state's land by the state if no one else was interested in its cultivation. His objective was to make good use of all uncultivated land and increase crops.

Waqf properties: As mentioned earlier, the entire foundation of the early Islamic public finance system was built on voluntary services and charitable donations. Besides bearing the cost of constructing general-use buildings, early Muslims also made provisions for their ongoing maintenance. A masjid is one typical example. Such provisions are known as a *waqf* (endowment). Voluntary establishment of *waqf* properties supplemented the state's requirement in fulfilling its obligation towards the Muslim community.

This overview illustrates that the main objective of the early Islamic public finance system was to provide for the economic and social welfare of its citizens. The Qur'ān and sunnah provided the necessary guidelines, and Islamic thinkers developed specific methodologies for specific periods and nations.

1. A public finance system must have three different elements to be functional. Which of the choices below is correct?

    A.   Revenue, income, and cash flow.
    B.   Budgeting, income, and expenses.
    C.   Budgeting, balancing, and developing.
    D.   Income, expenses, and taxes.
    E.   Collecting taxes, earning money and taking out loans.

2. Based on the lesson, what is the main economic reason the Moghul Empire in India lasted for over 300 years?

....

3. The seventh century Muslim nation extended its boundaries in various directions. Which territory was NOT conquered during the first 100 years of its history?

    A.   Spain.
    B.   Iraq.
    C.   India.
    D.   Egypt.
    E.   Morocco.

4. Which of the following statements is correct about the early Islamic economic system?

    A.   It resembled the present-day fiscal policy of a government in elementary form.
    B.   It had defined revenue collection and taxation mechanisms.
    C.   It had a functional revenue system covering public and governmental sectors.
    D.   It was developed based on the ethical and social philosophies of Islam.
    E.   All of the above.

5. Which of the following statements is NOT true about the elements of the early Islamic public finance system?

    A.   Revenue was disbursed for the welfare of the public.
    B.   Revenue was spent for the comfort of the ruler.
    C.   Revenue was spent for the improvement of the economy.
    D.   Collecting taxes was in accordance to the Islamic values.
    E.   The early public finance system established a consistent and functional tax system.

6. Define in one sentence what is meant by *fard kifāyah*.

....

7. Which of the following statements is true regarding the formulation of public finance policy in the early Islamic era?

    A.   The Qur'ān provided detailed instructions about fiscal policy.
    B.   The Qur'ān provided basic financial guidelines and economic principles.
    C.   Rasūlullāh (S) provided all of the details about public finance policy.
    D.   Public finance policy in early Islam covered the concerns of Muslim citizens only.
    E.   Public finance policy was aimed at creating a gap between the rich and the poor.

8. Who was the first to institute monthly rations and grants for the poor?

    A.   Rasūlullāh (S).
    B.   Abū Bakr (R).
    C.   'Umar ibn Al-Khattāb (R).
    D.   Uthman ibn Affān (R).
    E.   Ummayad rulers.

9. Some of the sources of public finance are specifically mentioned in the Qur'ān. Which of the choices below is NOT a public finance concept?

    A.   *Khumus.*
    B.   *Jizyah.*
    C.   *Zakat.*
    D.   *Riba.*
    E.   *Kharaj.*

10. Which of the following choices correctly identifies some of the revolutionary public finance policies instituted by khalīfah 'Umar ibn Al-Khattāb (R)?

    A.   Muslim soldiers who fought in a war were given a monthly ration.
    B.   Citizens who suffered from famine or had a bad harvest were given assistance.
    C.   Old age pensions were given to those who could not earn a livelihood.
    D.   All of the above.
    E.   None of the above.

Islamic Architecture

Objective of the Lesson:

Whether it is the very first House ever built to worship Allāh, or the newest *masjid* built today, the construction features a vast range of architectural designs. This lesson provides a brief overview of Islamic architecture. Many of the architectural designs are intricate and display the astounding skills of the architect.

One of the earliest acts of the first Muslim, Ādam (A), was to build a house of prayer. This house went to ruins, and was rebuilt by two other great Muslims, Ibrāhīm (A) and Ismā'īl (A). Use of a house as a symbolic center toward which one would face during prayer is a fascinating concept. It is not an idol, a mountain, a rock or a living thing, such as a tree. This First House, the Ka'bah, remains the center of prayer for all Muslims all over the world. For a religion that recalls a great event like the construction of a House, it is no wonder that it continues to develop and perfect the technology of construction. The construction and architecture of buildings by Muslims contributed to the knowledge of architecture and design used for other structures in the world.

The first house ever built, the Ka'bah, is a simple house and retains its simplicity even today. This house was rebuilt several times after damage from aging or flooding. Even today, it remains the same plain cube-like house without any decoration or intricate design. The only decoration that we may see is on the door and on the *kiswah*, the covering of Ka'bah. The House is kept simple because no man-made design, motif, pattern, ornamentation, or decoration can ever match the grandeur or majesty of Allāh. The simplicity diverts the attention of the devotee from admiring a man-made structure to the actual purpose of prayer—worshipping the Almighty Allāh.

Fig. Two of the several minarets in the Masjid Al-Harām, Makkah.

Islamic architecture, or architecture by Muslims, embraces several kinds of buildings. The foremost is the masājid. Other structures, such as the Madrasah, have also played important roles for Muslims. Palaces and forts are also examples of some grand designs by Muslim architects.

Fig. Round domes help eliminate the need of pillars in the main hall of the masjid.

The tombs of some of the Muslim royals and some religious leaders also show the skills of the architects. Architecture for the benefit of the common masses were the bazaar or *suq*, communal baths, and the *caravanserai* for travelers. All these structures have their unique features.

The masjid at the time of Rasūlullāh (S):

When Rasūlullāh (S) first arrived in Madīnah without any worry of persecution, he initiated construction of a masjid at Qubā'. This illustrates the importance of masjid in the life of a Muslim community. The first masjid was basically an open space with a surrounding wall.

His masjid in Madīnah was a simple structure, to emphasize the need for a simple life shunning extravagance. The simple masjid served all the practical and spiritual needs of the Muslims, without any display of power or wealth. The major feature of the masjid was its direction towards *qiblah*. For the comfort of the people, a roof of palm leaves coated with mud gave some shade at the front part of the masjid. When the masjid was first built, this part was not shaded. On one side of the masjid was the dwelling quarter of Rasūlullāh (S), highlighting that *deen* and *dunya* are two sides of the same coin.

The simplicity of this masjid inspired the simplicity of other masājid in Arabia. The architecture that flourished in Islamic lands was mostly outside of the Arabian Peninsula. Thus the title of the lesson refers to Islamic architecture instead of Arabic architecture.

The masjid:

Apart from the home, the masjid is the most important structure for a Muslim. A masjid can be anywhere—a clean space devoid of any images of other gods is sufficient. Therefore, technically, it is not necessary for a specially built house to be a masjid. Yet, specifically designed masājid are always built for the purpose of the community—a place where many people may gather for the regular prayer. There are no specific demands for the shape, size, or components of a masjid. Yet, some building features are commonly incorporated in a masjid. For example, *mihrāb*, *mimbar*, dome, minaret, and so forth. However, none of these structures are necessary components of a masjid or make a masjid spiritually better than another.

Entrance:

As we enter a traditional masjid building, we find an entrance passage that leads to a courtyard. The passage serves two purposes: providing a sense of entering a space beyond the hustle of worldly affairs, and providing a place to remove one's shoes. Most masājid that have a leading entrance path will also contain shelves for the storage of shoes.

Courtyard:

The courtyard of a typical masjid is surrounded by a wall and is open to the sky. The size of the courtyard varies. The courtyard provides an unobstructed view of the masjid proper. As expected, most masājid are in the middle of a busy marketplace or in a neighborhood full of houses. This open courtyard provides the architect an opportunity to display the shape and grandeur of the masjid. On the practical side, the open courtyard provides useful extra space for the overflow of devotees, space for holding a feast during Eid or the breaking of the fast in Ramadan. After sunset in a hot and dry climate, the walled space open to the sky also provides comfort to the people. In cold regions of the world, the open courtyard does not exist. Even if a courtyard is present in a cold climate, it is covered with a roof to protect worshippers from the weather.

Fountain: Many masājid that have a courtyard also have a circular fountain for performing wudu before entering the masjid. Some masājid preserve the open space and place the water faucets on a sidewall. Compared to a water fountain at the center of the courtyard, faucets on the sidewalls eliminate any disruption by late comers when the courtyard is already full of people.

Fig. Circular fountain in the courtyard of a masjid for making wudu.

Mihrab and mimbar: At the front of the masjid is the niche for the imam, to define the direction of qiblah. Many times, the Mihrāb projects outside the main wall of the masjid. A masjid that holds congregational prayers will also have a space for mimbar on the right side of the mihrāb. This raised position is used for delivering khutbah.

Dome: In pre-Islamic times, domes were built on top of round houses in the Middle East. Layers of bricks were placed in smaller circles to form the roof of a house without any pillars. The Romans improved the dome-building technique when they occupied parts of the Middle East. During the Byzantine Empire, large buildings had domed roofs. The dome can support a roof without any columns. In a large masājid, the dome became a preferred structure as fewer columns made the congregational prayers easier. In addition, large wooden pillars were difficult to find in the desert of Arabia. The first masjid built with a dome is probably the Dome of the Rock. This is also the first building by Muslims that adopted an intricate architectural design instead of the simple structures in Arabia. The geometric patterns of this building combine a circle and an octagon—the circle at the center of the building surrounds the rock, the circle is then surrounded by an octagon, and then there is an octagonal outer wall.

Domes continued to flourish throughout Muslim lands. Masājid built by different rulers or in different lands had slightly different dome shapes. Building a circular dome on top of a square or rectangular masjid was difficult. This problem was solved by building an octagonal frame, which allowed for easy merging into a rounded dome. In the 10th century, Muslim architects developed a technique of supporting the round dome by using interlocked arches.

Minaret: The origin of the minaret is obscure. The purpose of a minaret, calling worshippers to the prayer, was first performed by Bilal (r) from the rooftop. The earliest minarets were probably Syrian or Egyptian in origin. Similar to the dome, the minaret provides a visual signal from a distance about the location of a masjid. As Muslims occupied new land, the construction of minarets often provided a sign of presence and visibility. The minarets, or manār served as a watchtower in early periods. Most early minarets were not a physical part of the masjid, but a detached structure. The Qutb Minar in Delhi, built between the 12th and 14th centuries, is about 72 meters tall and is the tallest brick minaret in India.

Fig. Mimbar in the masjid of Al-Azhar in Cairo.

Elements of decoration: As Islamic civilization flourished, so did the introduction of mathematical calculations in building construction. Specifically, geometry played a role not only in the structural design of a building, but the repeated geometric patterns arising from a central circle formed a style of decoration for the walls and roofs. Islam forbids portraying living objects, so Muslim artists transformed geometry into a major art form. Squares, rectangles, triangles, pentagons, hexagons, or octagons were repeated in intricate designs to cover the wide walls or tall minarets. Colored tiles, marbles, woodwork, ivory, or precious stones were used to create patterns and optical effects.

Another artistic skill that continued to develop was calligraphy of the Qur'ānic āyāt. In chapter 6 on calligraphy, we learned the characters of *kufi* and *nakshi* had geometric patterns. Particularly, *Thuluth* scripts were used to decorate the walls of masājid. Some of the scripts were so complicated that only an expert calligrapher could decipher the text.

Similar to the use of geometric patterns, floral patterns were also used in decorating the walls and frames around the doors. The floral patterns are

Fig. Muqarnas or interlocked vaulted niches provide support to the domes, and reflect light and sound.

Fig. Lamps with frosted glass and chandeliers provide sufficient light without glare to read the religious texts.

repeated in an interwoven fashion using colored ink, precious stones, marbles, or carved into the walls of the building. The arabesque patterns used the geometric patterns and repetition of interlacing work.

The need to illuminate the large halls led to the use of lights in decoration. Designs were created to reflect and refract light. Windows had intricate geometric and floral patterns. Hanging glass lamps were another surface used to display calligraphy and geometric patterns. The interplay of light and shade was achieved by placing windows in locations that exploit the location of the sun as the day progresses. Chandeliers hanging from the center of the dome also illuminated the masājid.

One of the challenges the Muslim architects had was the acoustics in the masjid. The voice of the khatib or the imam should reach the last row of worshippers. Before the invention of loudspeakers, vaulted ceilings and steep walls were designed so that an imam would not have to scream to reach every corner of the masjid. The same acoustic design principle allowed the Iqāmah to reverberate throughout the masjid. In many masājid, a raised platform or *dikka* provided an advantageous position for the *muadhdhin* to repeat the *takbir* during salat.

In designing a masjid, flowing water was used both for wudu and to complement the gardens and courtyards. Shallow water passages were used to reflect the beauty of a building. The courtyard of the Taj Mahal is one example of such a masterpiece of architectural design. Even where water was scare, fountains were used. In Spanish Muslim buildings, flowing water around gardens was an innovation that surprised rest of Europe.

As Islamic lands expanded, architectural designs took widely different forms based on the availability of the raw materials and on the climate. In several corners of the Muslim world, the designs often incorporated local building traditions. Distinct architectural designs can be classified as Arabian, Persian, Egyptian, Indian/Moghul, Ottoman, North African, Chinese, Central Asian, Al-Andalusian, and Far Eastern. Some newer masājid incorporate key features of several existing designs, while others use contemporary design features.

1. In what types of buildings can one see the most elaborate and intricate designs of Islamic architecture?

....

2. Explain why it is appropriate to say "Islamic" architecture rather than "Arabic" architecture.

....

....

3. What are some of the reasons geometry played a significant role in Islamic architecture, ?

....

....

4. What are some the reasons minarets were incorporated into the architecture of many masājid in the past and present?

....

....

....

5. What were some of the ways Rasūlullāh (S) used the masjid in Madinah?

....

....

....

6. Why did the construction of domes become a preferred method in building many masājid? Circle all the correct statements.

   A.   Domes can support a roof without any columns.
   B.   The use of domes requires fewer columns, which allow a larger space for the congregation.
   C.   Scarcity of wooden pillars in Arabia made dome the preferred structure.
   D.   Domes provide space to write Islamic calligraphic āyāt.
   E.   Domes were preferred by Rasūlullāh (S).

7. What type of Arabic scripts were used in many masājid to write the āyāt of the Qur'an? This script is particularly notable in the Kiswah over the Ka'bah

....

8. Technically a masjid can be built using any design. However, historically, certain components were regularly added to many masājid. List the components.

....

....

....

Islam in Spain and Portugal

Objective of the Lesson:

This lesson describes the spread of Islam in Spain and Portugal, provides brief histories of the rulers and their achievements, and explains the reasons for the fall of the Islamic empire in this part of the world.

Within a few decades after Messenger Muhammad (S) passed away, Muslims spread out and occupied the land from current-day Afghanistan in the east and Morocco in the west. This land expansion and concurrent spread of Islam made the khalīfahs the most powerful rulers of the world. In an age without automobiles and telephones, to administer this vast land and to maintain law and order, the khalīfahs appointed trustworthy governors in smaller provinces. Each governor depended on an efficient and full-time army who was instrumental in suppressing revolts and preventing attacks. As the soldiers became full-time employees, the governors created different ways to generate income in order to pay their salaries. As farming was not a viable option in the northern deserts of Africa, the governors continued to spread their territories westward until they reached Atlantic Ocean. Another natural option was to travel north of Morocco, by crossing a thin body of water to Spain.

In the eighth century, Spain was occupied by a group of invaders, the Visigoths, who were economically and culturally under developed compared to native Spaniards. Under the harsh rule of the Visigoths, the elites of Spain were looking for an escape route. It is assumed that some of the elites invited the Muslims to overthrow the Visigoths. Muslim governors were also willing partners in this endeavor, not necessarily to help the elites of Spain, but to primarily support the needs of the ever-growing army.

First settlement: The governor of Al-Ifriqiyah (Tunisia), Musa ibn-Nusayr, selected a Berber army officer, Tariq ibn-Ziyad, to lead a group of soldiers to discover if Spain could be occupied. In the spring of 711 C.E., Tariq-ibn Ziyad and his soldiers arrived in several small ships, which may have been provided by the Spanish elites. The historical account narrates the fascinating leadership and foresight of Tariq. As King Roderick of Spain was away in northern Spain, Muslims easily established a base in the South. Roderick tried to recover the land, but was quickly defeated by the Muslims. Tariq continued to expand towards Cordova. Meanwhile, Musa ibn-Nusayr himself brought another army and within a few years, they occupied major parts of Spain. After Spain fell under Muslim control, both Tariq and Musa were called back to Damascus by the khalīfah. Spain was briefly ruled by Musa's son until he was assassinated in 716 C.E.

Rule of the Amirs: The Umayyad khalifate extended from Afghanistan and Punjab in the East and Morocco and Portugal in the West. This was the largest empire that the world had ever seen. The Iberian Peninsula was called al-Andalus, which is probably a modification of the term 'Vandalicia' or the occupation of the Vandals. Initially, Spain was ruled by amirs, who were under direct control of the governor stationed in Ifriqiyya. The governor was almost independent, but he had to answer to the khalīfah in Damascus. Because of difficulty in effectively managing such a vast country the amirs in al-Andalus were frequently replaced. They were replaced partially as a cautionary measure to curtail any chance of the amirs claiming independence. In the short period of 711–756 C.E., 21 amirs ruled the land—some for only a few months.

In the meantime, changes were happening in Damascus, too. The Umayyad khalīfahs were facing internal discontent and revolt. Umayyad khalifa Yazid earned strong disapproval for his killing of Husayn, the grandson of Rasūlullāh (S). Umayyads were distant relatives of Rasūlullāh (S). From the immediate family of Rasūlullāh (S), particularly from the descendants from his uncle Abbas ibn al-Muttalib, rose a group of leaders who ultimately overthrew the Umayyad khalifate. With this overthrow, a new khalifate of the Abbasids began. The capital was moved from Damascus to Baghdad. Most of the Umayyad clan members were killed. Only one clan member, Abd-ar-Rahman survived.

The Umayyad Amirs: Abd-ar-Rahman escaped from Iraq and moved westward toward his Berber mother's land. While there he gathered together members who were still loyal to the Umayyads. Abd-ar-Rahman progressed toward Spain and proclaimed himself as the amir of al-Andalus. He was thus different from the previous amirs of al-Andalus. The previous amirs were subjects of the khalīfahs at Damascus. The new amir Abd-ar-Rahman had no loyalty to his enemies, the Abbasids. He and his three successors, known as the Umayyad amirs, ruled al-Andalus for almost 100 years (756–852 C.E.). They successfully subdued revolts and firmly established their rule in al-Andalus. During the rule of the fourth amir, Abd-ar-Rahman II, al-Andalus was prosperous and witnessed many new types of building construction.

Decline of the Umayyad Amirs: The next 60 years (852–912 C.E.) were a time of internal crisis. Three Umayyad amirs who ruled the land were not equally successful in controlling revolts. The revolts were mainly by Muslims, and the successful ones had created independent emirates. Technically, most of Spain was still under Muslim rule, but it was fragmented. Some of the Muslim rulers were more interested in land-grabbing than in religion. They had matrimonial ties with Christians. Therefore, the land-grabbing was not viewed as an Arab or Muslim invasion, but as occupation by the wealthy. As the Umayyad amirs became weaker, two dangers for them were looming. In the north, the Christian Kingdom of Leon became stronger, and in the south, the Fatimid Khilāfa was establishing itself in Tunisia.

Golden Age of the Umayyad Rule: The Umayyad emirate was revived in the form of a new amir, Abd-ar-Rahman III. Within a few years of his accession to power in 912 C.E., he was able to crush most of the opponents in Spain. His five decades of rule saw successes and failures. Initially he was successful against the northern Christian Kings of Leon and Navarre. However, he also faced defeat at the hand of king of Leon Ramiro II. When Ramiro II died, Abd-ar-Rahman III regained his power and solidified Umayyad rule to its peak in al-Andalus. The territory of Muslim Spain was largest at this time. However, Muslims were not interested in progressing further north toward France. As the Fatimid dynasty was gaining power in Tunisia and Egypt, Abd-ar-Rahman III adopted the title of khalīfah. The Umayyad in Spain were not amirs any more, they were independent khalīfahs. Abd-ar-Rahman III also adopted the title of *Amir al-Muminin,* or 'commander of the believers.' After the death of Abd-ar-Rahman III, his son, al-Hakam, assumed the power of the khilāfa. He was able to maintain the superior status of the region. When he passed away in 976 C.E., his 11-year-old son, Hisham II, became the khalīfah.

Amirids: As the boy Hisham II assumed the role of khalifa, he was guided by a minister who was appointed by his father before his death. However, an ambitious man, Ibn-Abi-Amir, ousted the minister and he himself took the position of the khalīfah's guardian. Technically, Ibn-Abi-Amir became the most powerful person in the khalifate, although he never adopted the title of khalifa. Ibn-Abi-Amir and his sons virtually ruled the country while the Umayyad khalifas were almost puppet rulers. Ibn-Abi-Amir and his sons' rule was termed as Amirid. Ibn-Abi-Amir adopted a title of al-Mansur bi-'llah (one made victorious by Allāh), or known locally as Almanzor. During this time of Amirid rule, several Umayyad khalīfahs were in 'power,' but the kingdom was almost falling apart. Cordova ceased to be the capital. By 1031, Arab rule in Spain almost ended. Muslim rule continued for a few more centuries in the form of Berber Muslim tribe rulers.

Taifa Kingdoms: As the Umayyad Khilāfa of Cordova broke down, several small factions of independent and antagonist rulers created their own kingdoms. These factions were collectively called *muluk al-tawa'if* (kings of factions) or Taifa kingdoms. The kingdoms were based in a) Seville, b) Granada, c) Cordova, d) Toledo, e) Badajoz and f) Zaragoza. None of these kingdoms were big enough to be termed as khalifate. While the Muslim rulers were divided, Christian rulers in the north were gaining ground and consolidating power.

Rule of the Almoravids: In North Africa, a group of Berbers were beginning a movement to save al-Andalus from the Christian kings. Under the guidance of their spiritual leader, ibn-Yasin, and military leader, Yahya ibn-Umar, Almoravids (al-Murabitun or 'the ones who retreat to learning and studies') regained parts of Spain. They were able to occupy these lands not only because their military skills were rooted in harsh nomadic tribal upbringing, but also because of the limited defense of the Taifa kingdoms. Although the Almoravid movement started around 1050 C.E., major advances were made by Yusuf ibn-Tashufin in 1086. After defeating the Christian king Alfonso VI, Yusuf ibn-Tashufin occupied a land where Muslims were still divided. He and his descendants ruled Spain for about 60 years, until 1145 C.E. when the Almoravid rule ended.

Almohad Khilāfa: The fall of the Almoravids was due to Christian advances, public discontent, and the growth of another power in North-West Africa. This new Berber power was Almohad, a group supported by Berber tribesman and rooted in religious values. The early leader of this group was ibn-Tumart, who studied under Imam Al-Ghazzali in Baghdad. As ibn-Tumart reached Morocco, he attempted to abolish the corruption and *bida'at* that had crept into the society. His followers insisted on the tawhid of Allāh and were called *al-Muwahhidun*. This name was later Hispanised as Almohade. This group was attacked from various fronts by Almoravids. As ibn-Tumart tried to organize his group with the support of his own tribal leaders, he claimed to be the Mahdi—a divinely guided and inspired leader. This newly acquired title earned him solid support from his followers. Almoravids tried to stop the Almohad movement by conducting many battles, and ibn-Tumart was killed. However, the movement did not collapse with the death of the spiritual leader.

From the leader's immediate circle, Abd-al-Mumin established the Almohad Empire in 1130 C.E. His expansion reached Tunisia and Tripoli. While he was establishing his empire, Almoravid rule was crumbling in Spain. Christian rulers were occupying land in Spain. The Muslims of Spain were looking for support as the small local rulers were not strong enough to resist the Christian invasion. Abd-al-Mumin remained busy with his North-West African issues and only small areas of Spain were under his control. After his death in 1163, his son, Abu-Yaqub Yusuf became the new khalīfah.

Abu-Yaqub was able to regain parts of al-Andalus, and he occupied Toledo for some time. After Abu-Yaqub's death in 1184, his son Abu-Yusuf Yaqub became the khalīfah. He paid more attention to al-Andalus than his father. He agreed to a truce with king of Leon, controlled parts of Portugal and established law and order in al-Andalus.

The descendants of Abu-Yusuf were not as good administrators as the early Almohad khalīfahs. They were not able to defend their land from well-organized Christian attempts to occupy Spain. After about two centuries of rule, the Almohad Khilāfa collapsed around 1269. In the last two decades, several khalīfahs ruled for a brief period. Most of the Spain was not under Muslim rule at this time.

Nasrid (Banu'l Ahmar) rule from Granada: While the Almohad Khilāfa was collapsing, an Arab man from Madinah, Muhammad ibn-Yusuf ibn-Nasr, was establishing a small state from his capital in Granada in 1235. Ibn-Nasr was also known as ibn-al-Ahmar. His dynasty is known as Nasrid, or Banu'l Ahmar. About 20 rulers of this dynasty ruled from Granada for almost two centuries. These rulers were not strong enough to counter the well-organized Reconquista of the Christians. In the later part of the 14th century, Nasrid rule was at its peak with such construction as the Alhambra.

In January 1492, the last Muslim ruler surrendered to the Spanish Catholic rulers Ferdinand and Isabella. This effectively ended the Muslim rule in the al-Andalus.

Muslim contributions: During the eight centuries of rule in al-Andalus, Muslims contributed to many advancements. Many examples of these advancements are in architecture, literature, poetry, science, and medicine. Muslims in al-Andalus were trying to develop a flying machine, and in 875 C.E., an engineer named Abbas ibn Firnas remained afloat in his flying device for about 10 minutes. Many surgical procedures were developed by Muslim surgeons from al-Andalus. Abu al-Qasim and Ibn Sina were two of the major surgeons at that time. Water mills and domestic water systems were available to the people of Cordova. Under Muslim rule, Spain became one of the most progressive nations in the world, including the countries of Europe.

1. Before Muslims entered Spain in the eighth century, which group of people lived there?

    A.   The Amelikites.
    B.   The Visigoths.
    C.   The Hebrew Jews.
    D.   The Greeks.
    E.   Nomadic Arabs.

2. In the eighth century, Muslims were contemplating entering Spain. They were helped and encouraged by some local people. Who were these people?

....

3. Which Muslim governor entered Spain for the first time to establish Muslim rule in the country?

    A.   The governor of Syria, Mu'āwiyah.
    B.   Khālid Ibn Walīd.
    C.   The governor of Al-Ifriqiyah, Musa Inb Nusayr.
    D.   'Uthmān Ibn 'Affān.
    E.   Abd-ar-Rahman III.

4. When the Muslims began to rule Spain during the period of Umayyad khalifate, how was the administration structured?

    A.   Khalīfahs were stationed in Spain and they ruled independently.
    B.   Governors ruled Spain under the supervision of Amirs.
    C.   The Khalīfahs ruled Spain under the direct supervision of the Governors.
    D.   Amirs ruled Spain under the direct supervision of the Khalīfahs.
    E.   Amirs ruled Spain under the direct supervision of the Governors in Ifriqiyyah.

5. When Abbasids toppled the Umayyad rulers, one of the Umayyad rulers escaped and helped establish a successful Umayyad rule in Spain. Who was he?

    A.   Abd-ar-Rahmand.
    B.   Ibn Abi Amir.
    C.   Yahya Ibn 'Umar.
    D.   Yusuf Ibn Tashufin.
    E.   Hisham II.

6. Who was the most successful Muslim ruler of Spain at the time of Umayyad khilāfa?

....

7. All of the following statements except one indicate some of the challenges and problems Umayyads faced during their rule in Spain that ultimately weakened them. Which statement is incorrect?

A. The fragmented emirates lacked unity.
B. Some of the amirs revolted against the Umayyad rule.
C. The land-grabbing approach dominated rather than spreading Islam.
D. They had an alliance with the Christians.
E. The Christian kingdom of Leon was weakened.

8. Which event ended Muslim rule in Al-Anddalus?

A. Cordova ceased to be the capital of Muslim empire.
B. The Almoravids occupied Spain.
C. Muluk al-Tawa'if established in Spain.
D. The Christian kingdom of Leon defeated Abd-ar-Rahman III.
E. Muslim rulers surrendered to Ferdinand and Isabella.

9. What step did Ibn Tumart take in Morocco that earned him solid support from his followers?

....

10. List some of the advancements and contributions of Muslims in Spain during their eight centuries of rule.

....

....

....

....

Appendix - 1
Steps of Salāh

The description provided here is the commonly accepted way of performing salāt in Hanafī madhhab. There may be minor variations, which are allowed. All the variations should have supporting proof that Rasulullah (S) had occasionally practiced that variation. The teacher and parents are requested to show the ideal practice according to their madhab. The salāh must to be performed in the Arabic language only.

Physical preparation for salāh:

Physical cleanliness: Before performing salāh, make sure you have a clean body. You must have completed *wudu*, and be in the state of *wudu*.

Clean clothes: Your clothes should be clean and should cover the body. For boys, clothes should cover the body at least from the navel to the knees. For girls, clothes should cover the body from the neck to the ankle, and to the wrist. The head is covered, but the face can remain uncovered. Clothes should not be transparent. Avoid any clothing that has pictures of people, animals, or offensive writings.

Clean place: You should find a clean place to make your salāh. A prayer rug is not necessary. A prayer rug should always be clean, so it ensures a clean place while you are praying.

Direction of face: You will be facing *Qiblah*, which is the direction of Ka'bah in Makkah.

Time: *Fard* (compulsory) prayers are performed at the proper and appointed times. It is preferable to perform the prayer as soon as the *Adhan* (call to prayer) is announced or as soon as the time for salāh comes in.

Mental preparation: We begin the prayer with full mental and physical attention. During *salāh*, we are worshipping and talking directly to Allāh, therefore, we must give our total attention. Avoid any place or object that diverts your full attention. At any time during the salāh, do not look sideways, do not look at others, and do not talk to others during the salāh. Do not make unnecessary movements. Do not scratch, yawn, laugh, or smile. If you must sneeze or cough, that is fine, but try to minimize noise.

	Sunnah raka'at before Fard raka'at	Fard raka'at	Sunnah raka'at after Fard raka'at
Fajr	2	2	
Dhuhr	4	4	2
'Asr	4	4	
Maghrib		3	2
'Isha	4	4	2, then 3 (wajib)

What is a raka'ah? Each salāh can be divided into cycles of physical postures or raka'at. Each raka'ah involves the positions of *qiyam* (standing), *ruku* (bowing), *sujud* (prostration), *jalsa* (sitting), another *sujud* (prostration), all with their associated recitations. Following chart shows the specified number of raka'at for the five daily salāh. Some variations in the number of Sunnah prayers exists among the madhhab.

Description for a salāh with two raka'at:

The following description of steps is for a salāh with two raka'at (e.g., the Fard prayer of Fajr). At the end of this description, there are brief notes about how to perform three or four raka'at of salāh.

Step 1 (Figure above)

Make an intention to perform the salāh for the sake of Allāh. Say to yourself (in any language) that you intend to offer this *Salāh* (*Fajr, Dhuhr, Asr, Maghrib,* or *Isha*), *Fard, Sunnat,* or *Witr,* and the number of raka'ahs (example—"I intend to offer two *raka'ah* of *Fard, Fajr* prayer for Allāh").

Position: *Qiyam.* You are standing upright. Raise both hands up to the ears (palms facing the *Qiblah*—body facing the direction of the Ka'bah).

What to say: *"Allāhu Akbar"* (Allāh is the Greatest).

Step 2 (Figure 2)

Position: Place your left hand over your belly, place your

Figure 2

right hand on top of the left hand, and grip the wrist of the left hand.

What to say:

1. "*Subhanaka Allāhumma wa bihamdika, wa tabārakasmuka, wa ta'āla jadduka, wa lā ilāha ghairuka.*" (This part is known as *thana*. It means "Glory be to you, O Allāh, and praise be to You. Blessed be Your Name, exalted be Your Majesty and Glory. There is no god but You").

2. "*A'ūdu billāhi mina ash-Shaytānir rajim.*" (I seek the protection of Allāh against Shaitān, the condemned.)

3. "*Bismillāhir rahmānir rahīm*" (In the Name of Allāh, Most Gracious, Most Merciful.)

4. Now recite Sūrah Al-Fātihah now. We must recite Sūrah Al-Fātihah during each raka'ah. A salāh is not valid if Sūrah Al-Fātihah is not recited.

"*Al humdu li-llahi rabbi-l 'alamīn. Ar-rahmāni-r rahīm. Māliki yawmi-d dīn. Iyyāka na'budu wa iyyāka Nāsta'īn. Ihdina-s sirāta-l mustaqīm. Sirātal ladhīna an'amta 'alaihim, ghairil maghdūbi 'alaihim, wa la-d dāllīn. (Āmīn).*"

(The Praise belongs to Allāh, The Lord of all the worlds; the Rahman; the Rahim. Malik of the Day of Judgment. You alone do we worship, and to You alone we seek help. Guide us on the Right Path—the path of those upon whom You have bestowed favors; not of those upon whom wrath is brought down, nor those gone astray.

5. After reciting sūrah Al-Fātihah, you now recite any short sūrah or a few āyāt from the Holy Qur'ān. This

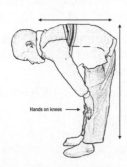

Figure 3

additional recitation of a part of the Qur'ān is done during the first two *raka'ah* only. It is always good to memorize as many sūrah as you can, so you can recite them during your *salāh*.

Step 3   (Figure 3)

What to say: "*Allāhu Akbar.*"

Position: This position is called *ruku*. Bow with your back perpendicular to your legs. Place your hands on your knees. Do not bend the knees.

What to say: "*Subhana rabbiyal 'Adhīm*" (Glorified is my Lord, the Great.) (say this three times)

Step 4   (Figure 4)

While moving back to *qiyam* (standing) position,

What to say: "*Samia Allāhu liman hamidah.*" (Allāh listens to him who praises Him.)

Position: In *qiyam* position.

What to say: "*Rabbanā wa laka al hamd.*" (Our Lord, praise be for You only.)

Figure 4

Step 5   (Figure 5)

What to say: While moving to the next position of *sujud*, say "*Allāhu Akbar.*"

Position: This position is *sujud*. Place both of your knees on the prayer rug. Try not to move the position of your feet, that is, do not move your feet away from the position of *qiyam*. After placing the knees, then you will place your two hands on the rug with palms touching the rug. Do not glide your hands on the rug. Your elbows are not on the rug. Your hands should be sufficiently apart to leave room for your head. Now place your forehead on the rug. Both

your nose and forehead should touch the rug. Your hands are on the side of your head. Your stomach will not touch the floor. You should be the most humble in this position.

Figure 5

The most powerful part of our bodies is our brain, the site of our intelligence. We submit our full selves, with full understanding, to Almighty Allāh. We realize that our strength, power, wealth, and everything that we have is from Allāh. To confirm this physical and spiritual humility, we repeat the *sujud* again in Step 7.

What to say: "*Subhana rabbiyal A'ala.*" (Glory be to Allāh, the Exalted.) (say this three times) .

Step 6 (Figure 6)

The next position is *jalsa*.

What to say: While moving to the *jalsa* position, say "*Allāhu Akbar.*"

Position: To move to the *jalsa* position, rise from *sujud*. First you will raise your head off the floor, then you will raise your hands. Now you are sitting on the floor—this posture is called *jalsa*.

What to say: "*Rabbi-ghfir lī wa arhamnī.*" (O my Lord, forgive me and have mercy on me.)

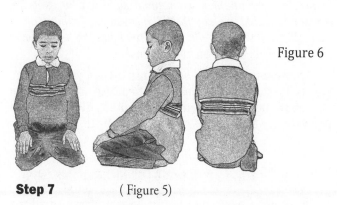

Figure 6

Step 7 (Figure 5)

You will repeat the *sujud* again. Every *raka'ah* has two *sujud*.

What to say: While moving to the position of *sujud*, say "*Allāhu Akbar.*"

Position: *Sujud.* Place your palms on the floor, and then your forehead. Both the nose and the forehead should be touching the floor.

What to say: "*Subhāna rabbiyal A'ala.*" (Glory to Allāh, the Exalted.") (say this three times)

This completes one raka'ah

Beginning of second raka'ah

Step 8 (Figures 1 and 2)

Rise to *qiyam* (standing) position. The movement should be in a systematic, graceful manner. First you will raise your forehead from the floor, then you will raise your hands and then you will raise your knees. Try not to move your feet, that is the position of your feet should be the same as it was during the first *raka'ah*.

What to say: While moving to the position of *qiyam*, say "*Allāhu Akbar.*"

Position: You are standing upright. Hold the left hand with the right hand on top.

What to say: Sūrah Al-Fātihah, and then any short sūrah or a few āyāt from the Qur'ān.

Step 9 (Figures 3)

What to say: "*Allāhu Akbar.*"

Position: *Ruku.* Bow with your back perpendicular to your legs. Place your hands on your knees.

What to say: "*Subhāna rabbiyal 'Adhīm.*" (say this three times.)

Step 10 (Figure 4)

Position: While moving back to *qiyam* (standing) position

What to say: "*Sami'a Allāhu liman hamidah.*"

Position: In *qiyam* position. You are upright.

What to say: "*Rabbanā wa lakal hamd.*"

Step 11 (Figure 5)

What to say: While moving to the next position of *sujud*, say "*Allāhu Akbar.*"

Position: *Sujud.* Follow the same sequence in Step 5.

What to say: "*Subhāna Rabbiyal A'ala.*" (say this three times.)

Step 12 (Figures 6)

What to say: While moving to the next position of *jalsa*, say "*Allāhu Akbar.*"

Position: Rise from the *sujud* position. Now you are sitting in *jalsa* position.

What to say: "'*Rabbi-ghfir lī wa arhamnī.*" (O my Lord, forgive me and have Mercy on me.)

Step 13 (Figure 5)

What to say: While moving to the next position of sujud, say "*Allāhu Akbar.*"

Position: *Sujud.* First place your hands and then your forehead on the floor.

What to say: "*Subhāna Rabbiyal A'ala.*" (say this three times).

Step 14 (Figure 6)

What to say: While moving to the next position of *jalsa*, say "*Allāhu Akbar.*"

Position: Rise from the *sujud* position. Now you are sitting in the *jalsa* position.

What to say: You will say the *Tashahud, Durūd*, and a short prayer, as follows:

"At-tahiyātu lillahi was-salawātu wattaiyibātu. Assalāmu 'alayka ayyuhan-nabiyu wa rahmatullāhi wa barakātuhu. Assalāmu 'ainā wa 'ala 'ibadi-llāhis-sālihīn. Ashhadu an lā ilāha illallāhu wa ashhadu anna Muhammadan 'abduhu wa rasūluhu."

(All these salutations, prayers, and kind words are for Allāh. Peace be on you, O Rasūlullāh, and the blessings of Allāh, and His grace. Peace on us and on all the righteous servants of Allāh. I bear witness that none but Allāh is worthy of worship, and I bear witness that Muhammad is the servant and messenger of Allāh.) This is known as the *Tashahud*.

Position: Raise your right index finger, so it is pointing upward while reciting the last part of this prayer.

Next you will recite the *Durūd*, (also called Salatul Ibrāhīm)

"Allāhumma salli 'ala Muhammadin wa 'ala āli Muhummadin, kamā sallayta 'ala Ibrāhima, wa ala āli Ibrāhima, innaka hamidun majid. Allāhumma barik 'ala Muhammadin wa 'ala āli Muhummadin, kama barakta ala Ibrāhima, wa 'ala āli Ibrahīm, innaka hamīdun majīd."

(O Allāh, send your Mercy on Muhammad and his followers as you sent Your mercy on Ibrāhīm and his followers. You are the Most Praised, The Most Glorious. O Allāh, send your Blessings on Muhammad and his followers as you have blessed Ibrāhīm and his followers. You are the Most praised, The Most Glorious.)

You may add a short prayer, such as:

"Rabbanā ātinā fi-d dunyā hasanatan wa fi-l ākhirati hasanatan, wa qinā 'adhāban nār"

(Our Lord, give us the good of this world, and good in the Hereafter and save us from the chastisement of Fire.)

Step 15   (Figure 7)

Position: Slowly turn your head and face to the right. This is called *Taslim.*

What to say: "As-salāmu 'alaikum wa rahmatullāh." (Peace and mercy of Allāh be on you.)

Step 16   (Figure 7)

Position: Slowly turn your head and face to the left. This is called *Taslim.*

What to say: "As-salāmu 'alaikum wa rahmatullāh."

This completes the two raka'at of salāh.

How to pray three raka'ats (Maghrib)

In order to perform a three-raka'at Salāh, use all the postures and prayers up to step 13. In step 14, recite only "At-tahiyātu lillahi was-salawātu wattaiyibātu. Assalāmu 'alayka ayyuhan-nabiyu wa rahmatullāhi wa barakātuhu. Assalāmu 'ainā wa 'ala 'ibadi-llāhis-sālihīn. Ashhadu an lā ilāha illallāhu wa ashhadu anna Muhammadan 'abduhu wa rasūluhu." This is known as *Tashahud*.

After saying "Allāhu akbar," return to the *qiyam* position, step 8. This time recite only Al-Fātihah, (in step 8), but do not recite any sūrah or part of the Qur'ān. All prayers and postures are the same as shown in step 9–16.

How to pray four raka'ats (Dhuhr, 'Asr and 'Isha)

In order to perform a four-raka'at prayer, use all the postures and prayers up to step 13.

In Step 14, recite only the prayer of "Tashahud," and resume the *qiyam* position—step 8.

In step 8, recite only Al-Fātihah, without adding any sūrah. Steps 8–13 complete the fourth raka'ah. The *qiyam* position in step 8 will be resumed.

In step 8, recite only Al-Fātihah, without adding any sūrah. Steps 8–16 complete the fourth raka'ah.

Figure 7

Appendix - 2
The Compulsory Acts of Salāh

Different madhāhib have different lists of compulsory acts of salāh. Based on the manner in these acts are classified, the list can have thirteen acts or fifteen acts. The Farā'id or Compulsory acts of salāh according to the Shāfi'ī Madhhab are sometimes considered Wājibat or Required acts of salāh in the Hanafī Madhhab. The purpose of the list is the same—to enumerate these acts as integral in salāh. Students of Fiqh can study the variations in minute details. Our purpose here is to list them for general understanding.

Conditions before salāh:

1. The body must be clean.

2. The clothes must be clean.

3. The place where the salāh is performed must be clean.

4. Covering the *satr* (for men, parts of body from the naval to the calf, and in women, the whole body except face, hands, and feet).

5. Performing salāt at its appointed time.

6. Facing the Qiblah.

7. Intention of salāh.

Conditions during salāh:

1. Say the takbīrāt al-Ihrām.

2. Stand for the salāh.

3. Recite sūrah al-Fātihah in each rak'ah.

4. Make rukū.

5. Make two sujud.

6. Make Jalsah i.e., to sit on knees during the salāh.

These steps are further elaborated with additional details. Some of the details are classified under the Sunnah Acts of salāh.

The Wājibāt (required acts) of Salah:

The wājibat are those acts that are required to be performed in salāh. Some of the wājibāt are as follows:

1. To recite a portion of the Qur'ān in the first two rak'ah of the Fard salāh.

2. To recite sūrah al-Fātihah in the first two rak'ah of the Fard salāh and in all the rak'ah of the other salāh.

3. In the first two rak'ah of a fard salāh, after reciting sūrah al-Fātihah, to recite another sūrah or a passage containing one long āyah or three short āyāt. In all other salāh, a sūrah should be recited after reciting sūrah al-Fātihah in all the rak'ah.

4. To observe Qiyam, i.e., to stand upright after rukū.

5. To observe Jalsah, i.e., to sit upright between the two sujud.

6. While sitting down after two rak'ah, to recite Tashahhud. This has to be recited once in any two-rak'ah salāh, and twice in three- or four-rak'ah salāh.

7. To finish the salāh by saying the salutation: As-salāmu 'alaikum wa rahmatullāh.

8. To perform the acts of salāh without rushing, at a steady speed.

9. To perform the Farā'id or Compulsory acts of salāh in their correct order.

Appendix - 3
Praying Behind an Imām

When we pray behind an Imām, we have to stand and follow certain orders. Imām is the leader, therefore, he leads the salāh.

Imām and one person: When there are two people in a group salāh, the Imām leads the salāh, and the other person stands to the right and a few steps behind the Imām.

Imām and one woman: When there are two people, and one of them is a woman, the male leads the salāh. The woman stands to the right of the Imām and several steps behind, such that her place of sujud is distinctly behind the feet-line of the Imām.

Imām, one man, and one woman: When there are three people in a group and one of them is a woman, the woman will stand behind the Imām, but her place of sujud is distinctly behind the feet-line of the second man. The second man will stand to the right and a few steps behind the Imām.

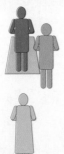

Imām and two men or women: When there are three people in a group and all of them are men or two of them are women, the individuals will stand behind the Imām, such that their places of sujud are distinctly behind the feet-line of the Imām.

Imām, one man, and two women: When there are four people in a group and two of them are women, the women will stand behind the Imām, but their places of sujud are distinctly behind the feet-line of the second man. The second man will stand to the right and a few steps behind the Imām.

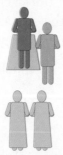

Imām, several men and women: The Imām will stand in front. Men will stand behind the Imām in one or several rows, and the women will stand distinctly behind the row or rows of men.

Appendix - 4
Salāh for Latecomers

If a congregational salāh has already started, a latecomer can join the salāh and complete it. However, there are some rules that a latecomer needs to know and follow.

First of all, a latecomer should join the congregation in the position he finds them. For example, if the congregation is in the standing position, the latecomer should start his salāh in the standing position. If the congregation is in rukū, jalsa or sujud position, the latecomer should join the congregation in the position he finds them. Below are some details.

1. First the latecomer should take his place in the row where he wants to join the congregation. He makes the intention of salāt and does the Takbirātul Ihrām. It simply means he says, "Allāhu Akbar", and by saying so he formally enters the state of salāt.

2. Immediately after saying Takbirātul Ihrām, the latecomer joins the congregation in the state he finds them, as mentioned above.

3. If the latecomer joins the salāh **at or before** the rukū position, he should count that as his first rak'ah. If the latecomer joins the salāt **after** the imām has completed the rukū, he should not count that at his first rak'ah.

4. After the Imām ends the salāh by saying Assalamu 'Alaikum wa rahmatullāh, and turns his face to the right and then to the left, the latecomer should not turn his face to the right or to the left, because he is not ending his salāh. He should stand up and complete the remaining rak'at of his salāt individually.

5. If there are several latecomers who joined the salāh, each person should complete the remaining missed rak'at individually. The latecomers should not form a mini-congregation of their own.

Scenarios:

Missing the first rak'at: A latecomer has joined the salāt after the rukū of the first rak'at was completed. In that case, after the Imām ends the salāh by saying Assalamu 'Alaikum wa rahmatullāh, and turns his face to the right and then to the left, the latecomer, instead of ending the salāt with the Imām, should stand up to complete the missed rak'at. He recites sūrah al-fātihah and another sūrah. Then he will go to rukū, sujud and sit down to recite tashahhud and durūd to end the salāh.

Missing the first two rak'at: If a latecomer misses first two rak'at of a four-rak'at salāh, as in dhuhur, 'Asr or 'Isha prayer, he should follow the procedure given below:

Latecomer has joined the salāt after the rukū of the second rak'at was completed. In that case, after the Imām ends the salāh by saying Assalamu 'Alaikum wa rahmatullāh, and turns his face to the right and then to the left, the latecomer, instead of ending the salāt with the Imām, should stand up to complete one by one the first and the second missed rak'at. He should recite sūrah al-fātihah and another sūrah in both the rak'at. Then he will go to rukū, sujud and sit down to recite tashahhud and durūd to end the salāh.

Joining the salāh after the last rukū: If a latecomer joins a salāh after the last rukū of the salāh, the latecomer will require to do the entire salāh from the beginning. Instead of ending the salāt with the Imām, the latecomer should stand up to complete the entire salāh.

Appendix - 5
The Du'ā Qunūt

The du'ā-e Qunūt is recited in the third rak'ah of witr salāh after 'Isha Prayer. It is suggested that you raise your hands to the ear lobe to say takbir and then recite the Qunūt. There are two forms of the du'ā-e Qunūt, one according to the Shāfi'ī Madhhab and the other according to the Hanafī Madhhab. Mālikī Madhhab suggests that this du'ā should be recited in the salāt-ul Fajr, in the second rak'at, however, according to many scholars, there is no clear evidence that Rasūlullāh (S) recited du'ā-e Qunūt in salāt-ul Fajr all the time, in all circumstances.

Du'ā-e Qunūt in Shāfi'ī Madhhab:

اَللّٰهُمَّ اهْدِنِيْ فِيْمَنْ هَدَيْتَ وَ عَافِنِيْ فِيْمَنْ عَافَيْتَ وَ تَوَلَّنِي فِيْمَنْ تَوَلَّيْتَ وَ بَارِكْ لِي فِيمَا أَعْطَيْتَ وَ قِنِي شَرَّ مَا قَضَيْتَ فَإِنَّكَ تَقْضِي وَ لَا يُقْضَى عَلَيْكَ وَ إِنَّهُ لَا يَذِلُّ مَنْ وَّ الَيْتَ تَبَارَكْتَ رَبَّنَا وَ تَعَالَيْتَ

Allāhumma ihdinī fī man hadayt, wa 'āfini fī man 'āfayt, wa tawallanī fī man tawallayt, wa bārik li fī ma a'tayt, wa qinī sharra mā qadayt, fa innaka taqdī wa lā yuqdā 'alayk, wa innahu lā yadhillu man walayt, tabārakta Rabbanā wa ta'ālayt.

O Allāh, guide us among those whom You have guided, pardon us among those whom You have pardoned, turn to us in friendship among those on whom You have turned in friendship, and bless us in what You have bestowed, and save us from the evil of what You have decreed. For it is You who decree and none can influence You; and he is not humiliated whom You have befriended, nor is he honored who is Your enemy. Blessed are You, O Lord, and Exalted.

There are minor variations in how the du'ā is recited, in singular or plural appeal, or with an additional line at the end.

In the Shāfi'ī Madhhab, one does not raise hands to the ear lobe to say takbir, instead, he/she brings his/her hands to chest level in supplication format and recites the du'ā.

Du'ā-e Qunūt in Hanafī Madhhab:

اَللّٰهُمَّ إِنَّا نَسْتَعِينُكَ وَ نَسْتَغْفِرُكَ وَ نُؤْمِنُ بِكَ وَ نَتَوَكَّلُ عَلَيْكَ وَ نُثْنِي عَلَيْكَ الْخَيْرَ. وَ نَشْكُرُكَ وَ لَا نَكْفُرُكَ وَ نَخْلَعُ وَ نَتْرُكُ مَنْ يَّفْجُرُكَ. اَللّٰهُمَّ إِيَّاكَ نَعْبُدُ وَلَكَ نُصَلِّي وَ نَسْجُدُ وَ إِلَيْكَ نَسْعَى وَ نَحْفِدُ وَ نَرْجُوْا رَحْمَتَكَ وَ نَخْشَى عَذَابَكَ. إِنَّ عَذَابَكَ بِالْكُفَّارِ مُلْحِقٌ

Allāh humma innā nasta'īnuka wa nastaghfiruka wa nu'minu bika wa natawakkalu 'alaika wa nusni 'alaikal khair, wa nashkuruka walā nakfuruka wa nakhla'u wa natruku mai yafjuruka, Allāh humma iyyāka na'budu wa laka nusallī wa nasjudu wa ilaika nas'ā wa nahfizu wa narju rahmataka wa nakhshā 'azābaka inna 'azābaka bil kuffāri mulhikun.

O Allāh we seek Your help and beg Your forgiveness and we believe in You and praise you and we are thankful to you and we are not ungrateful to You, and we turn away and forsake those who deny you. O Allāh, You alone do we worship and for You alone we pray and prostrate and we betake to please You and present ourselves for the service of Your cause and we hope for Your mercy and fear Your chastisement. Indeed, Your chastisement is going to overtake the disbelievers.

Appendix - 6
The Salāt al-Janāzah

Salāt Janāzah is performed on a deceased Muslim person. Before we discuss the salāh, let us learn the du'ā we need to say when we hear a death news.

إِنَّا لِلَّهِ وَإِنَّآ إِلَيْهِ رَاجِعُونَ ۝

Innā lillāhi wa innā ilāihi rāji'ūn. (2:156)

Surely we belong to Allāh and to Him surely we do return.

Salātul Janāzah

Salātul Janāzah is fard kifāya. The term fard denotes it is a compulsory Islamic duty imposed upon the whole community. However, kifāya indicates it is a "sufficiency duty", that means, as long as sufficient number of community members perform the duty, an individual is not required to perform it. However, if nobody performs the duty, then all Muslims of the community are accountable for missing the duty.

All the conditions of regular salāt are also required for salātul janāzah, for example, wudū, clean clothes, facing the Qiblah. However, there are no adhan, rukū or sujud. Entire salāh is done in standing position.

It is better that all participants stand in at least three rows, behind the Imām. The body of the deceased is placed in front of the Imām. If the deceased is a man or a boy, then the Imām will stand by the middle of the body, if the deceased is a woman or a girl, then the Imām will stand by the shoulder of the body.

First takbīr: After making niyah or intention of salāh, raise your hands in the usual manner with the Imām, and say, Allāhu Akbar. Then fold your hands in the usual manner. The Imām will read sūrah al-Fātihah silently. All participants should read the sūrah silently.

Second takbīr: Without raising hands, the Imām will loudly say Allāhu Akbar. If Imām raises his hand, then the participants should follow him. This time the participants will recite durūd Ibrāhīm.

"Allāhumma salli 'ala Muhammadin wa 'ala āli Muhummadin, kamā sallayta 'ala Ibrāhima, wa ala āli Ibrāhima, innaka hamidun majid. Allāhumma barik 'ala Muhammadin wa 'ala āli Muhummadin, kama barakta ala Ibrāhima, wa 'ala āli Ibrahīm, innaka hamīdun majīd".

Third takbīr: Without raising hands, the Imām will loudly say Allāhu Akbar. If Imām raises his hand, then the participants should follow him. The participants will now make special du'ā for the deceased. The following du'ā is usually recited.

اللَّهُمَّ اغْفِرْ لِحَيِّنَا وَمَيِّتِنَا وَشَاهِدِنَا وَغَائِبِنَا وَصَغِيرِنَا وَكَبِيرِنَا وَذَكَرِنَا وَأُنْثَانَا اللَّهُمَّ مَنْ أَحْيَيْتَهُ مِنَّا فَأَحْيِهِ عَلَي الْإِسْلَامِ وَ مَنْ تَوَفَّيْتَهُ مِنَّا فَتَوَفَّهُ عَلَى الْإِيْمَانِ

Allāhumma ghfir lī hayyinā was mayyitinā wa shāhidinā wa ghā'ibinā wa saghīrinā wa kabirinā wa dhakarinā wa unthāna. Allāhumma man ahyaitahu minnā fa ahyaihi 'alāl islām, wa man tawaffaita hu minnā fatawaffahu 'alāl īmān.

Oh Allāh! Forgive those of us that are alive and those of us that are dead; and those of us that are present and those who are absent; and those of us who are young and those who are adults; and males and females. Oh Allāh! Whomsoever You keep alive, make him live as a follower of Islam and whomsoever You cause to die, then let him die in the state of imān.

Fourth takbīr: Without raising hands, the Imām will loudly say Allāhu Akbar. If Imām raises his hand, then the participants should follow him. The participants will now make du'ā for all the Muslims. Recite any du'ā for overall good for all.

Salām: The Imām will end the salāt by saying salām. Some madhhab says salām to be made only in the right side (Hanafī and Mālikī). In Shāfi'ī Madhhab, salām is made on both sides, like in a regular salāt. Follow your Imām.

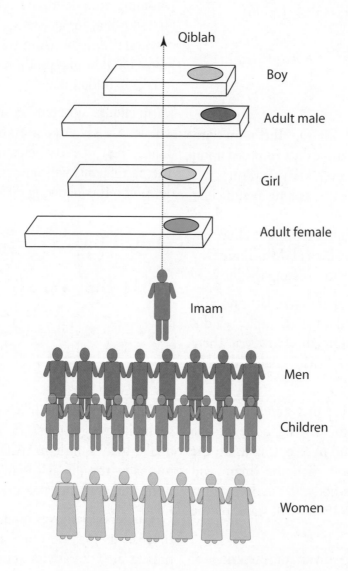

Fig: Graphical representation of Salātul Janāzah and position of the deceased body.

Appendix - 7
Conditions that Nullify Wudū

The Qur'ān clearly instructs us to make wudū before salāt.[5:6] The instruction in this āyah is fairly clear.

O you who believe! when you stand up for salāt then wash your faces, and your hands up to the elbows; and wipe your heads and your feet up to the ankles. And if you are unclean, then purify yourselves... (5:6)

We should never undermine the importance of doing wudū. If at anytime we are in doubt whether wudū is nullified or not, it is better to make fresh wudū.

Different madhāhib have formulated different conditions that nullify wudū. All of them agree to the following incidents or conditions that nullify wudū. If wudū is nullified, one must make wudū before proceeding to make salāt.

The conditions that nullify wudū are as follows:

1. Defecation, urination or passing gas.

2. Deep sleep, whether for a short time or long time.

3. Loss of one's senses due to fainting, sedation, drinking or insanity.

4. Emission of semen.

5. Vomiting a mouthful.

6. Touching one's private parts with bare hands.

7. Flow of any liquid from body: e.g., blood, pus, or other fluid.

There are several additional factors that can nullify one's wudū. If interested, please verify with an imam or a person well versed in fiqh.

Appendix - 8
Adhān, 'Iqāmah and Response

The Adhān is a call to prayer. It is recited in a melodious tone by a person, who is called the Mu'adhdhin. The call is given out loud, five times a day, before each of the five fard salāh. It should be given by facing the direction of Qiblah, the direction of salāh. Adhān reminds the believers that it is time for salāh. When a believer hears the adhān, he/she need to respond by saying some du'ā.

An 'Iqāmah is a call similar to Adhān, but given right before salāh starts. It is a call to start the salāh. 'Iqāmah is not necessary when a person prays alone, however, in a group salāh, any member of the group should call it out loud.

Recitation of Adhān and 'Iqāmah: The wording of the Adhān and 'Iqāmah are essentially the same. A small difference exists between them depending on the adherence of one or the other madhhab.

'Iqāmah: The 'Iqāmah is pronounced loud, but not in a melodious voice. According to Shāfi'ī Madhhab, in 'Iqāmah, except for Allāhu Akbar, everything is recited one time. According to Hanafī Madhhab, the number of recitation is the same as in the Adhān.

According to all madhāhib, after saying "Hayya 'alā-l falāh", the phrase "qad qāmatis salāh" should be recited twice. It means the salāh has started.

Replying to Adhān: When the Mu'adhdhin recites Hayya 'alā-s salāh and Hayya 'alā-l falāh, the listeners reply by saying "lā hawla wa lā quwwata illa billhai 'aliyyil 'azim," meaning, there is no power and might except from Allāh, the most High, the most Great.

Adhān for Fajr salāh: According to all madhāhib, the Adhān for Fajr salāh should include "As-salātu khairum min-an-nawm," recited twice. It means salāh is better than sleep. This phrase is recited after "Hayya 'alā-l falāh."

Du'ā after Adhān: The following du'ā is made after the Adhān.

Allāhumma rabba hādhi-hid da'wa-tit-tāmma wa-salātil qā'ima. Ati muhammadan-il wasilata wal fadīla wab ath-hu maqāmam-mahmuda-nil alladhī wa 'ādthahu innaka lā tukhlifu-l mī'ād.

Arabic	Meaning	In Adhān	In 'Iqāmah
		times recited	times recited
Allāhu Akbar	Allāh is the Greatest	4 times	2 times
Ashhadu 'an lā ilāha illa-llāh	I testify there is no god but Allāh	2 times	1 time
Ashhadu 'anna Muhammadar rasūlullāh	I testify that Muhammad is the messenger of Allāh	2 times	1 time
Hayya 'alā-s salāh	Hasten to salāh	2 times	1 time
Hayya 'alā-l falāh	Hasten to success	2 times	1 time*
Allāhu Akbar	Allāh is the Greatest	2 times	2 times
Lā ilāha illa-llāh	There is no god but Allāh	1 time	1 time

* In 'Iqāmah, after saying Hayya 'alā-l falāh, the reciter says "qad qāmatis salāh" twice. It means the salāh has started.

Appendix - 9
A Few Du'ā to Learn

رَبَّنَا عَلَيْكَ تَوَكَّلْنَا وَإِلَيْكَ أَنَبْنَا وَإِلَيْكَ ٱلْمَصِيرُ ﴿٤﴾

Our Rabb! upon You do we rely, and towards You do we turn, and towards You is the eventual coming (60:4).

رَبَّنَا ءَاتِنَا فِى ٱلدُّنْيَا حَسَنَةً وَفِى ٱلْأَخِرَةِ حَسَنَةً وَقِنَا عَذَابَ ٱلنَّارِ ﴿٢٠١﴾

Our Rabb! give us good in this world, and good in the Hereafter, and save us from the chastisement of the Fire (2:201).

رَبِّ ٱغْفِرْ وَٱرْحَمْ وَأَنتَ خَيْرُ ٱلرَّاحِمِينَ ﴿١١٨﴾

My Rabb! forgive and have mercy; because You are the Best of the merciful ones (23:118).

رَبَّنَا ظَلَمْنَآ أَنفُسَنَا وَإِن لَّمْ تَغْفِرْ لَنَا وَتَرْحَمْنَا لَنَكُونَنَّ مِنَ ٱلْخَٰسِرِينَ ﴿٢٣﴾

Our Rabb! we have done wrong to ourselves; and if You do not forgive us and have mercy on us, we shall surely become of the losers (7:23).

رَبِّ ٱشْرَحْ لِى صَدْرِى ﴿٢٥﴾ وَيَسِّرْ لِى أَمْرِى ﴿٢٦﴾ وَٱحْلُلْ عُقْدَةً مِّن لِّسَانِى ﴿٢٧﴾ يَفْقَهُوا۟ قَوْلِى ﴿٢٨﴾

My Rabb! expand for me my breast, and make my affair easy for me, and release the knot from my tongue, they may understand my speech (20:25-28).

رَبَّنَآ إِنَّنَآ ءَامَنَّا فَٱغْفِرْ لَنَا ذُنُوبَنَا وَقِنَا عَذَابَ ٱلنَّارِ ﴿١٦﴾

Our Rabb! we have certainly believed; therefore forgive us of our sins, and save us from the punishment of the Fire (3:16).

Family Tree of Rasūlullāh (S)

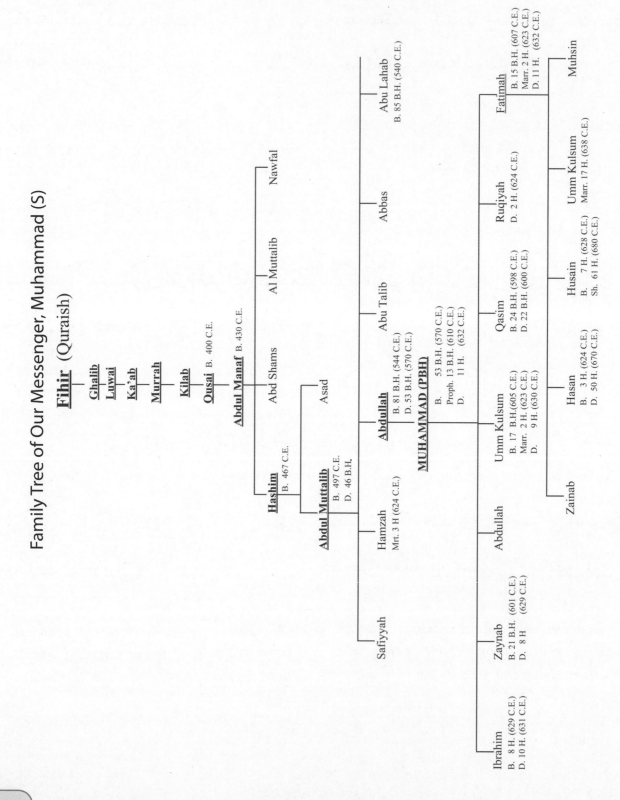

Outline of Curriculum—Grades 1, 2 and 3

Each year the curriculum begins with a few topics on Allāh, the Qur'ān, the Prophet (S), the Hadīth, or Sunnah. In the early years, the emphasis is placed on the 5 pillars, and each year, this emphasis increases. Each year, a history of some of the prophets is introduced in an age-appropriate manner. Several lessons are devoted to Islamic manners, values, and morals so that children grow up with a good understanding of Islamic culture. Each lesson includes a homework assignment.

Week	1st Grade	2nd Grade	3rd Grade
1	Allāh	Allāh the Creator	What Does Allāh Do
2	Islam	Blessings of Allāh	Some Names of Allāh
3	Our Faith	The Qur'ān	Allāh: the Merciful
4	Muhammad (S)	Muhammad (S)	Allāh: the Judge
5	The Qur'ān	Sunnah and Hadīth	We Are Muslims
6	An exam is recommended this week		
7	5 Pillars of Islam	5 Pillars of Islam	Other Names of the Qur'ān
8	Shahādah	Shahādah	Hadith
9	Salāt and Wūdū	Salāt	Shahādah
10	Fasting	Sawm	Types of salāt
11	Zakah	Charity	Why Do Salāt
12	An exam is recommended this week		
13	Hajj	Hajj	Sawm
14	Saying Bismillāh	Wūdū	Charity
15	Angels	Four Khalīfas	Hajj
16	Shaitān	Ibrāhīm (A)	Prophet (S) in Makkah
17	Adam (A)	Ya'qūb (A) and Yūsuf (A)	Prophet (S) in Madinah
18	Nūh (A)	Mūsā (A) and Harun (A)	How Rasul (S) Treated Others
19	An exam is recommended this week		
20	Ibrāhīm (A)	Yūnus (A)	Ismā'īl (A) and Ishāq (A)
21	Mūsā (A)	Angels	Dāwūd (A)
22	'Isā (A)	Food That We May Eat	'Isā (A)
23	Makkah and Madinah	Truthfulness	Being Kind
24	Good Manners	Kindness	Forgiveness
25	Kindness and Sharing	Respect	Good Deeds
26	An exam is recommended this week		
27	Allāh Rewards Good Works	Responsibility	Cleanliness
28	Respect	Obedience	Right Path
29	Forgiveness	Cleanliness	A Muslim Family
30	Love of Allāh	Honesty	Perseverance
31	Eid	Day of Judgment and Hereafter	Punctuality
32	Thanking Allāh	Muslims from Different Nations	Jinn
33	An exam is recommended this week		

Outline of Curriculum—Grades 4, 5 and 6

By 5th grade, a summarized biography of the Prophet (S) is completed, including an understanding of the events that shaped his life and early Islam. By 6th grade, students will have studied the biography of most of the prominent prophets at least once. At this stage, students will have learned all the fundamental principles and key concepts of Islam. Even if the students do not enroll in weekend schools after 6th grade, they will have gained significant age-appropriate knowledge about Islam.

Week	4th Grade	5th Grade	6th Grade
1	Rewards of Allāh	Allāh: Our Sole Master	Attributes of Allāh
2	Discipline of Allāh	Why Should We Worship Allāh	The Promise of Allāh
3	Some Names of Allāh	Revelation of the Qur'ān	Objectives of the Qur'ān
4	Books of Allāh	Characteristics of Prophets	Compilation of the Qur'ān
5	Pre-Islamic Arabia	Battle of Badr	Previous Scriptures and the Qur'ān
6	An exam is recommended this week			
7	The Year of the Elephant	Battle of Uhud	The Importance of Shahādah
8	Early Life of Muhammad (S)	Battle of Trench	Hadīth, Compilation, Narrators
9	Life Before Prophethood	Hudaibiyah Treaty	Nūh (A)
10	Receiving Prophethood	Conquest of Makkah	Tālūt, Jālūt, and Dāwūd (A)
11	Makkan Period	Adam (A)	Dāwūd (A) and Sulaimān (A)
12	An exam is recommended this week			
13	Pledges of Aqaba	Ibrāhīm (A) and His Arguments	Sulaimān (A) and Queen of Saba
14	Hijrat to Madinah	Ibrāhīm (A) and Idols	Mūsā (A) and Fir'awn
15	Madīnan Period	Luqmān (A) and His Teachings	Israelites After Their Rescue
16	Victory of Makkah	Yūsuf (A)—Childhood and Life in Aziz's Home	Mūsā (A) and Khidir
17	Abū Bakr (R)	Yūsuf (A)—Life in Prison and His Dream Interpretation	'Isā (A) and Maryam (ra)
18	'Umar al-Khattāb (R)	Yūsuf (A)—Dream Fulfills	Khadījah (ra)
19	An exam is recommended this week			
20	'Uthmān ibn 'Affan (R)	Ayyūb (A)	'A'ishah (ra)
21	'Ali Ibn Abu Tālib (R)	Zakariyyāh (A) and Yahyā (A)	Fātimah (ra)
22	Compilers of Hadīth	Maryam	Al-Qiyamah: The Awakening
23	Shaitān's Mode of Operation	Major Masjid in the World	Rūh and Nafs
24	Hūd (A)	Upholding Truth	The Angels and Jinn
25	Sālih (A)	Responsibility and Punctuality	Shaitān: The Invisible Enemy
26	An exam is recommended this week			
27	Mūsā (A)	My Mind, My Body	Taqwā
28	Sulaimān (A)	Kindness and Forgiveness	My Friend Is Muslim Now
29	Truthfulness	Middle Path	Friendship: With People of the Same and Opposite Gender
30	Perseverance	Significance of Salāt	Reading Salāt vs Performing Salāt
31	Day of Judgment	Significance of Fasting	Muslims Around the World
32	'Eid and Its Significance	Zakāt and Sadaqah	People of Other Faith
33	An exam is recommended this week			

Outline of Curriculum—Grades 7, 8 and 9

In these grades, the application of knowledge is gradually emphasized by using carefully selected topics. Details about some of the prophets are introduced to highlight the abiding morals in their lives. In 8th grade, several battles and early Muslim struggles are discussed in detail. Increased depth and emphasis of the lessons require focused attention from students. Age-appropriate moral lessons, for example, gossip, friendship, peer pressure, dating, indecency, encouraging good and forbidding evil, and so forth are covered.

Week	7th Grade	8th Grade	9th Grade
1	Why Islam? what is Islam?	Divine Names	Signs of Allāh in nature
2	The Qur'ān—other names	Objectives of the Qur'ān	Pondering the Qur'ān
3	Seeking the Forgiveness of Allāh —Istighfar	Hadīth	Preservation and Compilation of the Qur'ān
4	Allāh: Angry or Kind	Madhhab	Ibadat—Easy Ways to Do It
5	Islamic Greetings	Hope, Hopefulness, Hopelessness	Why Human Beings Are Superior
6	An exam is recommended this week		
7	Ādam (A)	Trial	Is Islam a Violent Religion?
8	'Ad and Thamūd	Friends and Friendship	Peer Pressure
9	Stories of Ibrāhīm (A) - I	Friendship With Non-Muslims	Choices We Make
10	Stories of Ibrāhīm (A) - II	Dating in Islam	Dating in Islam
11	Sacrifice of Ibrāhīm (A)	Duties Toward Parents	Alcohol and Gambling
12	An exam is recommended this week		
13	Lūt (A)	Islam for Middle School Students	Permitted and Prohibited Food
14	Yūsuf (A)—The Story of Overcoming Temptation	Battle of Badr	Food of the People of the Book
15	The Dwellers of the Cave	Battle of Uhud	Khadījah (ra)
16	Dhul Qurnain	Banu Qaynuka	Prophet's (S) Multiple Marriages
17	Abū Sufyān	Banu Nadir	Marriage to Zainab (ra)
18	Khālid Ibn Walīd (R)	Battle of Khandaq	The Prophet: A Great Army General
19	An exam is recommended this week		
20	How to Achieve Success	Banu Qurayzah	God's Chosen People
21	The Character of the Prophets	Surah Al-Ahzāb on the Battle of Khandaq	Mūsā's Personality
22	The Prophet's (S) Marriages	Hudaibiyah Treaty	Prophecy of Muhammad(S) in Bible
23	Purification	Tabūk Expedition	Essentials of Salah
24	Permitted and Prohibited	Farewell Pilgrimage	Muslims in North America
25	Lailatul Qadr	Performance of Hajj	Life Cycle of Truth
26	An exam is recommended this week		
27	Fasting During Ramadan	Paradise and Hell	How Ramadan Makes Us Better
28	My Family is Muslim Now	Finality of Prophethood	Indecency
29	Amr Bil Ma'rūf	Origin and History of Shī'ah	Allegations Against the Prophet (S)
30	Guard Your Tongue	Ummayad Dynasty	Family Values
31	Lessons from Past Civilizations	Abbasid Dynasty	Shariah
32	Science in the Qur'ān	Permitted and Prohibited Food	Justice in Islam
33	An exam is recommended this week		

Outline of Curriculum—Grade 10

In 10th grade, Islamic topics increasingly prepare youths to fine-tune their spiritual and social lives. Significant issues that have real-life implications are introduced. The application of knowledge continues to be emphasized. Age-appropriate moral lessons, such as Racism in Islam, Superstition, Marriage with Non-Muslims, Difficult questions on Marriage, Secular and Religious Duties and so forth are introduced.

Islamic Studies books for Level 11 and 12 will be published in course of time.

Week	10th Grade
1	History of Allāh
2	An Analysis of Fātiha
3	Fātiha vs. The Lord's Prayer
4	Muhkam Mutashabihat Verses
5	Al-Asr—The Formula of Success
6	An exam is recommended this week
7	Qur'ānic Calligraphy
8	The Bible and the Qur'ān
9	The Ten Commandments and Islam
10	Adam and Eve in the Garden
11	Women in the Qur'ān
12	An exam is recommended this week
13	Muslim Family
14	The Status of Women in Islam
15	Marriage to Non-Muslims
16	Marrying Four Women
17	Difficult Questions on Marriage
18	Who is Khalifah on the Earth
19	An exam is recommended this week
20	False Piety
21	Superstition
22	Do Not Transgress Limits
23	Secular and Religious Duties
24	Racism in Islam
25	Principles of Islamic Economy
26	An exam is recommended this week
27	Public Finance in Early Islam
28	Islamic Architecture
29	Islam in Spain and Portugal
30	Independent project
31	Independent project
32	Independent project
33	An exam is recommended this week